TERRAN V

what's
so
amazing
about

scripture?

HOW TO READ IT RIGHT AND TAP INTO ITS POWER

The Spiritual Bakery Publications
Cape Town, South Africa
Copyright © Terran Williams, 2020.

ISBN: 9798581424636

With deep and heartfelt gratitude,
I dedicate this book to you, my reader—
who either doubts the Bible is anything to go by,
or knows it to be true, yet longs to understand it better
and prize it even more.
You have been in my mind and prayers all along.

CONTENTS

FOREWORD

When I was a student at Rhodes University, I attended a local Pentecostal church. I was struck by how almost all the members turned up to Sunday meetings, or midweek meetings, with Bible in hand. This was quite new to me, coming from my historical church background. There were big ones, small ones, and "zippy" ones, but whatever the look, if a preacher referred to a text, Bibles would be flipped open. Further, they actually read them a lot, becoming biblically literate (though not always theologically schooled) and taking its words as God's very voice.

Today the situation is different. We now read the text on our devices with endless online resources on tap. But my impression is that the average Christian is not biblically literate. Far fewer trust every word. We make use of the Bible, yes, but in small bite-size moments. Our Scripture intake competes with so many other demands on our time: entertainment, media exposure, and social media engagements. So much is forfeited.

This is of great concern to me. How can we restore biblical literacy, skill, enthusiasm, and engagement in the Christian population?

This book intentionally addresses this problem. It seeks to provide its readers with a profound appreciation for the Bible (part one), a deeper comprehension and trust in its message (part two) and real tools for engagement with the text (part three).

I first heard of Terran Williams as he and Julie, parents of five young children, planted and led a vibrant church near to my home. Terran's zest for life, love of people, and his energetic yet thoughtful preaching ministry had resonance with the young and the old, reaching out to the unchurched and the de-churched with the gospel and discipling believers in the Word.

He also created weekly sermon content and devotional resources for thousands of people in eight other churches, and an intensive two-year church-planting course that was rolled out in South Africa, the UK and the USA.

My friendship with Terran commenced at a nearby restaurant as he showed great interest in the two decades of my focused field of study, lecturing and writing: the kingdom of God in the Gospels as the central lens for interpreting Scripture. During our hours of banter, I discovered firsthand that his love for his kids, surfing and good coffee was matched by his love for Jesus, the Bible and biblical theology.

Having handed over leadership of his church, and now giving himself full-time to a more voracious habit of study and to creating resources to serve the wider church, he asked me to preface his first work in this new venture.

Five things stood out for me when I read this book. First, Terran is a really good writer. Purely from a literary point of view, he communicates well. I have read many manuscripts of would-be authors over the years. Seldom do I read one and I think: this needs hardly any editing.

Second, as he declares his intent to be, he writes in an easy and accessible style. It flows. It never gets difficult, or heavy. It will not tire you out as you read.

Third, he writes comprehensively. He has included a remarkable array of relevant topics and important insights. The result of this and the previous point is that he really *does* equip the ordinary person to grasp the Bible and read it with new eyes.

Fourth, while it is easy and accessible, behind it lies an up-to-date reading of important theological literature. You can see that from the footnotes. There is depth underneath the simplicity.

Finally, he writes with passion. One can sense in every chapter, that he just loves his subject. He loves the Bible, he loves the grand story and he loves the central hero. I pray you will "catch" his passion as you read.

—Derek Morphew

PhD in New Testament Studies; author of 'Breakthrough' and 'The Kingdom Reformation' and founder of the international Vineyard Bible Institute.

INTRODUCTION

They say that you should write the book you wish you could have read. For the first decade of my faith especially, I longed for *this* one—the one you hold before you.

This is a book all about *that Book*—Scripture, The Holy Bible, God's Word, call it what you will.

Setting out on my faith journey as a 16-year-old new believer, with no real church background, in a cosmopolitan, secular enclave on the tip of Africa, I knew almost nothing about the Bible. Having recently trusted in Jesus, my initial escapades into it seemed to parachute me into another world entirely, with long lists of strange names and outlandish cultural practices, apostles and epistles (the apostles wives? I wondered), as well as weird warnings and wild commands.

Reeling from these confusing biblical passages, trying to find some kind of bearing, I asked fellow-believers for help, but was struck by how few of them could answer my questions. Who's who? When's when? Where's where? Why's this in here? How does it all fit together? How do I find myself an epistle? And most importantly: How do I get closer to God through it? Indeed, if I can be honest, at times I felt further away from him after reading my Bible.

As an adult, I would go on to study theology and, on the way, make more and more sense of the Scriptures. Slowly but surely the strange world of the Bible became my second home and my heart language. So awe-inspiring is its vast and intricate landscape, I've happily spent decades, week-in and week-out, guiding a growing number of God's people deeper into the Bible, watching them make it their home too. In this book, I've distilled all the help I have been privileged to get and give.

Divided into three parts, my hope is that by the end of reading it, you'll have come to see just how amazing Scripture is, how to really read it right and trust it fully, and finally, how to practically tap into its life-changing power.

Just *how* important are these topics for people to grapple with?

Very, very important. Essential even. Here's why. The other day, I overheard a young person ask a well-read, older friend of mine what books he recommended. He said, "There's a ton of books that you should read, but the first and most important one is the Bible."

"Yes, yes," she nodded, but then pressed him some more, "but what's *the second* most important book to read?"

He thought a bit and then answered, "Far behind the first one, it would have to be a book that *helps* you to read the Bible. The Bible, after all, requires an extensive introduction."

This conversation triggered an internal one in me. Having read many excellent books about the Bible, which one would I recommend as the ultimate introduction? Instead of just one, I thought of ten which I shortened to five with difficulty, each covering very different material—one about interpreting the Bible, another about its storyline and themes, one about its credibility, one that explored the Bible's teaching about the Bible itself, and another about the many ways to use it to grow closer to God. I wondered, can we really expect the average person to read all those books? And to my knowledge—no single one covered it all.

It was then that I knew *I had to write this book.*

In it, I have attempted to take the best biblical and theological insights I can find and make them more accessible to all, regardless of your current grasp of Scripture. Whether you're a beginner or a seasoned scholar, my goal is not to bring you to the end of your questions about the Bible, but rather, to equip you for all your subsequent adventures into the Bible.

One last analogy: think of your reading of this book as your *Spiritual Driver's License* for engaging Scripture. Just like you wouldn't climb into the driver's seat of a car before first learning how to drive, this book will provide you with the critical insights and skills you need to go wherever the many wonderful, winding roads of Scripture may take you—safely and smoothly, seeing all of what's really there.

So while a thousand transformative journeys through God's Word await you, *this* journey you're about to embark on over the page will equip you for all of the ones that follow.

Enough said—let's get going.

PART ONE

WHAT'S SO AMAZING ABOUT SCRIPTURE?

1

THE BIBLE'S IMPACT

God said, "Let there be light," and there was light.

Genesis 1:3

Is our life merely a random series of events in which we try to weave moments of happiness into a tapestry of atoms and molecules, briefly arranged together to give us our fleeting existence? Or is it something far more meaningful, perhaps even divinely premeditated?

To find the answer the Bible gives, let's start at the very beginning. On its first page, the first thing we discover is that there is a God and he is not silent. In fact, as we read on, we discover that we, along with all creation, owe our very existence to his words. Many times over we read, "God said 'Let there be' … and there was."

According to the Bible, outside of his light- and life-giving words, we would have remained truly in the dark—as formless and unanimated as the void that preceded life as we know it.

Contested as it may be, the Bible remains history's top contender as the revealer of life's true meaning. Not only does it begin by claiming that there is a God and that he spoke creation into existence, it then proceeds to go further still by claiming that God has continued to speak, each time with similar effect: bringing something out of nothing, and order out of chaos.

Has God really spoken in a book though?

If the Bible is to be believed—if a Creator not only exists but spoke existence into being, and whose later words were then recorded in a book—it is unlike any other book and would have made an indelible impact on the world, surely. So, has it?

Let's begin by exploring *the impact* the Bible has made.

A WORLD-CHANGING BOOK

Whether you resonate with its worldview or not, historians and philosophers agree on this fact: the Bible has changed the world more than any other book.

With a hundred million Bibles printed every year (and six billion copies currently in print), it is the best seller by far, year after year after year.[1] When a journalist asked a Bible printing company why that is, they answered, "It's just such a good book."

Given its long-running and wide-reaching influence, the Bible's words and underpinning concepts are the background song of so much of contemporary culture. Its phrases are on our lips, even if we have never read its verses: peace maker; glad tidings; scapegoat; hope against hope; hold out an olive branch; the eleventh hour; to wash one's hands of; a good Samaritan; a cross to bear; a labour of love; a sign of the times; a thorn in the flesh; a wolf in sheep's clothing; to fight the good fight; the skin of your teeth; the powers that be; the blind leading the blind; a law unto themselves; our heart's desire and on and on we could go.

Additionally, so many parts of it are also lodged into every imaginable crevice of society and culture: birth names and marriage vows; funeral rites and law contracts; classical art themes and orchestral inspiration; social justice declarations and history-altering constitutions; architectural engravings and archeological finds; best-ever literature and top-of-the-pops lyrics, to name a few. If all the Bibles were burned, there would be enough scraps of it in these artifacts of history and culture to piece much of it back together again.

---

[1] Source: www.econ.st/33tZkdW (accessed 08/20). Even the 400 million Harry Potter books sold come in a very distant second place.

Time Magazine once stated[2] that the most significant, future-shaping moment in the second millennium was the printing of the Bible at Gutenberg's Press—putting the good book into the hands and language of the common people proved to be the catalyst that led to more subsequent and radical societal changes than any other moment in our collective history.

Into a world long dominated by a shame-and-honour culture, where power was value and where people with more of it were more valuable than others, the Scriptures entered and turned society on its head. With the Bible came the idea, for the first time, that every human being is without gradations, an equally valuable image-bearer, worthy of fair treatment. With the Bible came the idea that morality is essentially about considering the wellbeing of the other, especially the downtrodden. And so, with the Bible, love and humility began to triumph over brute power for the first time ever. It is perhaps not surprising then, that so many great social reformers—Gandhi, Martin Luther King Jr, Nelson Mandela, Bishop Tutu, and the first Suffragettes—built their case for change in part on the teachings of Jesus.

These ideas did not come about during the enlightenment, as some suggest—they came about centuries before as the biblical worldview slowly soaked its way into the societal fabric of the world around it. Indeed, society's current passion for upholding human rights and protecting the marginalized has its conceptual roots firmly in Scripture, even if many activists and citizens do not realize this.

Whether or not one holds to its teachings, there's no denying the Bible's unrivalled impact on our world. Given its expansive reach and centuries-old proliferation, any truly open-minded person should at least give it a closer look before discarding it.

Not only has it had the furthest reaching impact, its significance has also been deeply personal for millions across the globe and the centuries. Let's explore this kind of personal impact now.

---

[2]Source: www.bit.ly/3lnnCfl (accessed 07/20)

5

A LIFE-CHANGING BOOK

As a teenager, I already suspected that the Bible had impacted *the* world, but I only began to regard it highly when I experienced it changing *my* world. Some critics of the church in its earliest years complained that the message the church believed "turned the world upside down."[3] From my perspective however, it turned my world the right side up. I am not alone in this conviction; it has done so for millions of others in at least four ways:

It Points You To Jesus

The Bible is not a book about heroes, but rather one Hero. As Martin Luther said, "Scripture is the cradle in which Christ lays." Like him, millions of others attest that they first encountered Jesus when they read the Bible. The Old Testament, written before his coming, is a red-carpet timeline laid out in prophetic anticipation of his arrival. The four Gospels describe his life, ministry, teachings, death, and resurrection. The rest of the New Testament reveals how the story of Jesus begins to spread further into the world and deeper into lives.

In the Bible, Jesus is the One to whom all roads lead. Scripture is the true *Route 66* to Jesus– or *66 Routes*. Start with any of the 66 books of the Bible, and you will find that each is a road that finds an onramp to the One who calls himself The Way.

It Reads You As You Read It

Multitudes attest that this book has had unparalleled power to awaken them, to startle them to life as it were. One explanation for this is that the Author of Life, who claims to have not only inspired the words you read but breathed you into existence too, is present with you as you read his words—breathing new life upon you as you do so.

The high point of the Bible's meta-story, the resurrection of Jesus, is also the key to understanding the power of Scripture: its central hero and author is alive—speaking into lives through the very words that

---

[3] Acts 16:7

tell us about him, by the very power that raised him from the dead.

A popular story circulates on my continent. It is often cited to explain Africa's positive reception of the Scriptures. It tells of an African woman who carried her Bible with her wherever she went. When people would ask her why, with so many other books to read, she answered, "It's the only book that can read me."[4]

Kethoser Kevichusa, an Indian theologian, tells of a Bible he was given before he came to faith. "For long, it just sat there," he said, "dead to me and me to it." Then one day, after hearing the gospel, he picked it up and began to read. "And then—it was different! Not unlike a piece of rock that suddenly comes to life, or a Labrador that suddenly begins to appreciate Beethoven, the miracle of Christ suddenly made me alive to its truth, beauty, and goodness. I was now alive to him as he was to me. I could not put the Bible down, reading it, marking it, clasping it, crying and singing with it."[5]

It Comforts, Fortifies, and Changes You

When life's calamities and complexities come crushing down upon you, when society's clashing viewpoints and clamouring demands churn around you, the Bible promises to be an unchanging true north, to give you a spiritual spine and an anchor to keep you from shipwrecking.

When God speaks, things happen. When we receive his words into our core, they "generate life, create faith, produce transformation, cause miracles, heal hurts, build character, transform circumstances, impart joy, overcome adversity, defeat temptation, infuse hope, release power, cleanse our minds, bring things into being, and guarantee our future forever."[6]

---

[4] S.V. Davidson, J. Ukpong, G. Yorke: 2010, "The Bible and Africana life" in *The Africana Bible*, Fortress Press, 40.
[5] https://bit.ly/2P8bqFe (accessed 02/2021)
[6] Quoted text adapted from Rick Warren: 2002, *The Purpose Driven Life*, Zondervan, 237.

It Invites You Into The Greatest Story

Some people think of the Bible as a disjointed patchwork of individual stories and other kinds of materials—memoirs, songs, discourses, and genealogies for example. In reality, like a string of precious pearls, each story masterfully holds together in a beautifully interwoven macro-narrative.

Though written by authors on varying continents in different epochs, it moves forward, each stage building upon the one before—creation, collapse, covenants, Christ, cross, church, consummation.

Of course, with a cast of thousands scattered over thousands of years, *it's clearly not a simple story*. But, see, that is what adds wonder and weight to the plausibility of its claimed supernatural orchestration.

What makes J.R. Tolkien one of the best authors of all time? Sure, there's a storyline of rings lost and found, Hobbits small sent out on quests large, fellowships created and dismantled, darkness rising and shadows growing, a ring finally destroyed and Middle Earth saved. Yet what makes Tolkien *great* is the way he creates "thousands of pages of narratives, poetry, articles, maps, and even lexicons over the course of decades"[7] through and upon which his story unfolds.

Taken as a whole, the Scriptures are the greatest story told by the Greatest Storyteller. This time the story is real—not imagined. Heaven's Tolkien weaves together a vast cast of real-life actors and thousands of surprising twists and turns, that move forward like a great tributary-fed river, growing larger and larger as it goes, all the while heading in one direction toward an epic, plot-resolving climax.

Most remarkably, as we read the story, we find that we are not merely bystanders. Instead, we each get swept into that eternal river. We become participants, each of us one more tributary, our small story connecting to that larger Story. Like no other book, millions of its readers attest to how the Scriptures possess a unique power to sweep them into the grandest of stories—one that is still being written.

---

[7] Quoted text from a 2015 Timothy Keller article, *The Story of the Bible: How the Good News About Jesus Is Essential*, www.bit.ly/3molS7j (accessed 09/20)

AN EDIBLE BOOK

Since I was 15-years-old, I have had only one hobby. Surfing. Though I live by the sea, this year because of the Covid-19 lockdown, I did not get to gaze upon the azure ocean for months. The more I longed to see it and paddle out into its waves, the more I also grasped just how much I had taken it for granted before. In the months before lockdown, I had passed by numerous opportunities to enjoy it, telling myself, "It's there and I'll get around to it… tomorrow."

Come to think of it, I have done the same with Scripture too many days of my life; becoming overfamiliar with the treasure in my possession. "It's there and I'll get around it to… tomorrow."

My fading wonder regarding the Bible becomes evident to me when I meet or hear of people whose appetite for Scripture far surpasses mine. There's the writer of Psalm 119, the longest chapter in the Bible, for example. Just this morning I read some of it with my children. Line upon line it spirals round and round a single theme: the Word of God, which it variously describes as God's statutes, precepts, word, teaching, instruction, decrees, promises and laws. When I asked my kids which verse they liked most, my oldest child selected, "My soul is filled with longing for your word at all times."[8] Another chose, "I delight in your decrees. I will not neglect your word."[9] As I mused over the combination of their choice of verses, it dawned on me: to neglect God's Word is to deprive my own soul of a deep relish only it can give.

There's also the story of a bomb victim, an American soldier in World War 2, who lost his hands and eyesight in an explosion. Yet his deepest grief was that he could not read the Bible anymore, for this was the book that had carried him through every smaller trial that had preceded this one. Then he caught wind of a potential solution. He heard of a woman in England who read a braille Bible with her lips, He tried the same, only to find that there was not enough sensation left on his lips. After much trying, he made a surprise discovery when *his tongue*

---

[8] Psalm 119:20
[9] Psalm 119:16

accidentally touched some raised characters. It worked! He could feel the braille with his tongue. He managed to read the whole Bible four times over like this, devouring every word as if it truly was his daily bread.[10]

There's simply no other book that carries the same power to sweeten and sustain a life. So says Scripture itself. I have found the best way to increase my hunger for it is to review its promises about itself, which often come in the form of *stunning metaphors* about the life-transforming contents of the book. For the remainder of this chapter I will explore seven of them:

A Revitalizing River

As we delight in and ponder its words, we are "like a tree planted by streams of water, which yields its fruit in season and whose leaf does not wither." [11] John of Damascus back in CE 740, while commenting on this verse, urges us to "draw from the fountain of purest waters in the perennial garden" where we can "luxuriate on the Scriptures which possess inexhaustible grace."[12]

Picture a tree planted by a river. Now imagine one planted in the desert. Which is more sturdy and fruitful? This is the spiritual difference between someone who draws wisdom from God's Word every day and the one who forfeits this privilege.

A Guiding Light

God's "word is a lamp to my feet and a light for my path."[13] It also sets our hearts ablaze. Peter the apostle describes the Old Testament prophetic Scriptures about Jesus like this: "You will do well to pay attention to it, as to a light shining in a dark place, until the day dawns and the morning star rises in your hearts."[14] God's word has the power to

---

[10] Source: Robert Sumner: 1969, *The Wonder of the Word of God*
[11] Psalm 1:2
[12] *De Fide Orthodoxa*, translated as *An Exact Exposition of the Orthodox Faith, Book 4, ch 17.*
[13] Psalm 119:105
[14] 2 Peter 1:19

light up the path we tread as well as the horizon up ahead.

Holistic Medicine

"Pay attention to what I say; turn your ear to my words. Do not let them out of your sight, keep them within your heart; for they are life to those who find them and health to one's whole body."[15] So says Solomon, the wisest man of his day. We moderns tend to fragment our health into physical, psychological and spiritual categories. The Bible not only presents a more integrated vision of our health and wholeness, it presents itself as a three-in-one physician, counselor, and pastor.

A Sharp Blade

The Scriptures are likened to a sharpened scalpel in the hands of a skilful surgeon, cutting out spiritual and moral cancers from our lives: "For the word of God is alive and active. Sharper than any double-edged sword, it penetrates even to dividing soul and spirit, joints and marrow; it judges the thoughts and attitudes of the heart."[16]

It is also a military sword, offering us protection from the onslaught of darkness and deception, and enabling us to set the captives free: "Stand firm then, with the belt of truth buckled around your waist … take the helmet of salvation and the sword of the Spirit, which is the word of God."[17]

Seed and Rain

God's Word carries new life and new possibilities in itself. In Jesus' own words, the Bible is life-giving seed[18] when humbly accepted and planted in our hearts.[19] As it is sown in our lives, wonderful things begin to happen. What does seed need to thrive?

Rain.

---

[15] Proverbs 4:20–22
[16] Hebrews 4:12
[17] Ephesians 6:14–17
[18] Mark 4:3,9,13–14
[19] James 1:21

In the same way, God's Word not only plants the life of God in us, it causes the life already planted in us to flourish. Now listen to God's astounding promise through Isaiah's voice:

"As the heavens are higher than the earth, so are my ways higher than your ways and my thoughts than your thoughts. As the rain and the snow come down from heaven, and do not return to it without watering the earth and making it bud and flourish, so that it yields seed for the sower and bread for the eater, so is my word that goes out from my mouth: It will not return to me empty, but will accomplish what I desire and achieve the purpose for which I sent it."[20]

According to Isaiah's prophecy, the words of God not only nourish the living seed already lodged in our lives—they span the distance between heaven and earth, *between God's mind and ours*, bringing immense life and revelation with them. They are the very means by which heaven invades earth.

A Foundation in the Storm

The Bible especially stabilizes us during hardships. Jesus teaches us that knowing his words, and building our lives upon them, is the secret to endurance in testing times, and hope on the darkest of days. He says, "Everyone who hears these words of mine and puts them into practice is like a wise man who built his house on the rock."[21] Much better to do that, says Jesus, than to send down one's foundation into the sand of transient values, only to come crashing down in the storms of life and future judgment.

After my children each selected their verse from Psalm 119 this morning, the verse I chose, the one that became luminous to me as I read it, was, "I have suffered much; preserve my life according to your word."[22] As I prayerfully think it over during this day, the message God gives me through it is that his Word will not only sustain me in the storm, it will carry me through the storm to a brighter future. This has

---

[20] Isaiah 55:0–11
[21] Matthew 7:24
[22] Psalm 119:107

been true to my experience for decades now—during the loss of loved ones, the dashing of dreams, through every financial and relational challenge, God's Word has given me the strength and perspective I have so desperately needed. Or as yet another passage affirms, "through the endurance taught in the Scriptures and the encouragement they provide, we ... have hope."[23]

Food for Our Soul

The Bible is edible, apparently. It is bread for our souls[24]—substantial, sustaining, satisfying—without which, we cannot fulfill our purpose. It is milk, meat and honey[25]—a three-course meal; containing the ideal nourishment for every stage of our spiritual development. Job could say, "I have treasured the words of his mouth more than my daily food."[26] In a vision, God instructs Ezekiel, "Son of Man, eat this scroll I am giving you. Fill your stomach with it." The prophet tells us of his obedient response and great surprise: "So I ate it, and it tasted as sweet as honey."[27]

What a tragedy then that, with more Bibles in print and on screens today than ever, the world and even many Christians are so spiritually malnourished.

In the 8th century BCE, the shepherd Amos prophesied about:

"A famine in the land, not a famine for bread or a thirst for water, but rather for hearing the words of the Lord. People will stagger from sea to sea, from the north even to the east, going to and fro to seek the word of the Lord, but not find anything."[28]

Read Amos' words carefully—the problem is not the *absence* of God's Word, but their (and our) unwillingness to *hear* it. The Israelites had rejected the prophets in their midst who delivered God's Word to

---

[23] Romans 15:4
[24] Matthew 4:4
[25] 1 Peter 2:2, 1 Corinthians 3:2, Psalm 119:103, Ezekiel 3:3
[26] Job 23:12
[27] Ezekiel 3:3
[28] Amos 8:11–12

them. Today we run the same risk. Though it is within reach, we fail to listen to it. We opt instead to seek light and truth in all the wrong places—from so-called experts or the latest philosophical trend. As exciting as new insights may be, they are a poor substitute for God's words.

Today's spiritual famine is the insanity of having a nearby storehouse filled with grain, a Bible or a church where the Bible is preached, yet we choose to look anywhere and everywhere else for food. Amos says Scripture-starved people *zig* this way and *zag* that way, staggering like a drunk person, kept distracted and disorientated throughout their entire quest, only to come up still empty and lost at the end.

If we truly desire spiritual health and vitality, feeding daily on God's Word is as beneficial and necessary as food is for our physical health. This is powerfully portrayed in Exodus 16, where God leads the rescued Israelites across a desert and supernaturally feeds them. Every morning God would pour out a bread-like substance called *manna* on the ground. "It was white like coriander seed and tasted like wafers made with honey."[29] God instructed the Israelites to each gather as much as they needed.[15] But there was one major condition: they were only permitted to take what they needed for *that single day.*[30]

After 40 years of eating manna, Moses preached to the desert-survivors about its meaning: "God fed you on manna *so that you might know that man shall not live on bread alone, but on every word that comes from God's mouth.*"[31] This is the passage of Scripture Jesus, when tempted, had been feeding and thinking upon. He knew what we must all know: God's Word does for our souls what bread does for our bodies: it sustains and it nourishes.

God still provides manna today. Yet, like the ancient Israelites, we too must discover that his manna does not fall into our mouths nor does it have a very long shelf life; we must go and gather it—each and every day. As we do so, we can expect the Word we ingest to metabolize into the energy we need to live a God-empowered life.

---

[29] Exodus 16:31
[30] Exodus 16:19, 16:21
[31] Deuteronomy 8:3

2

THE HUMAN-DIVINE BOOK

All Scripture is God-breathed.

2 Timothy 3:16

I personally had no interest in the Bible until a friend of mine introduced me to Jesus. Smitten by Jesus, I wanted to know everything I could about him. The Bible seemed to be the best way.

For most of us who come to trust the Bible's divine inspiration, we do not trust in Jesus because we first trust the Bible. Rather, we trust in the Bible because we *first trust in Jesus* who (as we are about to see) most definitely trusted the Bible.

JESUS' VIEW OF SCRIPTURE

The Scriptures, says Jesus, are God's words. Consider his wilderness fast. He is at his most vulnerable and Satan accosts him, trying to tempt him three times. Each time, Jesus counters his line of attack. Not by ignoring nor by out-arguing the fallen angel but by wielding the sword of the Spirit: "It is written… it is written… it is written."

His first defensive swing is to quote words given to a hungry people in a wilderness some 1300 years prior: "People shall not live on bread alone, but on every word that comes from God's mouth."[1] Notice that the three passages that Jesus quotes were written by Moses, yet Jesus

---

[1] Matthew 4:4, Deuteronomy 8:3

says they come "from God's mouth." So does Jesus simply overlook human instrumentality in the creation of Scripture? For that we go to another interaction of Jesus in the Gospels...

The Scriptures, says Jesus, are in people's words. On another occasion, he refers to Psalm 110, written by David a millennium before. He asks some of his critics, "Whose son do you think the Messiah is?"[2]

They think they know the answer: "David's."

Jesus corrects them, "But David, speaking by the Spirit, calls him 'Lord', so how can he be his son?" In this moment, he not only outmaneuvers these men but also articulates his understanding of Scripture as *human words in tandem with God's Word.* Or as he says: "David, speaking by the Spirit."[3]

Psalm 110, says Jesus, is "David speaking." It is human words. Yet notice the qualifying phrase: "by the Spirit." In Jesus' view, the Bible is not merely human words. It is not David speaking from his experience, or reaching some genius level of consciousness or creativity. It is also not merely God's words, as though David passively dictates or channels what he hears God telling him. Jesus' words are deliberate—he does not say, "The Spirit, speaking through David." No, when David writes or speaks Psalm 110, his whole personality is at work, his full agency is at play, but he does so "by the Spirit."

So we conclude from Jesus' statements that Scripture is *God's words through human words, yet also human words through God's words*—the human and divine meeting together in the co-crafting of Scripture.

ONE COMPOSER, MANY MUSICIANS

Spoken words result when breath passes over vocal cords. Athenagoras of Athens (born in CE 133) wrote, "Moses, Isaiah and the other prophets wrote things with which they were inspired, the Spirit making use of them as a flute-player breathes into a flute."

---

[2] Matthew 22:42
[3] This idea drawn from Andrew Wilson: 2014, *Unbreakable: What the Son of God said about the Word of God*, Kindle, ch 2.

Yet even this beautiful analogy overlooks *the variety* of instruments that make up the Scriptures. In comparison, the Quran, which Muslims believe is entirely the direct dictation from God to just one man, is a solo performance over a period of years. The Bible however is a *symphony*, in which each human author is a different instrument in the divine orchestra. One is a violin, another a horn, another a snare drum. Yet somehow, one heavenly conductor guides each of them in harmonized unity, across multiple centuries and continents. One Artist working through many artists, each of whom participate actively in their offering, each doing so distinctively, yet collectively creating something so wondrous and momentous that only a cosmic composer could have conceived of it in the first place.

Indeed, the 35 or so writers of the Bible's composite books were very different from one another. Consider Moses and John. Moses, an Egyptian prince-come-shepherd, compiled the book of Genesis in 1300 BCE in the Sinai wilderness. John, a fisherman-come-apostle, wrote his Revelations in CE 95 from the Isle of Patmos.

The Spirit did not bypass the biblical writers' level of education, culture, personality type, unique setting, vocabulary or writing style, but rather used each author's unique voice to write their unique portion.

Interestingly, in Christian theology the Bible's human-divine nature is not the only mysterious marriage of the divine with the human...

FULLY DIVINE AND FULLY HUMAN

If you are new to Christian theology, then I proudly announce one of its sweetest tenets: as unfathomable as this may sound, Jesus was fully human *and* fully divine *at the same time.*

As we read the Gospels, we bounce back and forth between the human and divine attributes of Jesus. Consider these verses:

"Waves swept over the boat. But Jesus was sleeping. The disciples woke him... he got up and rebuked the winds and the waves, and it was com-

pletely calm. The amazed men asked, 'What kind of man is this?'"[4]

One moment, Jesus is bone-tired in a boat, he is just like one of us. But the very next moment, he awakens and commands a violent storm to be still. Stunned along with the disciples, we must ask, "What kind of man is this?"

For here is a man who is clearly human, but apparently also divine.

But see, it's the same with our reading of the Bible. One moment we read how "the word of the Lord came to Jonah"[5] and the next moment, Jonah is rebelliously sneaking off in the opposite direction on a cruise liner of sorts. One moment we may uncover an ancient culture or story that feels so oddly out of step with our own, and in the next, God is speaking to our culture and story through it and we ask, "What kind of book is this?" For here is a book that is clearly human, but apparently also divine.

Generally, we tend to notice one of these aspects more than the other. For example, an early heresy called *Docetism* claimed that Jesus was too divine to truly take on human flesh. He only *appeared* to be human, hovering above the ground as a spirit being, so to speak. This heresy has spilled over at times into the church's perception of the Bible. It is tempting to underline only its divine elements, and bleach out (in our reading of it) its human elements.

So before we unpack the Bible's divine side, let's spend some time coming to terms with its human side.

THE BIBLE'S HUMAN SIDE

It is understandable that skeptics would deny the Bible's divinity, yet I find it curious that believers sometimes swing full pendulum to the other side and deny the Bible's humanity. I understand why: we fear that noticing these elements will somehow undermine the Bible's divine elements, perhaps eclipsing the possibility of its divine inspiration.

---

[4] Matthew 8:24–27
[5] Jonah 1:1

But as we are about to uncover, the human side does not destroy the concept of the Bible's divine inspiration. Rather, it beautifully enriches it in at least five ways:

Human diversity

Firstly, the Bible beautifully showcases human diversity. God's love for variety is shown in his visual creation—the red-lipped batfish, the thorny devil lizard, the poodle moth, and the Japanese spider crab. Isn't it just like God, then, to employ all manner of writers to compose his book—Joshua a military general, Daniel a prime minister, Amos a shepherd, Luke a doctor, and Nehemiah a cupbearer.

The 35 writers each have their own histories. Some of their life experiences may have similarities, but they are so different in the details. For example, both Jonah and John Mark fail in their mission at first, but one is consequently spat out of a fish while the other is kicked out of Paul's ministry team. Both Jeremiah and Paul are lowered by ropes, but the former drops into a make-shift cistern-prison while the latter escapes arrest by dropping down a city's wall.

They differ in personality types, local dialects, and cultural customs too. Some write in Hebrew, some in Greek. They possess a diverse range of preferred mediums—poetry, songs, parables, proverbs, psalms, sermons, sagas, letters, laws, visions, and lamentations. Some write with ecstatic joy, others with cutting sarcasm, and still others, with stoic reflection or heart-wrenching angst. Some are mesmerizing storytellers, others scrupulous chronologists. Some pride themselves on having lawyer-like logic, while others radiate raw emotion onto the page: bitter grief, zealous passion, or justice-seeking outrage.

Unaware Authors

Secondly, the Bible's divine inspiration may have been hidden from the biblical writers. In the same way God is with us whether we feel his presence or not, many authors may have been completely oblivious to the fact that they were writing Scripture. As David reflected on his shepherding days and wrote his song-prayer about the Lord as his shepherd, did he know that he was writing Psalm 23? As Luke wrote his biography of Jesus for Theophilus, or Paul wrote to the storm-tossed Timothy, did they know that these writings would one day form part of the New Testament? And even those who may have been conscious of writing Scripture surely had no idea how their writing would ultimately fit into the bigger tapestry that would come to be the Bible, as we know it today.

Unpolished Writing

Thirdly, the Bible's inspiration does not require polished or sophisticated writing. Although Isaiah, Luke, and the unknown writer of Hebrews were highly educated and wrote what they did with an extraordinary command of language and grammar, many of the authors were not as skilled. Hosea, an ancient farmer, writes like you would imagine an ancient farmer would—his grammar is so untidy that some of what he says is almost impossible to understand. John, a simple fisherman when Jesus called him, writes his Gospel with a vocabulary of only 360 words.

Even Paul, the brilliant mind educated before his conversion under the leading Jewish teacher of his day, Gamaliel, did not try to create literary masterpieces. Though he knew classical Greek, he used the more colloquial version in his writings. He is even forgetful at times. Once he tells a community that he only baptized two of them, then remembers that he also baptized a few more of them, then admits he can't remember who else he baptized.[6] Another time, he interrupts himself and shoots off on a tangent: "For this reason I, Paul, the prisoner of Christ Jesus for the sake of you Gentiles—Surely you have heard about the administration...'[7] He only comes back to his original train of thought some twelve verses later!

Far from undermining the evidence of divine inspiration, the fact that the Bible's writers and scribes did not perfect their writing or affect their speech points not only to their integrity and authenticity, but

---

[6] 1 Corinthians 1:14–16
[7] Ephesians 3:1–2

to God's commitment to human instrumentality despite all of its limitations. Only God could take such a diverse range of writings and still create a macro-narrative that demonstrates breathtaking, divine cohesion.

The Good, the Bad and the Horrid

Fourthly, the Bible's inspiration records it all. Over and above prophecies and anointed teachings, all kinds of voices are included—the speeches of Job's friends[8] which are riddled with theological error, numerous dumb things Jesus' disciples say, a letter by a pagan king,[9] a line from a poem by Aratus written to Zeus,[10] even the serpentine lies of Satan.[11]

Far from a collection of sugarcoated stories, the Bible does more than tell us how the world *should* be. It tells and reveals to us how twisted and broken the world really is—and in so doing shows why it needs the very redemption of which it speaks.

Consider the brutality of men against three biblical women: David's daughter, Tamar is raped by her brother;[12] Jephthah's daughter is sacrificed because of her father's ill-taken vow, all the while, her father blames her for his violence against her;[13] and most heinous of all, in the book of Judges, an unnamed woman is gang raped, murdered, and dismembered—an event which leads to the capture and rape of 600 more women.[14] I will come back to the significance of this particular story in a few pages time.

Imperfect Recipients

Fifthly, the Bible's divine inspiration does not require worthy recipients. Though some parts of the Bible are written for future generations and

---

[8] Job 4–23
[9] Daniel 4
[10] Acts 17:28
[11] Genesis 3:1–5, Matthew 4:3–9
[12] 2 Kings 13
[13] Judges 11
[14] Judges 10–21

to inspire the honest seeker,[15] most of the New Testament is written to people who are getting it horribly wrong. Just as well, perhaps otherwise much of the New Testament would not have been written at all. As examples, many biblical scholars think it took Paul's unjust arrest to motivate Luke to write Acts as a defense document. It took the Corinthian church's arrogance, disunity, sexual immorality, broken marriages, irrational worship, and despicable treatment of the poor for Paul to pen his first letter to them. In fact, Paul writes 11 of his 13 letters[16] specifically to deal with problems in churches.

Sinful Authors

Sixthly, the Bible's inspiration does not necessitate morally perfect writers. Contrary to adapted children's Bibles, the Bible is not a book about moral heroes. The authors of most ancient historical books tended to aggrandize themselves and the kings they wrote about, covering over failings. The Bible does not do the same: Moses cowers and vents; David takes another man's wife, then that man's life; Jonah rebels and hides; and Peter denies and flees. Far from the norm of inflating a nation's kings and military conquests, *1 and 2 Kings* honestly surveys 39 Jewish kings, with only eight coming up relatively clean. There's no propaganda here.

Perhaps therein lies the Bible's power. God makes it clear that the Bible's real hero is Jesus, its only sinless person, who rescues everyone else—imperfect writers and readers alike.

NAVIGATING THE HUMAN ELEMENTS

In all this—the diversity of writers, their unpolished writing, their personal flaws, and error-filled quotes—we must learn to do four things as we grapple with the Bible's human elements:

Refuse a simplistic understanding of biblical inspiration. Many believers have gone through needless crises of faith, by adopting a sim-

---

[15] John 20:31
[16] Only Ephesians and Romans may be the exceptions.

plistic idea about what inspiration is, then when they stumble upon these human elements, they doubt whether God really inspired the Bible at all. God's condescending to speak to us through other people, not via angels or direct dictation, does not negate the Bible's divine inspiration. Rather, it confirms it.[17]

Marvel at the miracle of God's grace. That God brought his fully human, fully divine Son into the world through an ordinary, imperfect young girl is one of the two great miracles in which divine life merges with humanity—*the miracle of incarnation.* The other is that he brought a fully divine, fully human book into the world through ordinary, imperfect authors—*the miracle of inspiration.* In both cases, God draws a straight line with skew sticks.[18] That's not only a miracle, that's grace.

Do not treat every passage as a direct utterance from God. Depending on the part of the Bible we are referring to, the term, "The Bible says" does not always mean, "God says." When I train Bible teachers, I tell them that as they explain certain passages, sometimes it is better to simply say, "David writes" or "Paul says" or "Satan said" or "the pagan king Nebuchadnezzar wrote," not always "God says", or even "the Bible says," if people will merely assume this to mean, "God says".

Ask why God included each part in the Bible. God weaves each part of the Bible into his unfolding drama of redemption. Only within that larger script, can we then ask the question, "What might God be teaching us by including this particular passage or book in the Bible?"

For example, there are powerful insights that come from contemplating why God would include lengthy genealogies in both Testaments.[19] Or consider the previously mentioned stories of the brutalized

---

[17] Bible teachers talk about the Bible being "infallible" which is true if by that we mean "fully reliable" or "as God intended it"—but not if we mean anything that leans towards "straight out of heaven" or "devoid of human elements." We will return to the Bible's truthfulness in chapter 10.

[18] The German Reformer, Martin Luther, first penned this phrase, saying, "God can use a crooked stick to draw a straight line."

[19] Many a Bible reader will simply jump over these strange parts of the Bible filled with tongue-twisting names. Yet when we ask why—in light of the larger story of the Bible—God includes these lists of names, some helpful insights emerge. For instance,

women in Judges. When we look at them in the scope of the entire biblical story that precedes and follows, much light is shed:

First, we look back from Judges to the first garden, to the first man who was instructed to protect not prey upon the first woman. In so doing, these small stories magnify how far human society, and even God's people at their worst, may fall from God's intended purpose— and we are then confronted with gender-based violence in our own day. One theology professor writes about these texts: "We will listen, how ever painful the hearing until there is not one last woman remaining who is a victim of violence."[20]

Then looking forward to Jesus, these stories serve as a backdrop to Jesus' treatment of women—his ground-breaking elevation of women, and the fact that he is the Heavenly Spouse who dies for his bride, and the Risen Christ who privileges a woman first to spread the good news of his victory over death. In so doing, he lays out a new path for both men and women.

A DIVINE BOOK

Though many believers may try to ignore the fact of its human side by hiding behind its divine side, many skeptics may conversely try to dismiss Scripture's divine side by hiding behind its human side.

Instead, having appreciated its humanity, let us now consider its claim of divine inspiration. Most of Scripture was not divinely dictated, yet it is permeated, 3,000 times in the Old Testament alone, with expressions like "the Lord said…" or "The word of the Lord came to…"[21]

---

that God cares equally about history, and about the individuals it was comprised of. We may not be interested in these ancient people, but God knows each by name, as he does you and me. By examining genealogies, we can also more fully appreciate how God uses imperfect people to fulfill his purposes. In Jesus' bloodline recorded by Matthew, there's Jacob the thief, Rahab the prostitute, David the adulterer and Solomon the idolater. Indeed, Jesus' genealogy highlights a complex, far-from-perfect family identity, just like each of our own.

[20] Nicola Slee: 2006, *Praying Like a Woman*, SPCK, 36–37.

[21] See Exodus 4:10–15, Deuteronomy 4:2; Jeremiah 1:7–9; Ezekiel 3:4 for example.

And if Jesus is divine, as he claims, then all his words are divine too. Likewise, the New Testament writers, commissioned by Jesus to pass on his teachings, also claim to speak God's Words. For example Paul writes, "This is what we speak, not in words taught us by human wisdom but in words taught by the Spirit, explaining spiritual realities with Spirit-taught words."[22] And Peter says, "I want you to recall the words spoken in the past by the holy prophets and the command given by our Lord and Saviour through your apostles."[23]

Still, the question remains, what of all the *other* parts of the Bible that do not claim to be the very voice of God? The answer comes in 2 Timothy 3:16: "*All* Scripture is God-breathed." The writer of Hebrews also reflects on Scripture as "God speaking in various ways."[24] Apparently, God likes to speak to us through his own words, but also through the words of others' too—through historical accounts, poems, prayers, stories and more. God has something to say to us in every part—from the parts where an author says, "Not I but the Lord give this command" right through to the parts which say, "To the rest, not the Lord but I say…"[25] The Bible is not a motley mix of divine inspiration and human utterances—with God's words here and human words there. No, all of it is human, and all of it is divine.

Although we may not know exactly how this process of inspiration worked with each author and book, we *do* know that the same Spirit who hovered over creation as it was taking shape and who overshadowed Mary as baby Jesus was conceived, also rested upon the mind and hand of each author as they wrote…

"Above all, you must understand that no prophecy of Scripture came about by the prophet's own interpretation of things. For prophecy never had its origin in the human will, but prophets, though human, spoke from God as they were carried along by the Holy Spirit."[26]

---

[22] 1 Corinthians 2:13
[23] 2 Peter 3:2
[24] Hebrews 1:1
[25] 1 Corinthians 7:10,12
[26] 2 Peter 1:20–21

THE BIBLE'S POWER

In a later chapter, we will consider how we come to discern the divine inspiration and thus trustworthiness of Scripture, outside of its own claim to be divinely inspired. But for now, let's consider that the concept of the divine inspiration of Scripture is not forced upon you, rather it is unveiled to you—a gift some people receive all at once, while for others, a little at a time.

I have a friend who did not believe the Bible was divinely inspired, but the more he read it and heard it preached, the more he came to believe it was. He said to me:

"Whenever one preacher would quote a Scripture and declare, "God says," I would take note of the preacher's bias and remind myself these were the words of ancient people, not God. But as I listened to the Scriptures being read and preached, I was struck time and again by the power in the words. I would find myself accepting that perhaps those few words were inspired by God, and on the next occasion, those too, and so on. After I had suspected this about enough passages in the Bible, I finally accepted that perhaps all of it is inspired by God."

My friend is not alone in his discovery. I have had the joy of seeing it happen again and again in open-minded people (and some close-minded people too). As a pastor, I sometimes have gently suggested to seekers and skeptics that they embark on an experiment:

"Jesus might not be God's Son, and the Bible might not be God's book, but then again, both of these claims just might be true. What if you were to commit to read a book or two in the Bible, say the Gospel of Luke then the book of Acts, and pray a simple prayer as you do? Something along the lines of: 'God, if you are there and Jesus is your Son and the Bible is your book, would you show me?'"

Discovering Scripture as the voice of God is just the beginning. No sooner have you realized *whose* words these are, then you begin to experience their supernatural power. This is because God's words do not merely express his ideas. They are conduits of his divine power. As the theologian Michael Horton so eloquently puts it:

> *"God speaks a creative word and the world exists; a word of judgment and life withers; a word of redemption and faith is born; a word of forgiveness and sinners are absolved; a word of new life and the dead are raised."*[27]

This is why Scripture is so good at changing not only our minds, but also our very hearts and lives.

And then going beyond merely bringing about a new state of affairs, it has the power to also *sustain* the difference it makes. As the Psalmist writes: the God who "sustains the humble" is also the One "who sends his command to the earth; his word runs swiftly ... (and it) melts (the ice and snow) so that the waters flow."[28] Our life, already unfrozen by the power of his *creative* word, now gushes forth, moment by moment, with divine energy by the power of his *sustaining* word.[29]

THE BIBLE'S AUTHORITY

I know of very few words that cause such a visceral reaction in my generation as the word "authority." Many of us are terrified and mortified that anyone should be allowed to tell us what to believe, and how to live. Having drunk in my surrounding culture's devotion to self-autonomy with my mother's milk, I understand the reaction.

Yet at some point we need to realize how immature and self-sabotaging this culture-wide reaction is. If indeed there is someone who knows better than we do, and cares enough about us to let us know, surely we would be fools to block our ears. A child who does this every time a parent gives an explanation, warning or instruction is bound to experience a lot more pain and unnecessary hardship than the child who listens to those who love him and know better than he.

---

[27] Michael Horton: 2013, *Pilgrim's Theology*, Kindle location 2386.
[28] Psalm 147:15,17-18
[29] Likewise, Hebrews 1:3 tells us that Jesus "holds all things together by his powerful word."

With God's parental love in mind, let's consider the nature and consequences of our resistance to God's authority in Scripture.

But did God *really* say?

The first strategy of Satan, whom Jesus calls the Father of Lies, to corrupt the human race is revealed in Genesis' third chapter. He whispers to Eve, "Did God *really* say?"[30] With both the goodness of God and his prior revelation to Eve now in question, Satan goes on to suggest that she is in fact perfectly capable of figuring things out for herself. You likely know the story: she falls for his so-called logic, distrusts God's heart, casts aside God's revelation, and pays for it *dearly*. Though Satan promises her freedom, he delivers bondage instead. Enticed with the promise of eyes that will truly see, Eve bites into forbidden fruit—only to discover that her spiritual vision becomes horribly distorted. Scales like cataracts grow and with them, confusion, anxiety, shame and fear.

The story is not all depressing though. Despite her failure, God declares that one day Eve's descendant will overcome the Liar. And he does! When Satan tempts Jesus, he uses the same tactics he used on Eve: "If you *really* are the Son of God…"[31]

Notice the duplicate use of the word "really" to Eve and Jesus: make no mistake about it, his goal is always to warp our perception of what's real, true, right, good, and beautiful.

This time however, Satan's target does not become Satan's victim. Eve's descendant *does not* take the bait. Instead, he crushes the serpent's lies by believing his Father's word, not Satan's. Where does he find words that wield such serpent-crushing authority? In Scripture alone. Three times Jesus replies, "It is written."[32]

The Truth That Sets You Free

Unlike Eve, Jesus stands on his Father's words, because he trusts his Father's heart. And by doing so, he shows *us* the way to liberty too.

---

[30] Genesis 3:1
[31] Matthew 4:3 and 4:6
[32] Matthew 4:4,7,10

Elsewhere Jesus says that as we embrace his revealed truth, we will enjoy his gift of freedom.[33] "Who the Son sets free is free indeed!"[34] Tragically, in the age of self-sovereignty that pervades Western culture, we have hungrily sought our freedom *in exactly the way Eve first lost hers*—instead of looking up to our Father on his throne, we distrust him and defy him, appointing ourselves to the throne, and looking within to our own desires, intuitions and preferences. This self-magnifying experience might create a momentary sense of euphoria, like the child who stumbles into a house of mirrors and discovers their endless reflection staring back at them, but seeing ourselves from every angle is not in fact as liberating or enlightening as we imagine it to be. If Eve's experience is anything to go by, we are left *more* spiritually blinded, not less, and more enslaved to the dark power of deception in the process.

Take heart weary friend, hope remains. In his victory over the Deceiver, Jesus shows us how "to stand firm in the freedom we have"[35]— not by assuming the autonomous role of arbiter of reality, but by lending our ears to God so that he can lend his eyes to us.

The Compass to Reality

In our attempts to comprehend reality, the authority of God in Scripture is a critically important factor for each of us to resolve. We will be tempted to find truth based on *anything but* God's inspired revelation as found in the Scriptures, but only God's Word, when properly understood, provides us with authoritative truth and ultimate reality.

We do not merely navigate by the commands God has given us. We live by the compass he has revealed. Accurately interpreted, the Bible is the one, true story, or compass of reality with four sequential points that act as our coordinates: creation, fall, redemption, and restoration. Creation is the answer to the question of why we exist. The fall is the answer to what is wrong with the world. Redemption is God's solution

---

[33] John 8:32
[34] John 8:36
[35] Galatians 5:1

to the problem. Restoration is the promised future we redirect our lives towards.

This four-point story of God at work in history serves as the compass points by which we can navigate all ethical decisions as well as critique the ways various cultures orientate to whatever false magnetic north that has taken them captive.[36] As Ellen Davies says, "Scripture's story is not a part of some larger narrative; it is itself the larger narrative of which all other true narratives are parts."[37]

Reason, Tradition, Culture and Experience

I do not want to create the impression that all we need to understand the world and make decisions is the Bible. We also have capacity for reason, the depth of conviction stored up in our church tradition, the insights generated by our experiences, and the surrounding cultural viewpoint in which we find ourselves.

But, though each of these can bring a meaningful contribution to our decision-making processes, they should only serve as junior conversation partners—the final say must be rooted in a firmer foundation. After all, each of us must humbly concede that our reason may be based on faulty arguments, or wrong or missing data. Traditions may be misguided relics. Experiences vary from person to person. And cul-

---

[36] When we speak of the authority of Scripture we do not merely mean that its commands are final, but that its story is the true story of the world, a story that definitively guides our perspectives, priorities and choices. Not wanting to confuse you, I must add that the four compass points of creation, fall, redemption and restoration are held together with a little bit of complexity, which I will try to articulate here: The story is that God made our world, which fell with humanity's failure, so that we now find ourselves in an age where evil, Satan and death prevail. God promised to redeem the world in and to the ancient nation of Israel, a promise that was wonderfully fulfilled in the coming, life, death and resurrection of Jesus, who launched the future kingdom age in the midst of this one. Though we live in the overlap of the future kingdom age and the present evil age, Jesus will return to bring the present evil age to an end, and the future kingdom age to its full blossoming when all will be restored. Already now the people Jesus calls (aka the church) are beneficiaries, citizens, ambassadors and agents of the future age. Simply believing this story goes a long way in determining how we live, even if no commands were given.

[37] *The Art of Reading Scripture*, iBooks, ch 2.

tural views come and go.[38]

In contrast "every word of God is flawless"[39]—the wisdom it provides is timeless. Its statutes and storyline still point to true North.

Though Scripture may sometimes undergird a prior assumption, conviction, ideology, or worldview, very often it may do the opposite—overhauling them entirely. Not just our understanding of what's right and wrong, or of what's illusory and real, but also even more importantly, God's Word has a way of upending our safe, tame and lame misunderstandings about God himself. Yes it comforts, but it is not always a comfortable book. Since the God of the Bible cannot be tamed, trademarked or boxed, it should come as no surprise that from time to time, those that seek to live on his words might find their lives and viewpoints interrupted, challenged, even shattered. Indeed, God's Word may at times break down our misconceptions and misalignments, only to rebuild us, this time the right way up.[40] In the process, we will also find the true liberty that is given to those who let God be God, and let his Word be final in their lives.[41]

---

[38] Church historians sometimes quip that when a church marries the present spirit of the age, it is soon enough made a widow in the next. Whilst Western culture's popular ideas of what's important, right and true change rapidly, our faith and convictions should not. Much better for the church to be Christ's messenger than culture's cracked mirror.

[39] Proverbs 30:5

[40] In Jeremiah 1:10, this is how God described Jeremiah's ministry of the Word.

[41] As an example of this "liberty," in his twenties, Billy Graham struggled with doubts about the Bible's authority. One night on a hilltop, he fell to his knees and told God: "If your Word says it, I believe it. That settles it." Though he would make more sense of God's Word as time passed, from that day on, his life and ministry was blessed with unusual power.

3

GOD'S SELF-REVELATION

In the past God spoke to our ancestors through the prophets at many times and in various ways, but in these last days he has spoken to us by his Son, whom he appointed heir of all things, and through whom also he made the universe.

Hebrews 1:2

How can we know God? Sure, God's Word plays a critically important part. But let's step back for a moment and appreciate how Scripture is only *one* aspect of God's self-revelation.

GOD CHOOSES TO REVEAL HIMSELF

It is very difficult to know a person unless they speak their thoughts. Take my relationship with my wife, Julie. As lovely as she was to look at, what made me really fall head over heels for her was getting to know the kind of person she was. To find that out, I listened to her words. The more I listened to her, the more of her I knew, and the more of her I loved.

When it comes to knowing an unseen, transcendent God, it's near impossible to know what he is like, unless he speaks. Thankfully, though God's dwelling is on high and he inhabits eternity, a realm we cannot access,[1] he has not been silent. In the opening chapter of the

---

[1] Isaiah 33,5; 57:15; see also Ecclesiastes 5:2

Bible, God speaks—bringing creation into being. Journey further into the Bible, and we discover that he *keeps* on speaking. Wonderfully, "he who forms the mountains, who creates the wind and treads on the heights of the earth..." also "reveals his thoughts to humankind."[2] Likewise, this chapter's leading verse states that, "God spoke through the prophets ... and has spoken to us by his Son."

But how does God make himself known? And how do we tend to respond to it? If in my previous chapter, I explained to you the tenet of Christian belief that affirms the human-divine nature of Scripture, in this one I will elaborate *the tenet of God's self-revelation and how that fits in with Scripture.* If you are new to Christian theology, you might find some of these concepts a bit abstract, but hang in there. Knowing this is crucial if you are to understand all of what makes the Bible so amazing.

Let's start with God's general self-revelation. The universe itself whispers and sometimes shouts out the immensity, power, creativity and intelligence of its Creator: "The heavens declare the glory of God, and the sky above proclaims his handiwork. Day after day they pour forth speech, night after night they reveal knowledge."[3] Paul concurs with the Psalmist in his letter to the Romans: "His invisible attributes—his eternal power and divine nature—are evident in what he has made."[4] Behind creation, there is a Creator. Looking up at the full moon last night, I saw and heard as much.

According to Paul, even the daily joys and provisions of everyday life point to a good God. To a pagan audience he boldly declares that, "God has not left himself without testimony: He has shown kindness by giving you rain from heaven and crops in their seasons; he provides you with plenty of food and fills your hearts with joy."[5] Behind goodness, there is a good God. As I contemplate the joy of a recent family lunch, that is obvious enough to me.

---

[2] Amos 4:13
[3] Psalm 19:1–2
[4] Romans 1:20
[5] Acts 14:17

Even our consciences, fallible as they may be and as shaped by our upbringing as they are, reflect that we have been made in the image of a righteous God. People who have never even heard the Scriptures, says Paul, "show that the requirements of the law are written on their hearts, their consciences also bearing witness."[6] By his argument, behind our moral sense, there is a moral God. His point seems true to me as I think of people who have flagrantly lived without reference to God, now on their deathbed pouring out confessions of dark secrets. Why is this? "As God created the universe, he left an imprint of himself upon it. Human beings, created in his image, are able to discern that imprint."[7] This is one reason that almost all cultures throughout human history have assumed the existence of a powerful deity or deities before whom they are accountable.[8]

Still following?

Now let's think about our general self-delusion. In the next two chapters, as we survey the biblical story, the theological tenet of *humanity's sinfulness* will make more sense. For now, allow me to simply state Paul's teaching on the matter: the fallen human race does not happily come to this knowledge of God's imprint on creation and claim to authority over them. Instead, we tend to resist the reality, leadership, and even the goodness of God. Speaking of fallen humanity, Paul writes, "By their unrighteousness they suppress the truth...

---

[6] Romans 2:15. This verse reveals that it is not only our upbringing and culture that etch a sense of right and wrong into us—the divine hand has inscribed not the entirety but at least something of God's own valuing of truth, justice and beauty upon the hearts of each image-bearer. This gives some explanation as to why almost all people, regardless of their faith or lack thereof, still value morality and ethics.

[7] Michael Bird: 2013, *Evangelical Theology*, Zondervan, Kindle location 3791.

[8] I am not arguing that there are not other reasons for the universal belief in God or gods, such as attempts in prescientific cultures to make sense of what science had not yet explained. Yet ignorance about science has never been the only reason for believing in God—there is in the human experience an intuitive readiness to do so, which is Paul's argument. I have heard many an atheist argue that "deep down inside you already know there is no God." Yet the sheer number of people (85% of the world's current population) who continue to believe in God, most of whom have access to scientific knowledge, attest to the exact opposite. Ask them and most will say that deep down inside, they always knew there was a God.

although they knew God, they neither glorified him as God nor gave thanks to him, but their thinking became futile and their foolish hearts were darkened."[9] Instead of thanking and worshipping God, we become entitled and worship created things. Yet we are, says Paul, "without excuse."[10]

Therein lies the rub—although creation points us to God's greatness, our failure to truly perceive God's glory and worship him accordingly points to how far we fall *short* of his glory, and thus how great our need for his mercy really is.

It turns out, God's general self-revelation in his creation and our conscience is not enough. Somehow the message of redemption is hidden from the vast galaxies, majestic mountain ranges and even the inner voice of our own heart. To hear it, to really hear it, we need God to make it known to us by other means.

This brings us to the best part of all: God's special self-revelation. God as mighty Creator is obvious enough, yet God as our personal Saviour is completely hidden from view. The Greek word for "reveal" (*apokalypto*) means, "the unveiling of something hidden." Human wisdom, especially one that is shaded over with spiritual blindness, can never of its own accord grasp what can only be known through God's unique and supernatural revelations. In essence, for us to experience true enlightenment and spiritual illumination, God himself must switch on the lights.

THE SIX LIGHTS OF GOD'S SPECIAL REVELATION

"The secret things belong to the LORD our God, but the things revealed belong to us and to our children forever, that we may follow all the words of this law."[11] We cannot comprehend God *completely,* for there are "secret things" which he has not revealed, but we can know him *very well* nonetheless. This is only because there are "things re-

---

[9] Romans 1:18, Romans 1:21
[10] Romans 1:20
[11] Deuteronomy 29:29

vealed." He has made himself known and know-able.

In fact, there are six lights of special revelation, all related to Scripture in some way, which combine together to pierce the darkness:

Revelation in History

The first light is that God revealed himself by speaking and acting in history. The Christian faith is not based on some philosophical seeker's abstractions. It is based on God's actions and words into a time-space world—most notably, the open sea of the Exodus, the open tomb of Easter, and the open heaven of Pentecost. Each of these events, and many more in the Bible, record the historical, revelatory acts of a transcendent God who chooses to reveal himself to a transient people and world. For example, Peter, writing about Jesus, says: "We did not follow cleverly devised stories when we told you about the coming of our Lord Jesus Christ in power, but we were eyewitnesses of his majesty."[12]

On this point, of all the things God said and did in history, one so surpasses them all that it deserves its own category of revelation:

Revelation in The Son

The second light is that God revealed himself by sending his Son. When the writer of Hebrews says that, "God spoke to us by his Son" they do not mean that Jesus merely *had* a message for us. No, he *is* the message incarnate. He does not merely speak the Word of God. He *is* the Word of God.

When the apostle John tries to describe God's greatest act of revelation, he does not write that the Word became a book. Rather he says, "The Word became flesh."[13] God's main gift to the human race is not a book, but a Person.

For those 33 years on earth, Jesus was (and continues to be) the living, breathing revelation of God, the most sublime and brightest of the special-revelation torchlights. He is God with skin on: God in the flesh.

---

[12] 2 Peter 1:16
[13] John 1:14

His embodied presence with us as a Palestinian Jew from Nazareth surpasses even the revelation of Scripture, for he is the direct, unmediated communication of God. Scripture is a sacrament and signpost to God, but Jesus is the substance and destination.

Revelation via Prophets and Apostles

The third light is that God revealed himself by calling prophets and apostles to witness to and interpret these acts of God. Before the time of Jesus, God spoke the defining interpretation of his acts "through the prophets at many times and in various ways." Abraham was the first prophet, then Moses. Other prophets follow after: Samuel, Deborah, David, Elijah, Elisha, Micah, Amos and many more. These prophets declared what no historian or social commentator of the day could have surmised—how the Exodus was not merely a migration of refugees but instead, God delivering a huge biological family of slaves and making them his very own people—in two places calling them, "my son."[14]

Centuries later, Jesus commissioned the apostles to teach others what he had taught them and to impart the defining interpretation of his identity, life, death, and resurrection. Just like the prophets of old, they saw beneath the historical events and were given eyes to perceive their deeper significance; preaching that the cross was not merely an unjust political execution, but a God-ordained sacrifice that would make it possible for slaves of sin and death to become his very own sons and daughters.[15]

The point is that, though the prophets and apostles speak about historical events like the Exodus and the resurrection of Jesus, they do not merely describe history. Rather they are enabled by the Spirit to give "prophetically interpreted history."[16]

---

[14] Exodus 4:22–23; Hosea 11:1
[15] Galatians 4:7
[16] I get this term from Oscar Cullman: 1962, *Christ and Time*, SCM, 100. A good analogy of this is a Christian sharing their "testimony" of God's work in their life. They point to actual events in their lives, but then interlace them with commentary of God being at work using words like, "God answered my prayers" or "I now realize the rea-

Many of the words and deeds of these prophets and apostles are lost to history, but by God's design not all were…

Revelation as Scripture

The fourth light is that God revealed himself in the writing of Scripture. For forty years, manna fell daily upon the ancient wilderness, disappearing like mist within that day. Yet God selected a sample of manna that apparently was divinely preserved in the golden ark of the covenant.[17]

This is a good analogy for Scripture. Not all prophets and apostles wrote Scripture. From Moses to Malachi, God spoke through prophets, some of whom wrote the books that make up our Bibles (such as Isaiah and Nahum) while others only spoke and did not write for God (such as Elijah and Elisha). The same can be said about the apostles. All preached and ministered, but only a few wrote letters (such as Matthew, John, Peter, and Paul) or authorized others to write (Peter likely commissioned Mark, and Paul did the same to Luke).

Still, like the sample of manna supernaturally preserved, enough of the prophets' and apostles' writings have been preserved so that the church is "built on the foundation of the apostles and prophets, with Christ Jesus himself as the chief cornerstone."[18] The Bible is God's choice words—kept for all generations like manna in the ark. These words are God's chosen foundation upon which every church is to be built.

Revelation through Preaching

The fifth light is that God continues to reveal himself by sending anointed preachers and teachers. God's plan was never merely to publish a book. The early church delivered to the world not only the words of Scripture, but also the words of preachers and teachers. Throughout most of history, people have first discovered the Bible to be God's

---

son God allowed this to happen was to show me that…"

[17] Hebrews 9:4

[18] Ephesians 2:20

Word not initially by reading it, but by hearing someone else who had read it preach its core message with God's accompanying power.

Contemporary preachers and teachers do well to learn from the first century ones, whose *priority* message was the gospel of Jesus Christ.[19] In the same way that God's highest revelation was the sending of his Son, so the leading edge in the preacher's swing of the blade is always Jesus Christ the Son of God and Saviour-king. Paul asks, "How can people believe in the One of whom they have not heard? And how can they hear without someone preaching to them? But faith comes from hearing the message... the word about Christ."[20]

Revelation by the Spirit

The sixth light is that God reveals himself by opening the hearts and minds of people who hear and read the gospel and the Scriptures. This is sometimes called divine *illumination*.

Jesus, the incarnate living word, was hidden in plain sight to most people. "He was in the world, and the world was made through him, yet the world did not know him."[21] Yet God has opened the eyes of many to see who he truly is, both while he lived on earth[22] and as the gospel has been preached ever since.[23]

In the same way, the Scriptures are the inspired written words of God in our midst regardless of whether we recognize them as such. Nonetheless, revelation reaches its goal only when we do—thankfully, God's Spirit can give us this recognition.[24] This is why, as we read and hear the Word, we pray, "Open my eyes so that I might see the wonderful things in your Word."[25]

In summary, these six torches can be grouped into three main movements of God's self-revelation:

---

[19] Romans 1:16, 1 Corinthians 15:1–3. Additional references are given in the footnotes of this book's final chapter.
[20] Romans 10:14–17
[21] John 1:10
[22] John 1:12
[23] 2 Corinthians 4:4–6
[24] Michael Horton: 2013, *Pilgrim's Theology*, Zondervan, Kindle location 4031.
[25] Psalm 119:105

The first movement: in torches one–three, he revealed himself in history through his words and deeds, through prophets and apostles, and supremely through his Son's incarnation. This is a past revelation, something that happened back then.

The second movement: in torches four–five, he revealed himself by orchestrating and inspiring people to write down and then preach the sample of all this which he deemed of lasting importance. This revelation is past-to-future.

The third movement: finally, in torch six, he continues to reveal himself in the hearts of people everywhere as the gospel and the Scriptures continue to be read and preached. This is a present revelation.

Now notice that each of these three movements are anchored in the Bible. In the first, the Bible records the past revelatory acts and deeds of God. In the second, the Bible not only records these revelations of God, but is also inspired by the Spirit and so is a revelation in itself. In the third, we find that we need more than the Bible to see what is in the Bible, we need the revelatory work of the Spirit. Pulling all that together:

- The Bible *records* revelation.

- The Bible *is* revelation.

- The Bible *needs* revelation.

The question I want to answer now is what this all means in terms of *what the Bible is.* There are at least three remarkable implications about Scripture in light of the reality of God's self-revelation:

A Top-down Book

The Bible is not the result of humanity reaching up to God, but God reaching down to us.

One famous philosophical argument against the claim of God's self-revelation in Scripture is the analogy of an elephant surrounded by three blind men trying to make sense of what is in front of them. One touches the side of the elephant and thinks the animal is a wall. One grabs hold of its tail and thinks the animal is a rope. Another grabs hold of its ear and determines that it is a banana leaf. Many people contend that each of these blind men are right in their own way, they are just restricted to their place in time and space, and to their limited experience and knowledge. The argument therefore is that the Bible (and indeed any truth claim) only captures the particular religious and spiritual experiences of some in history, and is hardly the whole picture of God.

Perhaps compelling on first hearing, this argument is fatally flawed on closer inspection. First, these men were all objectively wrong, not partly right. Second, by God's grace, we are not blind. The Scripture writers were given eyes to see what is really there, as we are given eyes to see what has been written. Third, the bigger problem with this analogy is that it assumes that the Bible writers were merely groping about to make sense of reality and God.

The truth is that God revealed himself of his own initiative. Through Isaiah, he said, "I revealed myself to those who did not ask for me; I was found by those who did not seek me. To a nation that did not call on my name, I said, 'Here am I, here am I.'"[26] The authors of Scripture were not intellectual giants, enquiring philosophers or spiritual sages operating on a higher wavelength who then discovered God as a reward for their diligent search. Rather God revealed himself, usually to unwilling and always undeserving people. The prophets and apostles were mostly rebels and ordinary people going about their lives when God called them. In most cases, they responded to this call not with immediate delight, but with a sense of unworthiness, distress, and trepidation.

The Product of Revelation

The Bible is not the product of our reason, but God's revelation.

Reason is a God-given faculty. "It is the glory of God to conceal a matter, and the glory of kings to search the matter out."[27] This verse written by King Solomon, a student of philosophy and a documenter

---

[26] Isaiah 65:1
[27] Proverbs 25:2

of a great variety of plants and animals, commends the intellectual and scientific quest to study and understand the material realm which God created. Some of this data lies on the surface for all to see and grasp, but much of it is only attained by centuries of accumulated enquiry. For example, only three millennia later would Einstein discern one of God's underpinning codes scripted into his creation, namely $E=MC^2$.

Still, as wonderful and noble as scientific discovery and exploration is, it has its limits. Limited to the physical realm, we cannot use the scientific method to verify anything that is metaphysical—the existence of God for example, or a spiritual realm, or the after-life, as well as the mind of God and the meaning of our lives and the universe. The opening verse of the Bible, "In the beginning God created…" cannot infallibly be proven or disproven by science. It is revelation. And whilst science can use reason to conclude, by current calculations, that 15 billion years ago the *Big Bang* happened, it can never calculate *why* it happened. (Or if there was or was not—excuse my term—a *Big Banger* who initiated the bang.) For that, we need revelation.

Even if science and philosophy *can* infallibly prove the existence of God (and many argue that it can and does), these fields of enquiry cannot tell us what *kind* of a God he is. Without revelation, if we are honest, the best we can do is follow what some Athenians did in the first century—worship an altar inscribed "to an unknown God."[28] Indeed, if God does not reveal himself, we can have no real idea of what God is like.

With regard to material things, the scientific method says that reason should precede faith. But when it comes to metaphysics, the order is reversed. "By faith we understand that the universe was created by the word of God."[29] Indeed, we cannot reason our way to faith using science, rather by faith we can begin to make sense of the meaning of life. We do not reason or do science in a vacuum of complete spiritual ignorance. Revelation is the God-given starting point upon which we reason.

---

[28] Acts 17:23
[29] Hebrews 11:3

A Particular Book

The Bible gives dignity not only to the universal truths, but also to the particular realities.

Many skeptics balk at the idea that God would identify with a particular place (ancient Israel), a particular person (Jesus) or a particular book (the Bible). But God does not factor in our preferences when he reveals himself.

It is true that God is *universally* in reach: "He is not far from any one of us. For in him we live and move and have our being."[30] Wherever we are, there is God. But this universal accessibility does not undo the importance of his *particular* self-revelations in time and space.

This unfathomably large and universal God has always been comfortable, apparently, pinning himself to the particulars—whether choosing one random moon-worshipper to become the father of his chosen people, or one brick-and-mortar location on Mount Zion to be his temporary house, or one Palestinian teenager's womb to knit his earthly body together, or a motley crew of 12 young men to be his representatives, or 35 authors to write the composite parts of a single book in their particular languages of Hebrew, Aramaic and Greek.

Again and again, the cosmic God selects a particular time, a particular people, a particular place in creation—all this fits squarely with a God whose mind is a trillion times greater than all other minds nevertheless publishing his secrets in one particular book, the Holy Bible. That's just part of what makes Scripture so amazing.

---

[30] Acts 17:27–28

4

THE BIBLE JESUS READ

For everything that was written in the past was written to teach us, so that through the endurance taught in the Scriptures and the encouragement they provide we might have hope.

Romans 15:4

Each of my children has a bookshelf in their room with a growing collection of books. Some of them have their own Bible on their shelf. It fascinates them when I tell them that the Bible is not a book, rather it is a mini-library of books within their mini-library. It was originally a collection of papyrus scrolls, I explain. The word Bible comes from the Greek word *Biblia* meaning "The Books." Only in the 13th century did the name "The Books" became "The Book," now hiding the fact that it is a collection of books.

Lately, I have been trying to explain to my kids that the Bible is not only a book filled with books, *it is a story filled with stories.* It includes hundreds of stories and yet all of them hold together in a larger story.[1] As I will show you in this chapter and the next, this larger story has at least fourteen stages: seven in the Old Testament and seven in the New.

Let's look at the Old Testament first. It details the story of God as it

---

[1] "The Bible is not, for a start, a list of rules, though it contains many commandments of various sorts and in various contexts. Nor is it a compendium of true doctrines, though of course many parts of the Bible declare great truths about God, Jesus, the world and ourselves ... Most of its constituent parts, and all of it when put together can best be described as story." N.T. Wright: 2011, *Scripture and the Authority of God*, HarperCollins, 24.

relates to ancient Israel. Perhaps a better name for it is *The Hebrew Bible,* because calling anything "old" suggests it is outdated or irrelevant, and nowhere does the New Testament describe it like that. This is, after all, the Bible Jesus read, memorized and pondered for decades—apart from which we cannot understand either Jesus or his mission.

Since its 39 books are not arranged chronologically, it can be difficult to piece together. The best way to make sense of it all is to understand where each of these books fit within the larger seven-stage story it tells:

STAGE 1: CREATION AND THE FALL

(PRE-2000 BCE)

In *Genesis 1-2,* the story starts with a glorious, unfallen creation in which God blesses a piece of real estate: our planet and, in particular, the Garden of Eden in it. He entrusts the garden and earth to Adam and Eve, the appointed overseers of creation who exist to love God, serve each other, and steward the rest of creation, eventually spreading Eden out into all of it. Short as this section is, its contribution to the storyline of Scripture is massive, for everything after it treats this first era as the stage being set for God's later redemptive drama, and also as the blue print of God's highest intentions for creation and humanity.

Sadly, in Genesis 3 a deceitful snake-like creature ensnares our first parents to distrust God and dethrone him from their lives. As they succumb to this temptation, a curse falls on the creation and the couple. Yet there is a glimmer of far-off hope—God promises that a future descendent of Eve will overcome this same deceiver.

Separated from the source of life, Adam and Eve are exiled from their idyllic garden into a hostile wilderness. Instead of living for God, loving their neighbour and stewarding all of creation well, humanity turns away from God and buckles in on itself—leading self-centered, self-sabotaging lives. Things go from bad to worse. Cities are built and tyrannized by violence and oppression. God's heart is broken. The known world is flooded. A family survives on an ark and a tower rises and falls in the city of Babylon.

Four major biblical themes emerge in this first stage:

- *Creation*—God makes a good world in a vast universe, which he plans to bring to its full potential.

- *Humanity*—We are made with the dignity of being God's image-bearers who are to reflect his good character. As his vice-regents, we are to enact his good reign and spread Eden into God's good earth.

- *Presence*—God's original plan is for heaven and earth to be the same place and for his divine presence to permanently and fully dwell in our midst. The fall of humanity splits the two asunder.

- *Salvation*—Though our corruption calls forth God's condemnation, he makes a promise to one day rescue those who trust in the serpent-crushing seed of Eve.

STAGE 2: THE PATRIARCHS

(2000–1700 BCE)

Genesis 12–50 outlines the stage wherein God creates a new family and gives them a new promise. Having left Eden, humanity's back is turned from God. Yet God still pursues us. He calls yet another couple, Abraham and Sarah to leave Babylon for a garden-like land they do not yet know. He promises that they and their offspring will be blessed and bless the world. From their son, Isaac, comes Jacob who fathers 12 sons, who father families that will eventually become the 12 tribes of Israel. Joseph, Jacob's favourite and second last son, is sold into slavery by his brothers, only to rise to power in Egypt. This is fortuitous as God guides him to stave off a famine in the region, and to provide for and preserve his brothers in the process. Looking back over this multi-generational story, our hopes for a better kind of humanity to emerge are dashed—every generation is as bad as the former (or worse). They lie, steal, hate, and nearly kill each other. The curse remains.

Three biblical themes manifest:

- *Gracious calling*—As Abraham discovers, we do not initiate or deserve any kind of relationship with God; as he did to Abraham, he still does to us. He calls us by grace, awakening our faith as a response to God's kindness and initiative.

- *International blessing*—Local as God's dealings may be, he promises Abraham, Isaac and Jacob that he will bless the entire world through their descendants.

- *God's sovereignty*—As Joseph learns, God can use even the terrible, unjust things that come upon his people to move his purposes forward.

STAGE 3: THE EXODUS AND DESERT JOURNEY

(1480–1400 BCE)

Centuries pass and God powerfully delivers, through Moses, this same family from slavery in Egypt. Now the populous Jewish people, he leads them toward the Promised Land. *Exodus, Leviticus, Numbers* and *Deuteronomy* tell this stage of the story. He confronts Pharaoh, sends ten plagues, and through the blood of a Passover lamb and the parting of the Red Sea, frees hundreds of thousands of Jewish slaves.

Then at Mount Sinai, God enters into a covenant partnership with his newly liberated people. He gives them 613 laws (including the ten commandments). Detailed over 2,000 verses, these laws set out to guide the Jewish nation in civil, ceremonial, and moral matters. At the heart of their worship henceforth will be a priest-run tabernacle or temple: the place where God's presence dwells. Yet despite all God's spectacular redemption and revelation, these people fail miserably and repeatedly to trust God. Four bitter decades spent circling around the Sinai desert follow, until almost all of the first generation of those led out from Egypt have died. With the Promised Land in view, Moses repeats the law one last time, then dies.

During this stage, four biblical themes surface:

- *Redemption*—By the blood of the lamb and by the powerful destruction of their enemies, God makes powerless slaves his free people.

- *The tabernacle/temple*—Like in the Garden of Eden, this is a place where heaven and earth fuse; a place where God's manifest presence dwells.

- *The sacrificial system*—Priests mediate between an ungodly people and a holy God by offering sacrifices.

- *Law-code*—God expects his people to live and abide by a set of laws that will make them distinct from the surrounding nations.

STAGE 4: THE PROMISED LAND

(1400–1050 BCE)

The books of *Joshua* and *Judges* narrate this stage. Picking up the reins from Moses, Joshua (who meditates on Scripture day and night) leads the Jewish people to finally enter the Promised Land. Little by little, they drive out the inhabitants and settle in as a loose federation of 12 tribes. But the shadow of sin and rebellion remains. Though initially obedient, they soon fall away from God just as the generations before them did. Becoming a law unto themselves, they then come under oppression from various pagan tribes, at which time they call on God who sends local deliverers or judges—Deborah, Gideon, Samson, and eight others. No sooner are they rescued, when they revert to their old ways again. Amidst this seemingly hopeless cycle, the book of *Ruth* offers a bright light of personal redemption. It tells of a non-Jewish woman who not only joins Israel's family but plays a crucial part in it: for she will be King David's great grandmother.

Three biblical themes come clear in this stage of the story:

- *Inheritance*—Though God's deliverance is entirely the work of God, he gives his people the promise of a Promised Land, something they will only enter as they actively and faithfully partner with God.

- *True worship*—Echoing Israel's earlier worship of the golden calf, God's people have a tendency to worship the idols of the surrounding people, idols that bring needless pain into their lives.

- *Deliverance*—Again and again, God sends unlikely saviours to rescue his people from their oppressors.

STAGE 5: THE MONARCHY

(1050–930 BCE)

The Jewish people demand a king "like the other nations." *1 and 2 Samuel, 1 Kings 1–11* and *1 Chronicles* tell the story of how a loose federation of tribes becomes a single political nation under a king. After warning them of the danger of exploitation, God complies with their demands and directs Samuel, the greatest of the local judges, to appoint Israel's first king: Saul, who devolves into a self-serving narcissist.

Samuel then secretly anoints David for kingship. This makes David a target for the threatened and insecure king Saul. David lives on the run and survives the manhunt. Once Saul is killed in war, David quickly gathers the tribes under his throne that he sets up in the capital city of Jerusalem. Better than Saul, David is nonetheless no saint—we watch his success-burdened character and family come undone. Many lives are ruined in the process. Nonetheless, God now adds to the two covenants already made to Abraham and Moses, a third: one of David's sons will eternally bless and rule the world in peace and justice.

The kingdom passes on to Solomon, who takes David's nation-building achievements to their zenith in this golden period of Israel's history. He packs away the tabernacle and builds a temple for God, something David only ever dreamt of doing. Then just as we wonder if Solomon is the one God had promised, he starts to worship false gods.

Flashes of godliness, faith, and wisdom aside, in all this we see that all earthly kings and even some prophets are susceptible to the same sins and rebellions of ordinary men: they lie, cheat, kill and worship idols—replaying their ancestors' failures over and over again.

Two biblical themes come into view in this stage:

- *Jerusalem*—God's plan is not only to put his people in a garden, but in a city. This speaks not only of a new humanity, but a new society too.

- *Kingdom*—God's plan is to provide a king in David's lineage who will eternally reign over his people for their blessing and for the blessing of the whole world.

THE WISDOM BOOKS

In this fifth stage of the story, the monarchy, five other books are written. Some scholars call them the Wisdom Books, others, the Poetic Books. They are full of imagery and are mostly written using the poetic device of two-line parallelisms.

Job is a poetic story about a good man who suddenly loses everything and must grapple with why bad things happen to good people. Without much help from his clueless friends, he learns that even in the confusing mess of life, God is still in reach, in charge and more than able to restore. We do not know for certain *when* Job was written—it makes no mention of Israel or its wider context.

Then there are the *Psalms*, 150 poetic prayer-songs, about half of which were written by David. They began to be compiled to guide Israel's enjoyment of and dependency on God through the triumphs and traumas of life.

Proverbs is a collection of life wisdom. Its opening verses say it well: "The proverbs of Solomon, king of Israel: for gaining wisdom; ... for receiving instruction in prudent behaviour, doing what is right and just and fair."[2]

Ecclesiastes is Solomon's poetic philosophy, an attempt to make sense of the world merely from an earthly point of view, only to show the futility of doing so without God: "'Meaningless! Meaningless!' says the Teacher. 'Utterly meaningless! Everything is meaningless.'"[3]

Song of Songs starts with, "Let him kiss me with the kisses of his mouth—for your love is more delightful than wine."[4] It is a collection of love poems, an unbridled and unblushing celebration of the heart-racing and sexual chemistry between a man and a woman.

At least three major biblical themes are evident in these five books:

- *Creativity*—As image-bearers of the Creator God, we utilize our imaginations not only our rationality as we worship, reflect, communicate, and create.

- *Faithful suffering*—Job's articulated suffering and over half of the Psalms, the prayers of lament, give voice to heartache on the road of trusting God.

- *Holistic spirituality*—God is interested in every aspect of life and how we live it: how we wrestle with suffering (Job), pray to God in desperation, trust or joy (Psalms), guide our children and leaders to live wisely (Proverbs), grapple with life's absurdity and complexity (Ecclesiastes) and indulge in sensual love (Song of Songs).

STAGE 6: DIVISION AND CAPTIVITY

(930–586 BCE)

1 Kings 12-22, 2 Kings and *2 Chronicles* tell this part of the story. The most complicated stage of Israel's history starts with a civil war that

---

[2] Proverbs 1:1–3
[3] Ecclesiastes 1:2
[4] Song of songs 1:2

occurs when Solomon dies, splitting the nation in two.[5] The Northern kingdom, with Samaria as its capital, consisting of 10 tribes, henceforth called Israel, and the Southern kingdom, with Jerusalem as its chief city, consisting of only two tribes, now called Judah. This stage spans 19 kings of Israel, all of which are corrupt, and 20 kings of Judah, only eight of which turn to God.

During this time God sends prophets in the mold of Moses to both the North and the South. In the North, the prophetic words of the authors *Hosea* and *Amos* and the wonder-working Elijah and Elisha all fall on deaf ears.

In the South, the preaching and writing of the prophets *Isaiah, Micah, Habakkuk, Zephaniah* and *Nahum* are more respected and received. The prophets warn that if the nation continues, by their idolatry, injustice, and immorality, to violate the covenant God had entered into with them through Moses, then, as he had originally stipulated, God will send an invading nation and take them into exile.

This is exactly what happens. In 722 BCE Assyria conquers the Northern kingdom,[6] leaving only Judah. All the exiled people of Israel are scattered throughout the Assyrian kingdom, never to return, making them "the ten lost tribes of Israel." The Southern kingdom hangs in there for another 136 years.[7] With only a few moments of spiritual revival (such as King Josiah's rediscovery of the Scriptures in 622 BCE) Judah's deep corruption means that it eventually succumbs to a prolonged invasion by the latest superpower, Babylon, which finally drags the Judeans into captivity in 586 BCE.[8] Now with centuries of persistent compromise in their blood, Abraham's family end up in the city they first began in.

Jeremiah's ministry and writing overlaps the years before and after[9] the Babylonian invasion. He watches God's people ignore his pleadings

---

[5] 1 Kings 12

[6] 2 Kings 17

[7] This massive time lag between the warnings and the doom is testament to a God who describes himself as "slow to anger."

[8] 2 Kings 25

[9] Before captivity: Jeremiah 1–24. After captivity has commenced: Jeremiah 25–52.

and pay for it. He is called "the weeping prophet." His book, *Lamentations* expresses the depth of his sorrow.

Both the prophets *Daniel* and *Ezekiel*, dragged as teens from their homeland, reach adulthood in Babylon and are called to prophetic ministries in the heart of darkness. Ezekiel's ministry is to the Jewish exiles, Daniel's is to a succession of pagan kings as their trusted advisor and administrator.

Five more themes crystalize during this stage:

- *Unity*—God's people are the strongest when they unite under the person God's selects to lead them, and weakest when they are divided by carnality.

- *Exile*—Echoing Adam and Eve's ejection from the garden, God's people learn that unfaithfulness to God can cause the loss of their God-given place in his world.

- *Mission*—The exiles are called to live in and influence corrupt pagan societies, by serving the common good while staying true to God and the revealed truth he has given them.

- *Prophets*—These men and women speak for God in the power of the Spirit, denouncing rebellion against God and the strong exploiting the weak, warning about the coming disaster and also catching glimpses of a future hope.

- *Kingdom*—Especially the prophet Isaiah sees a coming invasion, not by Babylon but by God himself, when a Moses-like prophet and David-like king will bring about a new exodus, a new kingdom, and a new creation. God will eclipse the present evil age with the coming kingdom age. Injustice and war will be eclipsed by justice, peace, and love of neighbour; the dark ignorance about God replaced by the shining light of God being known; oppression by salvation; guilt by forgiveness; sickness and brokenness by healing and wholeness; and distress and despair by comfort and joy. The nations will no longer oppress God's people but now flood in to pay tribute to their God and king. Death will be swallowed up, resurrection bodies will be given to all, and fallen creation will be revived and renewed.

STAGE 7: THE RETURN

(538–410 BCE)

Over fifty years after exile, when the Persian empire overthrows the Babylonian one, its king Cyrus releases the exiled Jews to return home.[10] The books of *Ezra* and *Nehemiah* tell the story. Many prophetic messages by *Haggai, Zechariah, Joel,* and *Malachi* are written down too.

Groups of exiled Jews return in three waves, led by Zerubbabel the governor, Ezra the teacher, and Nehemiah the administrator respectively. A smaller temple is rebuilt. The walls of Jerusalem are restored. Religious reforms are enacted. Many Jews, however, do not return. For example, the story of *Esther* tells of an exiled Jewish girl's marriage to a Persian king, just in time to foil a genocidal plot against the Jewish people still spread throughout the Persian kingdom.

Themes in this stage include:

- *The Spirit*—Echoing earlier prophets, Joel tells of a future lavish outpouring of God's immediate presence that gives speed to the nations calling on God for salvation: "I will pour out my Spirit on all people. Your sons and daughters will prophesy, your old men will dream dreams, your young men will see visions... And everyone who calls on the name of the LORD will be saved."[11]

- *Disappointment*—the people of Israel who started out centuries before with grand hopes of what they would become in themselves and in the world do not amount to much. When the smaller temple is unveiled, many who had seen the former temple burst out in tears. Nehemiah's final three prayers effectively

[10] 2 Chronicles 36
[11] Joel 2:28–32

amount to, "God, you know I tried with these people!"[12] The last prophet Malachi, in 410 BCE accuses the city's rebuilders of disobedience, arrogance, stinginess and the oppression of the weak. It ends with a strange promise of "the sun of righteousness rising with healing" and a prophet like Elijah to come before the Great Day of the Lord.

To conclude, there are at least seven stages that make up the bigger story unfolding over the entire collection of books that make up the Hebrew Bible (or Old Testament). In the second last chapter of this book, we will return to the major themes we've touched on in each of these stages:

Creation. Humanity. Presence. Salvation. Gracious calling. International blessing. God's sovereignty. Redemption. Sacrificial system. Law-code. Inheritance. Faithful worship. Deliverance. Jerusalem. Kingdom. Creativity. Faithful suffering. Holistic wisdom. Unity. Exile. Mission. Prophets. The Spirit. Disappointment.

These themes may seem a little fragmented for now, but they are in fact early signposts, pointing to something and Someone greater than all of them. Soon, they will find their center, converging like bicycle spokes on a single hub and axle. Then things will really get rolling.

---

[12] Nehemiah 13:14, 22, 29, 31

5

THE STORY OF THE NEW TESTAMENT

Fellow Israelites, listen to this: Jesus of Nazareth was a man accredited by God to you by miracles, wonders and signs, which God did among you through him, as you yourselves know. You put him to death by nailing him to the cross. But God raised him from the dead.

Acts 2:22, 24

If the Old Testament tells the story of God, ancient Israel and their failed witness to the surrounding world, then the New Testament tells the story of Jesus, the early church and their more successful witness to the world at large.

The New Testament starts and orbits around the identity and mission of Jesus, which is why we will start with the four Gospels. But in order to understand them, we must understand the political context into which Jesus was born.

BETWEEN THE TESTAMENTS: KINGDOM FEVER

In Jesus' time, Israel's hopes for the promised kingdom of God had reached fever pitch.

What history unfolded in the centuries between the Old and New Testaments? The late prophets had spoken of a new creation and new exodus, a delivering Messiah-king and the promise of the nations flooding in to worship their one true God at his new temple. Yet, despite the high hopes of the returning exiles for a land to call their own, the Jews found themselves under one oppressing regime after another.

The Greek emperor, Alexander, conquered Palestine and the surrounding areas (332 BCE), imposing Greek culture upon it, and leaving it, after his death, vulnerable to Egyptian (200–142 BCE) and then Syrian rule. Then in 167 BCE, a Syrian leader desecrated the Jerusalem temple by setting up an altar to Zeus in it. A successful military Jewish uprising under Judas Maccabee won a century-long, on-off independence for the Israelites who were then ruled by Maccabee's corrupt Jewish descendants.

The rising Roman empire, retaining Greek culture and gods, decisively put an end to Israel's autonomy in 63 BCE, when General Pompey marched into the Most Holy Place, saying mockingly that he found no God in there. Caesar stamped out Jewish uprisings and set up a brutal military presence to impose "order"—for example, when Jesus was a boy, the Romans crucified thousands of zealots near his home. Caesar crowned Herod in 44 BCE to rule and tax Palestine. Herod was a heartless, half-Jewish local warlord whom the Jews hated despite his attempts to win their favour by beautifully renovating their temple. This is the same Herod who executed his wife and three sons, and almost all infant boys in Bethlehem when he heard rumours that a Messiah had been born there.

Jewish scholar Joseph Klausner, writing in the 1920s, noted that in the centuries following their return to Judea, the devastated Jews failed to see the prophets' promises come to pass:

> "They experienced slavery to foreign governments, wars, tumults and torrents of blood. Instead of all nations being subject to Judah, Judah was subject to the nations. Instead of "the riches of the Gentiles," godless Rome exacted taxes and tribute ... Instead of the Gentiles "bowing down with their faces to the ground" and "licking the dust of their feet," comes a petty Roman official with unlimited power over Judea. Instead of Messiah the son of David, comes Herod."[1]

---

[1] Klausner, quoted in N.T. Wright: 2019: *The New Testament in Its World*, iBooks, ch

All of this to say: by the time of Jesus, the Jews desperately yearned for the Messianic kingdom (as they imagined it to be) to vanquish all pagan occupiers, and turn Jerusalem and its cleansed temple into the God-magnifying, nations-magnetizing, planet-renewing and history-rebooting seat of God's presence the prophets said it would one day be.

Like with the Old Testament story, the New Testament story can be divided into seven stages. To understand any part of it, we must know where it fits within the larger story.

STAGE 1: JESUS FROM BIRTH TO EARLY 30's

(6 BCE–CE 27)

After the birth of his cousin John in 6 BCE, Jesus is born in about 5 BCE[2] to a virgin, Mary, and his adoptive father, Joseph, in Bethlehem. The family soon flees to Egypt to escape the infant genocide ordered by Herod, who would himself die shortly after in 4 BCE. Herod's rule is divided up amongst his sons. Jesus' family then returns to a small town in the North of Israel, Nazareth in Galilee. 12-year-old Jesus mesmerises teachers in the temple on the tail end of an annual pilgrimage to Jerusalem, in which the Jews of all Palestine would swell the city from its normal number of 50,000 to about 150,000.

The oldest sibling of many others, Jesus is trained by Joseph to be a carpenter or stonemason and works in neighbouring Jewish villages and non-Jewish towns like Sepphoris, where an amphitheater for Greek plays is rebuilt. John the Baptist begins his ministry around the Jordan River in about CE 28, reaching his highpoint by baptizing Jesus, whom he accurately discerns as the Messiah. As Jesus comes out of the water, the Spirit descends on him in power, and then leads him into successful combat with the devil, launching him into his Messianic

6.

[2] Later historians proved an earlier historian to be wrong about his dating of Herod's death (and thus Jesus' birth), but only long after the dating of history had been reconfigured around the BC/AD date that we call year 0, at which time Jesus was already about 5.

ministry.

STAGE 2: JESUS' PUBLIC MINISTRY UNTIL DEATH

(CE 28–30)

The four Gospel writers record this time as the lion's share of their biographies. Like four artists interpreting the same subject from different viewpoints and with different styles, the Gospel writers render their distinctive takes on the same striking Jesus of history. Matthew and Luke absorb most of Mark's work—the three are called the Synoptic Gospels as they focus primarily on Jesus' work in Galilee. John's Gospel, written last, does not reference the earlier ones, instead focusing in on Jesus' work in Judea.

A harmonization of the four reveals at least seven phases between Jesus' baptism and his death:

- His first ministry in Judea[3]

- Setting up and launching his ministry in Capernaum, Galilee, which culminates in some murderous threats toward him[4]

- A second wave of Galilean ministry, which achieves enormous popularity for Jesus, ending in a trip to Jerusalem[5]

- The last days of ministry in Galilee and surrounding areas,[6] where he draws more opposition that leads him to be "on the run" avoiding capture, taking him and his disciples to Caesarea Philippi, where Jesus fully discloses to his disciples about his

---

[3] John 2–4
[4] Mark 1:14–3:6
[5] Mark 3:7–6:6a, John 5:1–6:1
[6] This phase includes his ministry to the Decapolis, the ten cities populated mainly by Gentiles. Though Jesus focused his ministry on the Jews, he anticipated through his brief ministry to them that the time would come when his gospel would go to all nations.

Messianic identity and path of suffering, and ministers to more people there[7]

- His final journey to Jerusalem, the cross looming in his mind already[8]

- Jesus' final week in Jerusalem and surrounds, culminating in his upper room discourse[9]

- Jesus' arrest, trials, floggings, and crucifixion at the order of Pontius Pilate, the Roman-appointed governor of Syria-Palestine[10]

Throughout, Jesus' primary message, especially in his parables, is the arrival of *God's kingdom*. He demonstrates this new creation and new exodus in his exorcisms and healings, his storm-taming miracles and Moses-like feeding of the thousands, the calling of 12 disciples,[11] his life-changing conversations with all kinds of people, his inclusion of society's outcasts at his table, and his taking up our sins and taking on the dark powers on the cross.[12] In all this, he opens up a new world, a door never to be closed, in the midst of the old one.

Despite their high Messianic hopes and his miracles, most Jews reject Jesus as the long-awaited Messiah. Failing to take on Roman oppression and instead critiquing Israel itself for its hardness of heart and misconceptions about the kingdom, he is not at all what they expected. Besides, who had ever imagined the Messiah would be crucified?

---

[7] Mark 6:6b–9:50
[8] Luke 9:51–19:27
[9] Mark 11:1–13:37, John 13–17
[10] Mark 14:1–15:47
[11] By calling 12 disciples, he was reconstituting the people of God, previously descendants of 12 patriarchs, under his leadership.
[12] Contemporary biblical scholars debate endlessly whether the death of Jesus was a substitutionary atonement (taking up our sins in our place) or a cosmic victory (taking on the dark powers of sin, Satan and death that oppress the world). Yet with so many biblical texts that support both, we do not have to choose.

STAGE 3: JESUS' RESURRECTION UNTIL ASCENSION

(CE 30)

Jesus rises from the dead, ministers to and further trains his disciples, prepares them for their imminent ministry-launching baptism by the Spirit, and then ascends before their eyes.[13] He makes it clear that his kingdom will manifest in the world not through the political liberation of biological Israel, but in the true Israel of God who, transformed by his gospel and Spirit, will spread the fame and name of their king. God has at last become king, taking up a peculiar throne—the cross. This empty cross is now the seat of true power: able to forgive sins, redeem all that has been broken, and utterly defeat death and darkness.

STAGE 4: THE EARLY YEARS OF THE FIRST CHURCH

(CE 30–33)

Recorded by Luke alone in his sequel to his Gospel, in *Acts 2-7*, we read of the birth and ministry of the first-ever church in Jerusalem. On the day of Pentecost,[14] Jesus' previous promises to send the Spirit to his people are fulfilled.[15] The Spirit's flames fall upon 120 believers in an upper room. At this moment, the Spirit who had empowered Jesus for his kingdom-advancing ministry comes upon his people. It's a succession of sorts, equipping them (and us) to continue the work he started.[16]

---

[13] Matthew 28, Luke 24, John 20–21, Acts 1

[14] Pentecost commemorated the day God gave Moses the law for Israel, some 50 days after the original Exodus Passover. The Spirit's arrival on this day, exactly 50 days after Jesus' delivering work on the cross, speaks of Jesus as the New Moses who ascends to heaven and sends down the Spirit who will supernaturally inscribe the ways of God not on tablets of stone this time, but into the hearts of the new Israel.

[15] John 14:16–18, 16:13–15

[16] Luke, writing both his Gospel and Acts, deliberately sets up Pentecost as a succession of the mantle of power for service that had previously rested upon Jesus. In the Gospel, Jesus' own experience of the Spirit's outpouring is the launch moment of his own ministry in the world. Thereafter, he is sent, guided and empowered by the Spirit to do all sorts of ministry and miracles. The same pattern then repeats itself with the church in

Newly empowered by the Spirit, and led by Peter and the apostles, the church functions within Judaism as an all-Jewish movement. At first, it grows wildly (adding 3,000 in one day!) and enjoys the city's favour. But then it begins to attract more and more persecution until it experiences its first martyrdom: a moment which scatters many in the church into the surrounding areas. As the sparks begin to fly, the fire begins to spread. Will it be quenched?

STAGE 5: THE GOSPEL IN JUDEA AND SAMARIA

(CE 33–37)

In *Acts 8–12*, Luke shows how this persecution moves the church, in the Spirit's power, to minister not only in Jerusalem, but now in Judea and Samaria, and then finally to the ends of the world.[17] Philip, Peter, Barnabas, and others are pioneers into these areas, reaching Gentiles for the first time—much to the shock of many Jewish Christians—thereby transforming the church into an international and even more diverse community. Saul, at the height of his church-persecuting fervency, encounters Jesus, who calls him to be an apostle. Also going by the name Paul, he cuts his teeth in ministry in Damascus and Syria.

STAGE 6: PAUL'S MINISTRY AND LETTERS

(CE 46–64)

Paul says of himself, "For I am the least of the apostles and do not even deserve to be called an apostle, because I persecuted the church of God. But by the grace of God I am what I am, and his grace to me was not without effect."[18]

Acts. Pentecost's power sends the church out, guiding and empowering it for world-changing ministry. The book of Acts recaps Luke's Gospel in its opening lines as "all that Jesus *began* to do and teach"—the implication is that, through the anointed church, the ascended Jesus *continues* to do and teach.

[17] Acts 1:8
[18] 1 Corinthians 15:0–10

As we have been discovering, we cannot understand any part of the New Testament until we understand how it fits in with the larger story. Before ascending, Jesus said to his apostles, "When the Spirit comes upon you, you will be my witnesses in Jerusalem, Judea, Samaria, and to the ends of the earth."[19] We have looked at the first five stages of the story, up until the gospel message going out to Judea and Samaria and Saul (aka Paul) being converted. In this stage, we see Paul lead the charge "to the ends of the earth."

In Acts 13–28, Peter moves off-stage and Paul takes centre-stage in Luke's account. Under his lead, the church rapidly progresses from the Jewish sect it once was to a Gentile-majority network of faith communities that rapidly spread further and further outward from its original starting point in Jerusalem. These faith communities experience persecution, but their newly adopted faith nimbly jumps over geographical and cultural barriers and continues to see them through the toughest of times. While travelling or in prison, Paul writes many letters to various faith communities. Of these, 13 of them are still preserved, constituting the bulk of the 21 letters in the New Testament.[20] About his own teachings, Paul says, "Brothers and sisters, stand firm and hold fast to the teachings we passed on to you, whether by word of mouth or by letter."[21]

---

[19] Acts 1:8

[20] Yet still we must not overstate Paul's contribution. It's common to hear preachers say, "Paul wrote most of the New Testament." Additionally, since the Reformation, Protestant theologians are in danger of seeing Paul, not Jesus, as their main source of theology. The truth is that if we count all the words, Paul wrote 23% of the New Testament. Luke, who authored two massive works, a Gospel and Acts, wrote even more, 25% to be exact. That said, next to Jesus, Paul is the most written about follower of Jesus—a quarter of Luke's words (in Acts 13–28) have to do with the ministry of Paul. If we add everything said about Paul and by Paul, its no wonder the high esteem the Bible-reading church gives to his example and theology. Yet even here we must be careful to keep Jesus central as we encounter him in the Gospels. The theology and example of Jesus and his kingdom ministry in the Gospels is the interpretive lens we use to make sense of Paul's example and theology, not the other way around. In a Christ-centered theology and practice, we do not come to Jesus via Paul. Rather we come to Paul via Jesus.

[21] 2 Thessalonians 2:15

THE FIVE WORLDS OF PAUL

Paul was uniquely poised for his missionary and theological contribution because he lived in five worlds:

First, Paul was Jewish by upbringing. His Hebrew name, Saul, is that of Israel's first king. As a teen he studied under the famed rabbi Gamaliel in Jerusalem. He describes himself as "a Hebrew of Hebrews; in regard to the law, a Pharisee; as for zeal, persecuting the church; as for righteousness based on the law, faultless."[22] He knew the Hebrew Bible inside out and was versed in the Messianic expectations of his time. A brilliant intellectual himself, he was able to take all of his years of training and knowledge and use it to articulate so much of the church's theology, which is itself built upon the Scriptures Paul knew so well.

With Jews inhabiting most cities in the Roman empire, Paul, once he converted, would visit the synagogue in whichever city he visited and be able to enthrall the Jews with his depth of biblical knowledge, showing them how Jesus fulfilled the Messianic promises. Typically, when some Jews would accept Jesus as their long-awaited Messiah, the synagogue would eject him and his converts. When this happened to Paul, he would turn his attention to Gentiles and the fledgling church—Gentiles and Jews mixed together—that would usually meet in homes.

Second, Paul was an apostle by calling. Outside of the original 12 apostles, the Risen Jesus directly called a few more to be "sent ones" to represent and suffer for him. Paul's encounter with Jesus and the Spirit caused him to reformat radically his understanding of the kingdom. He now realized God had kept his promises to send the saving king, but had done so in a way no one could have imagined. God had launched his reign and new creation not at the *end* of the evil age, but in the *midst* of it, where it would flower from within until this king would return to consummate it.

Driven on by a singular passion "to preach Christ where he is not

---

[22] Philippians 3:3

known" Paul went out to summon the world to Jesus' reign and salvation, with signs and wonders accompanying his ministry. As he implemented the victory of Jesus against the powers of darkness, he absorbed enormous backlash in the form of suffering. For example, in Lystra, Paul healed a cripple which almost caused the stunned crowd to worship him, but when some threatened Jews arrived, the citizens changed their mind and stoned him instead, leaving him for dead.[23]

Third, Paul was Roman by citizenship. Just over a decade younger than Jesus, Paul was born in CE 6, growing up in one of the empire's largest cities, Tarsus (in modern day Turkey). In the first century, the empire's fastest growing religion was this imperial cult—promoting the socially advancing belief that Caesar was a god and the Saviour of the world. Paul understood well this inflated claim and the idolatrous demand that all must bow their knee and declare, "Caesar is Lord." Against this backdrop, he subversively opted to use the term, "Jesus is Lord" rather than merely, "Jesus is king." He knew well the target every Christ-follower would draw on their back if they declared the same, but taught that faithfulness to Jesus was more important than good fortunes in a corrupt system.

On a collision course with Caesar, Paul nonetheless benefited from Roman citizenship, at times using it to appeal for more just dealings by authorities.[24] Rome had unwittingly prepared the world for Paul's missionary effectiveness: paved roads and set shipping routes connected its provinces and towns across thousands of kilometres; everyone spoke the same language; and a military presence secured the kind of order that made travel by land and sea much safer than it had been in centuries past. He learned tent-making too,[25] a common trade-skill in his home city, enabling him to set up shop and earn an income wherever he went.

Fourth, Paul was Greek by culture. Living in a predominantly non-Jewish and highly intellectual city (with a university) Paul was compe-

---

[23] Acts 14:8–20
[24] Acts 16:35–40, Acts 22:22–29
[25] Acts 18:1–4

tent at relating to people who knew nothing of the Hebrew Bible. Unlike the Jews in all-Jewish towns, he had grown up with them as his neighbours. This gave him a missional edge. He was adept at interacting with their Grecian philosophy and culture, which Rome had assimilated rather than rejected when it previously took over the vestiges of Greek rule. He could skilfully enter the minds and hearts of people; by using their language, metaphors, and foundational ways of thinking as a starting point. He was able to socialize with non-Jewish Gentiles, and pioneered church communities filled with Jews *and* Greeks, bonded together for the first time in history by a brotherly and sisterly love.

Fifth, Paul was a pastor by passion. From CE 44–46, Barnabas recruited Paul to help him to co-lead and teach the first ever multi-ethnic church in Antioch; with Jews and Gentiles joining in prayer, worship, communion, community, support, study, and mission. As Barnabas had done for him, he later learnt how to identify and train up other leaders whom he would affectionately call sons and brothers and partner with in mission. At Antioch he experienced firsthand the power of a community that functioned as the heavenly kingdom's outpost on earth: as the Father's family, Jesus' body, and the Spirit's true temple.

This is why Paul did not only preach the gospel, hoping for a convert here and there. Rather, in each location, his goal was to call a diverse *community* into existence who heralded Jesus as their Lord. He poured his life into these communities: teaching them, developing leaders, and strengthening them by keeping in contact with them, and helping them deal with the numerous problems they faced.

PAUL'S MISSIONARY JOURNEYS AND LETTERS

Paul wove together these five worlds in an unrepeatable way throughout his 18 years of ministry in Asia Minor and Europe, even while he periodically returned to his home-base church in Antioch and served the Jerusalem church where he could.

His first journey (CE 47–48) with Barnabas took him to Cyprus and four cities in Galatia. Soon after returning to Antioch, he participated in the CE 49 Jerusalem Council, led by James, which relieved the influx of Gentile believers from the need to follow Jewish law. His second journey with Silas (CE 49–52) took him through Asia Minor, then (guided by a vision) to Philippi in Greece, then via Athens down to Corinth, where he stayed for 18 months. At this point, he wrote his first two encouraging letters, both to the fledgling *Thessalonian* church.

After visiting Jerusalem and Antioch briefly, he embarked on a third journey (CE 52–55), which included a stay in Ephesus for two years, starting off with revival and ending with Paul fleeing for his life. There, he wrote to the *Galatians*, urging them not to listen to misled Jewish teachers who said that salvation is not only by faith in Christ, but also by the law of Moses, especially by circumcision and following Jewish food laws. He also wrote two letters to the *Corinthians*, which turned out to be the most heartbreakingly compromised and confused of the churches Paul had helped to birth. Thereafter he travelled to Greece and probably Illyricum (modern-day Yugoslavia), where he wrote his masterpiece letter to the *Romans*, showing how the gospel equalizes and unites Jews and Gentiles into the same community of grace and love.

During this journey, Paul collected an offering for the impoverished Jerusalem church, which he delivered to them in CE 57. Hated for his habit of summoning Gentiles to believe in the Jewish Messiah without practicing Jewish law, he was mobbed and nearly assassinated by Jews in Jerusalem. Roman authorities evacuated him, only to imprison him in Caesarea for two years thereafter. On trial, he made eloquent defenses to governors and the king there. He appealed to Caesar and was sent by ship with other prisoners to Rome, surviving a shipwreck, before finally arriving in Rome in CE 60.

Under house arrest in Rome, he wrote letters to the *Philippian*, *Ephesian* and *Colossian* churches, and also a short letter to *Philemon* urging him to reconcile as a brother with his runaway slave. As found in all of his letters, Paul lovingly and skilfully applied his theological grasp of the gospel to the complex and often rapidly changing situations faced by each of the recipients. In CE 62 he was released, then possibly travelled to Spain, and knowing his time left was short, wrote baton-passing letters to his trainees and delegates, *Timothy* and *Titus*, before returning to Rome where he was beheaded by the mad tyrant emperor Nero on false charges.

STAGE 7: GENERAL LETTERS AND THE REVELATION

(CE 60–95)

Paul's 13 letters to churches in our Bibles are not arranged in the order he wrote them, but from longest to shortest, with his three letters to individuals (Timothy, Titus, and Philemon) after that. Then come eight more letters, written by five other people.

These are commonly called *the general letters*. Unlike *Paul's letters*, which most often can be correlated to the narrative of Paul's travels outlined in Acts 13–28, we know very little about the story behind most of these letters, though we know that two were penned by Jesus' own brothers, and the other six were written by two of his very first followers.

James, written by the brother of Jesus, is likely written before Paul's first letter in CE 45. Heavily influenced by Jesus' Sermon on the Mount, it calls for practical faith and godliness.

Between CE 60–70, *Hebrews* is written by someone in Paul's circle (scholars argue it is likely either Barnabas, Priscilla, or Apollos). It is written to encourage a Jewish-majority church that was worn down by decades of persecution and were thus tempted to revert back to Judaism.

Peter, having relocated to Rome, writes *1 Peter* in CE 62 to help churches endure persecution faithfully. Two years later, *Jude* (another brother of Jesus) writes his short letter, and Peter writes a kind of farewell speech (*2 Peter*). That same year, Paul writes his baton-passing letter to Timothy (*2 Timothy*) and both Peter and Paul are martyred.

The first Christians paid the ultimate price as they refused to declare Caesar as Lord, reserving this acclamation for Jesus alone.

Soon after, John, the last living apostle, migrates to Ephesus, taking Jesus' aged mother with him. Between 85–95 AD, now an old man, John writes three letters (*1, 2 and 3 John*), his Gospel, and *the Revelation,*[26] which likens Roman tyranny to Babylon, and concludes the biblical canon in spectacular fashion. John, imprisoned on an island, writes down his series of visions in which the whole biblical story comes together in powerful symbolism and imagery. Jesus is portrayed as a slaughtered lamb who is exalted as the divine king of the world, leading his people out of slavery and exile from "Babylon", a symbol of Rome. As his people resist Babylon's influence, they may have to suffer alongside their slain leader. Ultimately, not even death can prevent the dawn of the New Creation which is here depicted as a New Jerusalem garden temple, the true home of humanity after its long, long exile.

And so, on the Bible's very last page, heaven and earth are finally united—just as they had once been on its very first page in the Garden of Eden. Renewed humanity now takes up the tasks first appointed to it: to rule the world together in the love and power of God. The story's end turns out to really just be the beginning of a new, yet to be told, story.[27]

---

[26] There's some scholarly debate about whether John the apostle who most likely wrote the Gospel of John is the same person as John the elder who wrote 1, 2 and 3 John and the same person still as John the seer who wrote the Revelation. In the very least, we can speak of them as all being part of the *Johannine* circle: the tremendous amount of distinctive theological overlap between the works means that either John or disciples of John wrote the various works.

[27] Wording of this paragraph adapted from www.bit.ly/3fRzqpi (accessed 09/20)

6

COPYISTS, CANON, CRITICS AND TRANSLATORS

Jesus ... went into the synagogue. He stood up to read, and the scroll of the prophet Isaiah was handed to him. Unrolling it, he found the place...

Luke 4:16-17

The old Bible heirloom that rests on many a home's bookshelf did not fall from the sky, leather-bound, written in Old English, with Jesus' words in red.

Let's go back in time to 150 AD, to an average town in Asia Minor. A Jewish synagogue has a compilation of papyrus scrolls written in mostly Hebrew, but also some translated into Greek—their sacred, inspired writings. A nearby group of Christian house churches has a similar compilation plus another pile of scrolls, all written in Greek—what will later be called "the New Testament". None of these scrolls have chapter or verse divisions.

Neither of these communities have the original manuscripts. Written half a millennium or more ago, the original documents of the Hebrew Bible have long since perished. Written up to a century beforehand, many of the original New Testament documents have perished or are kept elsewhere.

What the synagogue does have is copies of copies of the originals. So does the church, though it might just have copies of the originals. In fact, the synagogue has a professional scribe whose singular calling is meticulously to replicate the scrolls. In the early church, some lay people do the same job, thrilled to share the Scriptures with the many fledgling churches that are springing up everywhere.

Now let's return to our time. How things have changed! Today, we can click on a Bible app and select which language and translation we'd prefer to read. There are chapters, headings, verses, cross-references, and footnotes.

How did we get from snapshot one in 150 CE to the present form of the Bible? It is a truly wonderful five-phase story, which tells of many people for whom we should forever be grateful.

PHASE 1: COPYISTS MADE COPIES

Long before the printing press, Jewish rabbis and early Christian scribes exercised great precision in hand-copying the biblical texts, following detailed systems for counting letters and having multiple correctors read through their copies to check for errors. This accounts for the striking accuracy and consistency seen in most ancient copies of our Old and New Testaments.

Still, there are *variants* or differences in the thousands of ancient copies we have. For example, one manuscript says that Jesus is "the one and only Son" while another says he is "the only Son."[1] Or one quotes Jesus as saying that a demonized man will be freed only "by prayer" while another adds "and fasting."[2] About 95% of these discrepancies were mistakes of sight, hearing and writing, or poor judgment. The remaining 5% resulted from intentional changes, where scribes revised grammar or spelling, or tried to harmonize similar passages, or conflated the text.[3]

---

[1] John 1:18

[2] Mark 9:29

[3] Wikipedia offers a nice summary of the common causes for variants: "Most of the variations are not significant and some common alterations include the deletion, rearrangement, repetition, or replacement of one or more words when the copyist's eye returns to a similar word in the wrong location of the original text. If their eye skips to an earlier word, they may create a repetition. If their eye skips to a later word, they may

PHASE 2: THE RECOGNITION OF THE CANON SETTLES

Let's take a look at how the books of the Hebrew Bible and the New Testament came to be recognized as Scripture.

John says about the Revelation, "I warn everyone who hears the words of the prophecy of this scroll: If anyone adds anything to them, God will add to that person the plagues described in this scroll."[4]

Although this verse applies only to the book of Revelation, its figurative warning alerts us to how important it is that we know what God has and has not said to us, hence our attention to the Scriptures and an accurate interpretation of them.

The TaNaK Canon

In Jesus' time, the Old Testament canon was already in place. The word "canon" is a Greek term meaning "measuring stick" used by Judaism and Christianity to refer to a specific list of books deemed to be inspired by God and therefore included in Scripture.

The finalized contents of the Hebrew Bible went through a long process. Most of it had been written by Moses, David, Solomon, Ezra, and other named prophets. Some of the authors, however, remained anonymous and were simply called "scribes" or "prophets". Generations of prophetic scribes collected earlier writings, integrating them into larger compositions, and at times editing them (think of Moses' obituary at the end of his Pentateuch[5]). By the time of Jesus, most of the community of Israel had recognized the divine inspiration of their Hebrew compilation of 24 scrolls, calling it the *TaNaK*, an acronym of its three sections, the *Torah* (also called the Pentateuch), the *Neviim* (the Prophets) and the *Ktuvim* (the Writings). Some of these 24 scrolls

---

create an omission. They may resort to performing a rearranging of words to retain the overall meaning without compromising the context ... Spellings occasionally change. Synonyms may be substituted. A pronoun may be changed into a proper noun (such as "he said" becoming "Jesus said")." www.bit.ly/3mpjWey (accessed 09/20)
[4] Revelation 22:18
[5] Deuteronomy 34

were further subdivided to bring about the 39 books of the Old Testament we have today.

A popular Greek translation[6] of the *TaNaK* before Jesus' time also included the *Apocrypha,* which was written *after* the last books of the *TaNaK* and includes the historical accounts of the Maccabees, the poetic Wisdom of Solomon, and more. As important as these writings are as a source of history and for understanding the development of Judaism in the centuries before Christ, few Jews at the time and fewer in the early church deemed them as bearing the marks of inspiration. By CE 150, the Palestinian Jews had officially excluded them, and had settled on the same books included in the Protestant Bible's Old Testament.[7]

The New Testament Canon

The earliest churches were visited by travelling apostles and their delegates. When the number of living apostles began to dwindle, and the number of churches began to rise and spread further and further apart, receiving a letter from an apostle would have been relished. These letters could also be kept far longer than any visiting apostle, and shared between more than just one church and region too.

By CE 95, all the apostles had died. So what did the churches do? They carefully collected, copied, and shared these writings with other churches. For those early churches, the Gospels and letters were Scripture every bit as much as the Hebrew Bible. Since Jesus commissioned the apostles who wrote many of these, and the apostles commissioned the people who wrote the rest, the documents functioned as a God-given standard for what to believe and how to live. Even when they were still alive, Peter referred to a small collection of Paul's writings as

---

[6] Called the Septuagint or the LLX. It's important because mostly the New Testament authors, writing in Greek, quote from it rather than the Hebrew Bible.

[7] On the heels of the birth of Protestantism, at the Catholic Council of Trent in CE 1563, the Catholic magisterium decreed for the first time that the Apocrypha be treated as Scripture. This is why Catholic Bibles include Tobit, Judith, Wisdom, Sirach, Baruch, 1 and 2 Maccabees, plus additional sections of Esther and Daniel. Called the deuterocanonical books, they are included between the two Testaments.

Scripture.[8] And Paul, for example, recognized Luke's writing on a par with the Old Testament.[9] A post-apostolic leader, Clement in CE 96 wrote to the church in Corinth, "Take up the epistle of the blessed Paul the apostle. Truly he wrote to you in the Spirit."[10] And Ignatius soon after, in CE 110, wrote to another church, "Be eager, therefore, to be firmly grounded in the precepts of the Lord and the apostles."[11]

Between 100 and 200 AD, both Old and New Testament writings were copied, passed on, and collected by the churches. Though each church's library slowly grew to include a collection similar to our modern Bible, no widely accepted New Testament list existed. Hence, there was a growing need for an authoritative list.

With the apostles deceased, the later church fathers still wrote more letters, like the *Didache*.[12] People began to wonder if they were Scripture too. What's more, a teacher called Marcion chose a list that he deemed as canon which excluded most of the Hebrew Bible and anything that sounded Jewish in the more recent writings. Church leaders responded in CE 170 by listing books to be used safely in teaching and worship—the vast majority found in our New Testament, with the exception of Hebrews, James, and 1 and 2 Peter.

Only by the fourth century was there a prominent and final church-wide recognition of the New Testament canon. In CE 363 the Council of Laodicea stated that only the 39 books of the Old Testament and the 27 books of the New Testament are to be read in the churches. The church has abided by this ever since. To formulate and finalize their list, the council applied three tests to each book:[13]

---

[8] 2 Peter 3:16

[9] In 1 Timothy 5:18 Paul quotes not only Deuteronomy 25:4 but some words of Jesus recorded in Luke 10:7, referring to both texts as "the Scripture says".

[10] 1 Clement 3:1

[11] Magnesians 13:1

[12] Written in Greek toward the end of the first century, this collection of writings revealed how Jewish Christians saw themselves and how they adapted their practice for Gentile Christians.

[13] The articulation of these three tests is adapted from Michael Eaton: 2014, *The Plan and Purpose of God*, Africa Leadership School, 396.

The Test of Apostolicity

This first test asks, *"Is the author an apostle or do they have a connection with an apostle?"*

For example, Mark likely wrote under Peter's authority, and Luke wrote under Paul's authority. Someone in Paul's circle wrote Hebrews. This is also why no books written after John's death were accepted. Contrary to modern conspiracy theories, the only Gospels the church ever accepted were Matthew, Mark, Luke and John, all written while eyewitnesses were still alive. Unnamed Gnostics penned the so-called "Lost Gospels" of Thomas, Philip, Mary, and others, during the second and third century, attempting to reinvent Jesus as a teacher of their own religion. None were even considered for the canon.

The Test of Content

This second test asks, *"Does the book reflect consistency of moral values and doctrine[14] with what had been accepted as orthodox teaching?"*

This is why the false "Gospel of Peter" was rejected—its doctrine jarred with everything we know about Peter and truth as described in the rest of the New Testament. Though they did not even consider them, the same could have been said about the "Lost Gospels"—in stark contrast to the human, Jewish Jesus depicted in the Gospel of Mark for example, the gnostic "Jesus" seems to have no connection to Jewish Scriptures or historical reality.

The Test of Acceptance

This third test asks, *"Was the book accepted by the church at large?"*

It is important to note that the early church was *not* selecting or authorizing its Scripture. It was merely seeking to *recognize* the Scripture that God had given, and the writings through which God continued to speak through long after they were written. This is also the reason that it required time to settle upon a final list.

---

[14] By "doctrine" I mean what the Bible teaches about those subjects that loom large in Scripture and describe reality, such as God, Jesus, the Holy Spirit, Scripture itself, humanity, creation, salvation, the church, the kingdom, and the future of all things.

PHASE 3: COLLECTORS GATHER ANCIENT TEXTS

As is the case for every ancient document of religious or historical significance, we do not have the original biblical manuscripts. They have perished or been lost to antiquity. However, thanks to religious bodies, archaeologists and museums that have found, collected, and cared for ancient fragments, we have *thousands* of ancient copies—24,000 for the New Testament alone. This is a truly staggering amount when compared to the 10 ancient copies of Caesar's Gallic Wars or the 20 copies of Tacitus written shortly before and after the New Testament, and yet relied upon as major sources of historical record.

Unlike the vast time gap of over 900 years between the original and the oldest copies we have of Caesar's Gallic Wars, Tacitus, and even the first Buddhist texts, we have copies for the entire New Testament written within 350 years, and a fragment from John's Gospel within 130 years, of the original.

Over time, more copies have been found. As recently as 1947, a young Arab goat herder investigated a cave after throwing a rock in it and hearing pottery break. He dug in the dark, found a broken jar and uncovered within it the Dead Sea scrolls. These scrolls, amongst other things, contained the entire Hebrew Bible (except Esther and Nehemiah). Dated to some time between 250 BCE and CE 50, these scrolls were about a millennium older than the most trusted copies we had previously found. Their 99% likeness to the more recent copies showed just how meticulous and faithful the copyists over multiple centuries had been.

PHASE 4: TEXT-CRITICS SELECT VARIANTS

To solve the problem of variants in the collection of texts, textual scholars have, since the 16th century, developed a science called *textual criticism*. Through it, they seek to uncover what was written originally by comparing copies. With the discovery of older and older copies, this science has been refined and honed over the last two centuries.

Though scholarly debate continues on the numerous variants found in these copies, most scholars agree that textual criticism has served to confirm the reliable transmission of the Old and New Testament manuscripts. F.J. Hort, one of the most respected textual critics, concluded, "The text of the New Testament, in the variety and fullness of the evidence on which it rests, stands absolutely and unapproachably alone among ancient prose writings."

Additionally, most unsolved textual issues have little to no doctrinal significance. When it comes to solving the puzzle of variants, these scholars use tests that lead them to deem as correct those copies that are oldest, the best quality and whose text explains all the variants in other copies.[15]

PHASE 5: TRANSLATORS INTRODUCE NEW VERSIONS

Christians have translated their sacred texts from the very beginning. Jesus spoke and preached in Hebrew and Aramaic, a local dialect. Greek was his third language. Yet the Gospels, written for a wider audience than just Israel, quote him in Greek. Driven on by the apostle John's vision of all tribes and tongues worshipping God, missionaries and teachers have continued to translate parts or all of the Bible into over 3,000 languages (and counting). In major languages, there are multiple translations. In English alone, there are over 450 different translations of the Bible.

The main reason for different translations is that *translation theories differ*. These theories mainly have to do with the historical distance between the original language and the modern English language; in its words, grammar, idioms, and in its culture and history. Individual

---

[15] The gold standard for Old Testament scholars is to correlate the Masoretic Text, well-preserved medieval copies based on a very careful copying tradition, and manuscripts of the Greek translation, the Septuagint, dating back before Christ. As for the New Testament, those earliest copies found in Egypt have proven to stem from the most solid copying tradition.

translators or translating committees must decide where they want to be on the translation spectrum...

On the left-hand extreme is something called "formal equivalence" or "word-for-word" translation. This is the attempt to keep as close as possible to the original form of the words, the order of words, the idioms, and the grammar in the original. This theory is comfortable with maximum distance between original and modern readers of the text. The 1993 New Revised Standard Version (NRSV) and the 2001 English Standard Version (ESV) fit here.

On the right-hand extreme of the spectrum is "dynamic equivalence" or "thought-for-thought" translation, whereby translators try to keep the original meaning or thought intact, but are comfortable using words, sentence orders and grammar that is more attuned to modern readers. The goal is to create *the same effect and meaning in the mind* of the modern reader as would have occurred in the mind of the original reader. The 1992 simple-language Good News Translation (GNT) and the 1996 New Living Translation (NLT) fit here.

In between these spectral extremes is the 2011 New International Version (NIV), the English world's best-selling translation. More recent, and also in the middle of the spectrum, is the 2016 Christian Standard Bible (CSB), which is slightly to the left of NIV.

Falling off the spectrum to the right are the paraphrased translations. Spurred on by the aim of *speaking freshly and accessibly* to the modern reader, these versions have little concern with staying close to the original wording, even employing modern idioms and inserting the author's interpretations. The 2002 Message (MSG) is the most popular example of this.

To compare their differences, consider these versions of John 8:31:

- *"If you remain in the word, my truly disciples of me you are."* (Word for word from the Greek original.)

- *"If you abide in my word, you are truly my disciples." (ESV)*

- *"If you hold to my teachings, you are really my disciples." (NIV)*

- *"You truly are my disciples if you remain faithful to my teachings." (NLT)*

- *"If you stick with this, living out what I tell you, you are my disciples for sure." (MSG)*

An area of particular debate between translators is the word *adelphoi*, used over 100 times in the book of Acts and in Paul's letters when addressing faith communities. The word literally means "brothers" but the ancient world understood it to mean "brothers *and sisters*" when addressed to a mixed crowd. However, modern English readers, especially in the last few decades, no longer make that assumption. Those recent translations that continue to opt for "brothers" instead of "brothers and sisters" are certainly sticking to a literal translation, although they are unwittingly sending a *female-excluding* message to modern readers—this when the original readers would have heard it *inclusively*. This is an example of why dynamic translations are needed in the first place. It is also an example of why we need *continually updated* translations: modern language continues to evolve and meanings change.

Which Translation to Use

For the sake of absorbing and memorizing Scripture, it is good to use only one translation over many years. Choose a highly credible one created by a large body of scholars—I suggest the middle-of-the-spectrum NIV or CSB. To get a fresh reading of texts that one may have become overfamiliar with, read the NLT or MSG from time to time. For the sake of study, use not one but many different versions, including those on the left like NRSV or ESV, but I would suggest you don't use the 1611 King James Version (KJV) which has not benefitted from the more recent textual scholarship and the uncovering of the oldest copies. Thankfully, all these and other versions are free on *www.biblehub.com*, a web portal that also has the original Greek and Hebrew language for study.

PART TWO

HOW TO READ THE BIBLE RIGHT

7

THE AUTHOR'S INTENDED MEANING

Do your best to present yourself to God as one approved, a worker who does not need to be ashamed and who correctly handles the word of truth.

2 Timothy 2:15

In 1871, on a farm that my great- great- grandparents owned, someone found a diamond on a small hill called the Colesberg Kopje. A diamond rush ensued and everyone got digging. The deeper they drilled down the vertical vein of treasure, the bigger the diamonds they found. By 1914, the largest ever man-made pit—the 1,097 metre deep Kimberley hole—had unearthed three tons of diamonds.[1]

Scripture is something like this—there are seemingly endless diamonds of truth in this vein that holds God's revelation. "The words from your mouth are more precious to me than thousands of pieces of silver and gold." [2]Much of it is easily enough found on the surface. But some of it lies much deeper, and we need to do some digging. There is a name for this "digging"—it's called *exegesis*. Though to make matters simpler, I will speak of *proper interpretation*, or "correctly handling the

---

[1] If you're wondering how wealthy I am now, suffice to say that my ancestors, as digging began, swapped the farm for a small railway station in the Karoo desert, which didn't amount to much.
[2] Psalm 119:72

word of truth."

It is not enough to read Scripture; we must seek to understand it correctly. In this chapter and the next, I will teach you how properly to interpret the Bible.[3] I will show you the collection of digging tools that I took years of my life in theological education to gather, all so that you don't have to wait that long to start finding diamonds yourself.

A Call to Humility and Graciousness

Throughout this chapter, I will provide many examples of what I (now) understand to be incorrect readings of Scriptures.

Notice the word "now" in my previous sentence—not only as a reader of Scripture, but as a preacher, I must admit to having violated almost everything I will say in this chapter in a sermon at some point. I mention this caveat so as to avoid causing some of you who see things differently to feel threatened by any of my interpretations of passages, and also to undermine a prideful response in others of you who may agree with my readings, but then may unfairly evaluate teachers and preachers who may, at least at this stage in their theological journey, see things differently.

As important as Scriptural conviction is, it must be balanced with the humility and graciousness required for all of us, over time, to have better and better understandings of Scripture. None of us have a perfect understanding of the Bible. We are all on a journey toward clearer understanding. As we believe that we see aspects and passages of Scripture more clearly, we will also have to extend grace and patience to those who see it differently to us. Besides gentle, respectful conversation about points of divergent views, we can leave the matter in God's hands, using the counsel Paul abided by as he said to one church: "If at some point you see the matter differently, God will make that clear to

---

[3] A disclaimer up front: entire scholarly tomes are written on the subject of correct interpretation, so this and the next chapter are enormously selective. For further reading on the subject, I suggest these two books: G. Fee and D. Stuart: 2013, *How to Read the Bible for all its Worth*, Zondervan and J. Hays and J. Duvall: 2012, *Grasping God's Word*, Zondervan.

you."[4]

The point I want to draw attention to here is that it's not only possible but also highly *probable* that we will read our prior beliefs and preferences into Scripture. We do this in two ways: we distort the meaning or we deny the meaning.

Distorting the Meaning

Peter writes, "There are some things in (Paul's letters) that are hard to understand, which the ignorant and unstable twist to their own destruction, as they do the other Scriptures."[5]

Did you get that? Paul may confuse us, says Peter!

Or said another way, Scripture may confuse us, says Scripture.[6] Instead of running in the paths of God's true commands and experiencing freedom,[7] we may fall into the dangerous mud-pits of loopy interpretation and application.

Difficult as some texts may be, we must not settle for a twisted reading of them. We do not want to claim that we have found a diamond when we have actually found coal. More often than we realize, we may *think* we have read something and assume a particular understanding of a passage when it is in fact not saying that at all.[8]

It is not only Paul's words that are vulnerable to misinterpretation. Being such a large book comprised of so many smaller books, themes and sub-plots, the Bible is bound to have many passages that can be twisted and taken out of context to justify or support beliefs God never intended us to. Here are some false "doctrines" that people have held to, based on the twisting of biblical passages:

---

[4] Philippians 3:15
[5] 2 Peter 3:16
[6] Many theologians speak of a doctrine called the "perspicuity of Scripture" which says that God has seen to it that any person who reads Scripture will be able to understand it. Though that is true of much of the Bible, Peter suggests that it is not always the case.
[7] Psalm 119:32
[8] The same error applies in conversation. The speaker says one thing, but the hearer hears something else. The message encoded in the speaker's words is wrongly decoded in the hearer's mind. Good Bible reading runs parallel to good listening—we must do the hard work of really hearing and not jump to assumptions.

- the prosperity gospel, whereby people "name and claim" perfect health and plentiful wealth,

- the destruction or oppression of a people group, as Apartheid and European colonizers did,

- the keeping of slaves as the church in the American South once did,

- demoting Jesus, as the Jehovah's Witnesses do, by denying his deity, claiming he is actually only a very special angel,

- being baptized for the dead as the Mormons do, or embracing polygamy as a sect of Mormons do,

- cutting out an eye or limb or other body part to resist temptation as many a half-blind or limbless struggler has done,

- handling snakes in worship as some African sects do, and

- the anti-Semitism that once pervaded the Lutheran church[9] as it labeled Jews as "Christ killers" and unwittingly fed the discrimination that would lead to Nazi Germany's genocide of European Jews.

As is evident from this list, sadly, when we twist Scripture our lives, our communities and our witness to a watching world tend to get distorted and damaged too.

Denying the Meaning

Complicating the matter further, postmodern thinkers promote something called "a reader-response model" which sees all texts, but especially ancient texts, *not as a window to reality but rather as a mirror of fantasy.*

---

[9] Let's not only blame Luther for his proof-texted, anti-Semitism. Long before him, the "Glossa Ordinaria," the standard medieval one-volume commentary on the Bible had a steady theme of, through illustrations and commentary, showing the passing of God's favour from Synagoga, sometimes depicted as a woman skulking away in shame, to Ecclesia, who is crowned as a queen.

We are so subjective, this view says, that we can never know the original meaning of a text. We are unable, by this view, to separate our own reflection from what we think we see in the text.[10] The argument is that meaning is therefore something each of us uniquely must find for ourselves. This view concludes that all interpretations are equally wrong and equally right—all at the same time. With this view, no one can make assertions about anything—except the assertion that no one can make assertions about anything. This is a good example of a theory that disproves itself as soon as it is stated.[11]

ANCIENT MEANING, TIMELESS MESSAGE

Aware of all the dangerous distortions and our tendency to treat the text like a mirror instead of a window, we must learn to "handle the word of truth correctly." There are two most important aspects to this: *In every passage, first we must uncover the ancient meaning and then, only then, discover its timeless message.*

The Bible's message is *grounded* in ancient cultures. It speaks first to the cultures and situations in which it was first written. But its message is not *bound* to those ancient cultures. The wonderful thing about God's Word is not only that God spoke through it to people long ago, but also that he still speaks through it, to us and to generations to come. Precisely because it is *timeless* it is always *timely*. Despite all our advances over the march of time, reality itself has not changed—God is still the same God, human nature is still human nature, and our need

---

[10] Although postmodernists rightly challenge the dogmatic over-certainty about objective meaning found in modernists of a former age, I believe they allow the pendulum to swing too far to the other side—all the way to the loss of objective meaning. Somewhere in the middle of these extremes is a better way of reading texts called critical realism. It is self-critical of the subjective ways we easily read ourselves into texts. Yet at the same time it assumes that there *is* real objective meaning in the text and in the mind of the author. Difficult as it may be, we must learn to separate our reflection on the window from what can be seen through the window.

[11] A point nicely articulated by my favourite biblical scholar, Michael Eaton: 2014, *The Plan and Purpose of God*, Africa Leadership School, ch11.

for and the provision of salvation still stands.

And yet God's Word in the Scriptures does not fall out the sky upon us like rain. Rather it comes to us as a river that started a long way back. The flow of God's Word to us now finds its riverbanks in God's Word to them then.

This is why we ask two questions of each passage:

1. What did the human author say to the original audience? That's the ancient meaning, what it meant for them.

2. What is God saying to us here and now through these words of Scripture? That's the timeless message, what it means for us.

Written For Us But Not To Us

The sacred texts were not written *to* us, however by the Spirit's inspiration they were written *for* us.[12] We may not be the original recipients but nonetheless, with a careful reading involving some interpretative work on our part and the illumination of the Spirit, we can know what God is saying to us.[13]

We may ask if something that was not written to us is really meant for us. Let me answer this by referring to the example in Revelation chapter two and three, in which John, guided by Jesus, writes seven short letters to seven different churches. Each church, in a different city in Asia Minor, receives a separate message that addresses particular things in its unique situation. Yet, at the end of each of the seven messages, John writes, "Let him who has ears hear what the Spirit is saying to *the churches*"—one would think it would say, "to the church"

---

[12] Credit for this insight goes to John Walton who uses this distinction of "to" and "for" in his 2009 book, *The Lost World of Genesis One,* 7.

[13] Fee and Stuart write, "Because the Bible is *God's Word,* it has *eternal relevance*; it speaks to all humankind, in every age and in every culture… But because God chose to speak his Word through *human words in history,* every book in the Bible also has *historical particularity*; each document is conditioned by the language, time and culture in which it was originally written." (*How to read the Bible for all its worth,* Kindle location: 346)

(i.e. one's own church) but instead it says, "to the churches." In other words, each of the seven churches only have one letter written *to* them, yet they also have another six that are written *for* them. This serves as a model for accepting the whole Bible as written for all of God's people; the difference being that, though the seven churches were only divided from each other by distance of geography and situation, we are divided from the original readers of every book in the Bible by a distance of geography, situation and time. This model also lays stress in the right place: the Spirit is as eager to say something through Scripture to those of us *for* whom it was written as he was to say something to those *to* whom it was written.[14]

If God had inspired a letter directed specifically to us or to our church, no translation work would be required. We would understand instantly to what he was referring. But as it is, we need to essentially "learn another language"—do the hard work of entering into the foreign world of those to whom the letters were originally written. Is it worth the effort?

It's Like Learning Our Spouse's Language

Allow me to develop the analogy: *imagine learning another language for the sake of love.* Learning another tongue is difficult, but when we are motivated to do so, we put in the effort. So imagine falling in love with someone of another language. You would no doubt happily learn their language in order to connect with them and understand them more. Similarly, God has chosen to speak his words in an ancient language, culture, and situation, and it is our great privilege and joy to learn how rightly to hear and understand them in that setting.

---

[14] Another analogy that helps us think of how the biblical books are for us even if they were not written to us, is to think of a parent who, before passing away, writes five long letters, one to each of her five children. After the parent passes away the children gather to celebrate their memories, and make even better sense of what kind of person their mother was, what views she held, what she wanted her children to know, become and do. The children do this by sharing their letters with each other. As they read each other's letters, there are parts in each letter that, though addressed to only one child, contain statements that apply to all the children, And even those parts that speak to a particular situation shed light for the other children in quite different situations.

Our driving passion may be to know what God says to us, but the only way to hear it is to learn to decipher what he said to them.

Although this might require effort on our part, take heart that God did not try to veil the truth and encode his messages with hard-to-decipher meanings. The Scriptures were written to be understood, and mainly by simple people. Take John's Gospel: it has a vocabulary of only 360 words and uses simple Greek that translate into one-syllable English words like light, truth, love, word, God, and life. Compare that with Plato's sophisticated Greek writings in which many readers get lost on page one. That was certainly not the apostle Paul's heart, as evident in his words to the Corinthian church: "We do not write you anything you cannot read or understand. And I hope that, as you have understood us in part, you will come to understand fully."[15] Or take his letter to the Ephesians—it is written for children too; we know this because near the end it suddenly addresses the children directly who would have been present while it was being read.

So how should we go about interpreting any and every passage in Scripture? There are two guidelines as we interpret. The first guideline is to *start big then move to the small.* When we dive right into a verse without any consideration of its placing in the book or Testament it is in, or the genre of book it is, we end up not being able to tell the wood from the trees. Rather, first pan out and see the forest, then zoom in on the tree and then its particular branches.

A practical way to do this is to *ask the right questions, in the right order.* This is the second guideline. But what questions?

Seven Questions

I suggest seven of them. I will deal with six in this chapter and the seventh in the next. Here they are:

1. Its place in the story: Where does the book that this text is in fit within the 14 stages in the Bible's larger story?

2. Its genre type: What genre of literature is this text?

---

[15] 2 Corinthians 1:13–14

3. Its author's purpose: Why was this particular book even written and what situation does it address?

4. The flow of thought: Based on the section before and after, what is the author trying to say in this passage?

5. The cultural background: Are there any ancient cultural assumptions, situations, or practices referred to that are different than our own?

6. Word and sentence study: What do the words, phrases, and their grammatical relationship to each other mean?

7. Its timeless message: In this passage is there some wisdom to learn, instruction to obey, an example to follow, warning to heed, a principle to apply, promise to believe, or doctrine to grasp?

If you've learnt another language, you know how complicated it can seem at first. But what is difficult initially becomes second nature after some time and practice.

I say this to encourage you as you read this chapter and the next: when one of my friends first read them, she said that it made understanding the Bible seem more out of her reach, not less. "Do you really expect me to ask these questions of every text?"

I answered, "Not every text will require these questions to be understood, but as you get the hang of it, you will instinctively run through them, and other principles too, in your mind, sometimes giving no more than a second to each."

"But how will I remember all these principles and questions?" she asked.

"Well, you could write them down somewhere. Or keep coming back to them here. Eventually you will have absorbed them, and won't even need to review them."

So, don't be intimidated by the apparent *technicality* of this chapter and the next. Keep in mind that you are learning the rules of the language of the One who loves you most.

QUESTION 1: ITS PLACE IN THE STORY

Ask of each text: *Where does the book that this text is in fit into the 14 stages of the Bible's larger story?*

This is especially important as we read the 39 books in the Hebrew Bible. We must place them in the right part of the story for them to make sense. To help you recall, the first seven stages, all in the Hebrew Bible, are:

Stage 1: Creation and the Fall
Stage 2: The Patriarchs
Stage 3: The Exodus and Desert Journey
Stage 4: The Promised Land
Stage 5: The Monarchy
Stage 6: The Division and Exile
Stage 7: The Return

Here are some examples of correctly placing books of the Bible in their stage of the story.

The Psalms and the laws of Moses make no sense if we think they were written *before* the Exodus. Likewise, most of the 16 Prophetic books make no sense if we think they were written *before* the division of Israel into the northern and southern kingdoms.

Or think of Nehemiah. It makes no sense if we think it was written *before* the return of the exiles to Palestine. Only then would there be a destroyed wall for Nehemiah to repair, and only then would he need permission from a pagan king to do so. And none of the 39 works that make up the Old Testament make sense if we think they were written after Jesus' arrival—this is why Jesus' name is not found anywhere in them.

In all this, we interpret the earliest stages (the Hebrew Bible) in light of the later stages (the New Testament). That's why we don't kill Amalekites as Saul was instructed to do.[16] Rather, like Jesus, we pray for our

---

[16] 1 Samuel 15:3

enemies. The only thing we are called to put to death is our sinful nature.[17] It's also why we don't need to rebuild a temple like Zechariah did, instead we have the privilege of participating with Jesus as he builds his temple-church, not of brick and mortar, but of lives and love.

This quest for context is true of the New Testament too. To help you recall, there are another seven stages in the latter part of the Bible:

Stage 1: Jesus from birth to early 30s
Stage 2: Jesus' public ministry until death
Stage 3: Jesus' resurrection until ascension
Stage 4: The early years of the first church
Stage 5: The gospel in Judea and Samaria
Stage 6: Paul's ministry and letters
Stage 7: General letters and the Revelation

Jesus' commands to his disciples in the Gospel of Matthew to preach only in Israel,[18] or to leave our offering at the Jerusalem temple in order to reconcile to our brother[19] do not make sense after stage five in the above list, when the church spreads beyond the Jewish capital city. None of Paul's letters make sense if we place them *before* Jesus ascends to heaven, or *before* the church spreads beyond Palestine and comes to be populated mainly by Gentiles, in organic communities that are no longer a biological family or political nation but are now faith families made up of people from many nations and cultural backgrounds. The Revelation makes little sense if we place it *before* the martyrdom of Peter and Paul, when persecution against Christians first became state-sponsored.

Having said that, I need to clarify the difference between a "stage" in the biblical story and an "age" in God's redemptive work. Though I have divided the New Testament story into seven stages, when it comes to the way God relates to us, stages four through seven are in fact all

---

[17] Romans 8:13
[18] Matthew 10:5–6
[19] Matthew 5:23–24

the same "age" as each other, the age in which we live too.

Together with the first churches in the first century, we are in *the age of the church,* the time between *Pentecost* (the coming of the Spirit) and the *Parousia* (the second coming of Jesus).[20] Though there may be all kinds of cultural and situational distance between our church and any of the first century churches, the fact we are all in the same age means that God's Word to each of those churches (i.e. the epistles of the New Testament) more naturally applies to us now than God's Word to all God's people before the coming of Jesus.[21]

QUESTION 2: ITS GENRE TYPE

Next, we ask of each text: *What genre of literature is this?*

In the modern world, there are different kinds of writing. There are suspense, adventure, romance, and science fiction genres to name a few. We know we need to read these very differently. After all, the authors use these genres for different effects—a poet will seek to move you, while a textbook writer will try to inform you. A journalist will describe a crisis moment in history with an eye for facts, while an autobiographer will retell the same moment from the vantage point of their life's journey. We would not (and really should not) read a love

---

[20] To clarify the matter theologically, we are only in the first part of *the age of the church.* When Jesus returns, and the kingdom is unveiled in full, we will be promoted to "the church victorious," but for now we are in the age of "the church militant," embroiled in a spiritual battle with the unholy trinity of the fallen world, the sinful nature and the legions of hell. The kingdom of God is present in part, and is colliding with darkness as it spreads out into the unbelieving world through the Spirit's presence and power in the church and the preaching of the gospel. Though our church's circumstances may be different to Jerusalem's or Rome's first century churches (which in turn are different to each other) we must not overlook the foundational similarity between every church's experience of God. Together with them, we are beneficiaries and ministers of the new covenant in the midst of a world in desperate need of God's grace.

[21] I could say this more strongly: each of our current faith communities is an extension of the same people in every Christ-following community we read of in the New Testament. Although it is helpful to think of "them and there" and "us and now" when it comes to separating the ancient meaning from the timeless message, it is still helpful to remember that they are we, and then is now—this increases our conviction that God's Word to them is also God's Word to us.

letter like we would a legal marriage contract.

The Bible, likewise, consists of different kinds of genres, most of which were popular in their time: there's historical narrative, legal code, fables, wisdom poetry, prayer-and-song poetry, prophetic poetry, parables, letter-writing, teachings, and apocalyptic literature. We must read and interpret each differently.[22]

Let's consider just five of the Bible's genres:

Narrative

Almost half of the contents of the Old Testament (40% in fact) are historical narratives or stories. *A common error is to read these stories as allegories filled with hidden meanings.* When Abraham secures a bride for his son through a servant, this is not about God the Father securing a bride for his Son through the Spirit.

Another error is to assume every Old Testament story has a moral lesson. It's true that the story of Jacob and Esau show the damages of parental favouritism, but the reason for the story is primarily to tell of God's unlikely, grace-based choices: God chose Jacob, the deceptive second born rather than Esau who was by rights the first born heir. It's true that David's single-combat sling-stone victory over Goliath teaches us courage in the face of long odds, but when we read the tale in the context of 1 Samuel, we realize it is introducing David the future king whose trust in God and whose support from God shows up the present king Saul as a fraud.[23] Of course there *are* moral lessons in Old Testament stories, but they are usually inferred not stated. For example, nowhere does Genesis say that polygamy is wrong, yet each and every example of it results in relational disaster.

---

[22] "There are various kinds of literary forms in the Bible. Each of them possesses its own rules of interpretation ... Each author assumed that his readers would interpret his words according to the rules governing that literary form. If we are not aware of the rules under which the biblical author wrote, misinterpretation almost certainly will take place." (Robert Stein: 2011, *A Basic Guide to Interpreting the Bible*, Baker Academic, 75)

[23] When we read it in the context of the whole Bible, we realize David's representative victory over Goliath, points to Jesus the Son of God who single-handedly takes on the intimidating powers that oppress humankind.

They are great stories. Like all good stories, they have beginnings where the characters are introduced, middles where there is plot tension and endings when things resolve. For example, Joseph's story starts with his dream in which his brothers bow down to him[24] and ends with them actually doing so[25] but in-between they cast him down into a pit and sell him off into slavery. As a decades-long reader who knows the ending to each of the stories, I must admit to at times having lost a sense of just how good these stories are. I rediscovered their quality when I began to read them to my children, who were often so riveted that they refused to let me stop reading.

Are all the stories historically true? Most of the narrative biblical stories are not metaphorical or embellished, but literally true events. That said, we must not apply the standards of modern-day journalists or historians who are tasked with *objective precision* reporting. The biblical narrators, in contrast, recounted the stories as best as they could but with a particular concern to get across *what God was showing his people through these stories.*[26]

As a result, there is some debate amongst scholars about how often figurative elements may be included in some ancient biblical accounts. In particular, the earliest accounts such as Genesis 1-3 (and 4-11 less so), which reach back into the most distant past, may combine historical with figurative elements.[27]

Poetry in general

Totalling 30% of the Bible's contents, Job, Proverbs, Psalms, Song of

---

[24] Genesis 37:6–8

[25] Genesis 50:18

[26] Earlier, I called this "prophetically interpreted history."

[27] A leading Old Testament scholar, John Walton, helps us understand the genre of these chapters, as well as the way they were understood in the ancient world, in his books, "The lost world of Genesis 1", "The lost world of Adam and Eve," and "The lost world of the flood." Take Genesis 1 for example. Though laden with exquisite theological truth about God, creation and humanity it is unlikely that it is endeavouring to be a tight, factual history of the origin of all things. This is something the early church father Origen noted when he asked how light and day exist on earth on Day 1 while the sun is only made on Day 4?

Songs, Ecclesiastes, and most of the Prophetic writings use the genre of Hebrew poetry.

Like all poetry, it is image-rich, using metaphors and simile to evoke imagination and emotion. Compare for example a narrative and a poetic account of the Israelites crossing the Red Sea: the narrative version, in Exodus 14 says, "The Israelites went through the sea on dry ground, with a wall of water on their right and on their left," which is followed in Exodus 15, by a poetic retelling of the same event: "By the blast of [God's] nostrils, the waters piled up. The surging waters stood up like a wall; the deep waters congealed in the heart of the sea."[28]

Unlike much of our modern poetry that has meter and rhyme, Hebrew poetry is marked by its free form within a couplet structure: every thought conveyed is done so in a series of two connected lines.[29]

Reading figurative parts of the Bible in a literal way is a recurring mistake in the history of the church. When the Psalm says, "God is clothed in majesty... The world is firmly established—it cannot be moved,"[30] it is not a scientific text to be used against the likes of Galileo who argued that the world is spherical and spinning, any more than it is a statement of God's wardrobe.

When David writes, "I was sinful at birth"[31] he is not teaching the doctrine of original sin as much as he is highlighting his lifelong corruption. When Jeremiah says, "Cursed be the day I was born... cursed

---

[28] Exodus 14:22 and 15:8
[29] There are three kinds of parallelism used in the Old Testament—being aware of this gives us an interpretive advantage:
1) In synonymous parallelism, both lines say more or less the same thing:
'I have swept away your offenses like a cloud,
your sins like the morning mist.'
2) In antithetical parallelism, the second line (usually beginning with 'but') reinforces the first idea by contrasting it:
'Hatred stirs up conflict,
but love covers over all wrongs.'
3) In synthetic parallelism, the second line adds completely new information to the first line:
'Deliverers will go up on Mount Zion to govern the mountains of Esau.
And the kingdom will be the LORD's.'
[30] Psalm 93:1
[31] Psalm 51:5

be the man who told my father the news,"[32] he is not being literal. He does not literally want that man (if there even was such a man) to be cursed; he is rather poetically conveying a deep sense of grief.

Similarly, when we read of God "coming down" or having eyes, ears, hands, and feet, these are samples of God revealing himself to us in ways that we can understand. Biblical scholars call this *anthropomorphism*, in which God, for the sake of relating to us, either takes on human shape in his visitations or allows human authors to describe him in human terms.

In short, we should not take the figurative elements in Hebrew poetry literally.

However, I can't resist adding how remarkable it is that God not only figuratively takes on the shape of a human, but literally too. The Son of God literally "came down" and took on eyes, ears, hands and feet. And when it comes to Jesus' death, amazingly he takes David's *imaginative* description of severe abandonment in Psalm 22 and fulfills it *literally* on the cross: After crying out its first line, "Why have you forsaken me?" he then enacts its inked poetry in real space-time and with real blood:

> "All who see me mock me; they hurl insults, shaking their heads: "He trusts in the LORD," they say, "let the LORD rescue him. Let him deliver him, since he delights in him." ... I am poured out like water, and all my bones are out of joint. My heart has turned to wax; it has melted within me. My mouth is dried up, and my tongue sticks to the roof of my mouth; you lay me in the dust of death. A pack of villains encircle me; they pierce my hands and my feet. All my bones are on display; people stare and gloat over me. They divide my clothes among them and cast lots for my garment."[33]

Song poetry (Psalms)

Unlike the prophets, the songwriters do not mainly speak on behalf of God but *to* God. Even here we must be careful how we read them.

[32] Jeremiah 20:14–15
[33] Psalms 22:1, 7-11

They particularly guide us to relate honestly to God in whatever season we find ourselves. We can use them as our own prayers.

By recognizing what kind of Psalm we are reading, we will be able to interpret it and apply it more accurately. When we understand the different kinds, we can begin to see why some help us to worship God as a gathered church, while others help us to take our pain to God all on our own, or to live more wisely, or to celebrate the long-awaited Messiah-king. These are the ones to look out for: *Lament* psalms, for when we are discouraged or broken, are the largest group (over 60 out of 150). They are either individual or collective lament psalms. When in encouraging circumstances, we can find both individual and collective *thanksgiving* psalms. *Hymns of praise* focus more on God's greatness than on what he can or has done for us: some primarily celebrate him as our creator or as our protector or benefactor. *Salvation-history* psalms retell the story of God's great saving works in the history of his people. There are also *covenant renewal liturgies, David-celebrating* psalms, *king-exalting and -enthroning* psalms, *songs about Zion or Jerusalem, wisdom* psalms and *songs of trust* that implore us to rely on God in all circumstances.[34]

Especially because the Psalms are "the prayer book of the church," we need to read them through the eyes of the gospel. As glorious as these prayers are, laced with authentically expressed and artistically crafted

---

[34] Here is a list of many examples under each kind of Psalm, which I drew from Gordon Fee and Douglas Stuart: 2013, How to read the Bible for all its worth, 4th Edition, Zondervan, Kindle location 3785
Individual lament: 3; 22; 31; 39; 42; 57; 71; 88; 120; 139; 142
Collective lament: 12; 44; 80; 94; 137
Individual thanksgiving: 18; 30; 32; 34; 40; 66; 92; 116; 118; 138
Collective thanksgiving: 65; 67; 75; 107; 124; 136
Praise hymns to God as creator: 8; 19; 104; 148
Praise hymns to God as our protector and benefactor: 33; 103; 113; 117; 145–147
Salvation-history: 78; 105; 106; 135; 136
Covenant renewal liturgies: 50; 81
David-celebrating, king-exalting and -enthroning psalms: 89; 132; 18; 20; 21; 45; 72; 101; 110
Songs about Jerusalem: 46; 48; 76; 84; 87; 122
Wisdom: 36; 37; 49; 73; 90; 112; 127; 128; 133
Songs of trust: 11; 16; 23; 27; 62; 63; 91; 121; 125; 131

truths about God which we should graft into our prayers, and though they prophetically point to the future salvation of the coming Messiah, there is one limitation to using the Psalms as our own prayer book: we now know more about the gospel than these song-writers did.

We can learn to lace the gospel into them when we use them in prayer. For example, the Psalm-writers readily prayed for the destruction of their enemies[35]—Jesus' later teaching that we forgive our enemies, followed by his example of doing so on the cross, had not yet pierced the consciousness of God's people as it has ours. Also, if we compare Paul's prayers with David's prayers, for instance, we notice in Paul's prayers rich references to God the Father, the Holy Spirit, and the Lord Jesus Christ—these ideas about God are barely present in the Psalms, for God's fatherhood and triune nature had not yet been fully revealed at the stage in the story of God when the Psalms were written.

Wisdom poetry (Proverbs)

Proverbs are a collection of tried-and-tested, abridged wisdom to guide us in daily living, teaching us to live a life that does not cut against the grain of God's moral universe. They poetically articulate the basic attitudes and patterns of behaviour that will help a person grow into responsible and godly adulthood.

However, they are not to be taken as commands or as promises. For example, the proverb, "Train up a child in the way he should go: and when he is old, he will not depart from it"[36] is not always true, but most often is. It is a principle, not a promise.

They are also not to be taken alone. Each proverb usually has many other proverbs on the same topic, each highlighting a different nuance. For a larger understanding of a subject, we should hold these Proverbs side-by-side. For example, to clarify that our children will not automatically follow in our faith, we also hear the charge to children:

---

[35] For example we read Psalm 139 and find the most beautiful descriptions of God's attentive care for us, he is all-knowing and always-present. Yet in light of the gospel we need to re-interpret v10–22, in which the Psalmist asks God to slay the wicked even as he expresses his own hatred for those who hate God.

[36] Proverbs 22:6

"Hear, my son, your father's instruction, and forsake not your mother's teaching."[37]

Apocalyptic

This genre is employed partly in Ezekiel, Daniel and Revelation. No book has been more misunderstood than the Revelation because its basic genre is so unfamiliar to us. In the ancient world, if you were told that an apocalyptic scroll had been written, "you know before you even open it that there will be trumpets, plagues, stars, books, strange animals, lots and lots of numbers"[38] and also super-supernatural beings, cosmic battles, and kaleidoscopic imagery.

John is directed by the Spirit to use this genre to encourage churches being threatened by Rome. The book is awash with Old Testament references, apart from which so much does not make sense.

Some of the symbolism is clear enough—Jesus is the one who "was dead, and is alive for ever and ever!"[39] The golden lampstands[40] are the seven churches. The seven stars[41] are either the seven angels or the seven "pastor-messengers" of the churches. The great dragon[42] is Satan, the prostitute[43], the great city of Rome.

Clear symbols aside, we should view the series of visions as a whole and not press every detail to mean something—many are merely for dramatic effect.[44] Details of the sun turning black like sackcloth and the stars falling like figs need not literally mean that this will occur, they serve to make the vision of the earthquake more vivid.

As for the use of numbers, the Jehovah's Witnesses miss entirely what kind of genre this is by concluding that only 144,000 people will be admitted into heaven.[45] But the number symbolizes *all of God's peo-*

---

[37] Proverbs 10:1
[38] E. Richards: 2016, *Misreading Scripture with Western Eyes*, iBooks, ch 3.
[39] Revelation 1:18
[40] Revelation 1:20
[41] Revelation 1:20
[42] Revelation 12:9
[43] Revelation 17:18
[44] Revelation 6:12–14
[45] Revelation 14:1

ple. Do the math: 12 x 12 x 1000 = 144,000, or 12 patriarchs (representing those people of God awaiting the Messiah's first coming) x 12 apostles (those people of God who follow the Messiah, Jesus) x 1000 (which is generic for "a lot of people") = 144,000.

Instead of trying to read into every detail in the book, we would do better to hear its central, clear message: *Hang in there, for no matter what terrible things unfold on the earth and against the church, God is in control, and in the end the Lamb wins!*

QUESTION 3: THE BOOK'S PURPOSE

Next we ask: *Why was this particular book even written?*

Remember, first the forest then the trees. It is crucial we understand the purpose of the whole biblical book when wanting to understand better a particular passage within it.[46] The various authors wrote to specific people for specific reasons. Proverbs, for example, was a collection of collections of nutshell-wisdom, compiled during Solomon's thriving monarchy to pass down the necessary character required of young people for public roles in society.

Later, when reading the epistles, it is especially crucial to ask, "Who wrote it, to whom was this written, and why was it written?"[47] In every case, the author has one or more reasons for writing. Usually, there are one or more behaviours or doctrinal errors that need correcting, or theological misunderstandings that need clearing up.

This is what motivates the author to pick up pen in the first place. We should thus assume that everything in the letter will somehow be shaded by the author's intent. For example, as we read 1 Corinthians 1-4[48] we might at first think Paul is laying out a *random* set of theological

---

[46] The best single-volume resource to help you do this is Gordon Fee and Gordon Stuart's, *How to read the Bible book by book.*

[47] D. A. Carson is at pains to make this point: "The principal point to observe is that the nature of the letters requires that the interpreter make the effort to understand the historical circumstances surrounding the writing of each document" (D.A. Carson: 1994, "Reading the Letters" in *The New Bible Commentary,* IVP Academic, 1114).

[48] Specifically 1 Corinthians 1:10–4:21.

teachings, but they in fact deal with the problem of pride-based division in that church. When we realize that, every paragraph in that section takes on a different hue of meaning than if it was merely sporadic teachings about the cross, the Spirit, leadership, or judgment.

Similarly, does Luke write the book of Acts *primarily* as a universal manual for "how to do church" or "how to be filled with the Spirit"? If we believe that, we may interpret this entire book to teach things the author never intended to teach us. Luke writes Acts to tell how the Spirit of God and the gospel empowered what was at first a Jewish sect to become a vibrant, international community that worked its way, almost unstoppably, all the way to Rome. It is not therefore *primarily* a teaching about how to experience the Spirit or how to organize a church—though of course insights abound for these subjects too.

As for 1 Timothy, Paul writes to help salvage a once-healthy church that had imploded when some elders led the church into false teaching. Sure, there are implications here for how all churches can be organized, but in the main, Paul is teaching how a church in the snares of false teaching can be repaired.

Though most times the addressed problems are clearly stated in Paul's letters, there are times when we are not immediately sure what they are. Much like listening to one end of a telephone conversation, we try to figure out what the unseen party is saying. In Philippians for example, Paul repeatedly emphasizes unity, giving a gospel-centered and practical basis for it. But even this is addressing a situation—suddenly, near the end of the letter he comes out with it: "I plead with Euodia and I plead with Syntyche to be of the same mind in the Lord."[49] Apparently two prominent women in the small church were not getting on.

Forest-related questions aside, let's get to the tree and its branches—the actual passage in question.

---

[49] Philippians 4:3

QUESTION 4: THE FLOW OF THOUGHT

Next we ask: *Based on the section before and after, what is the author trying to say in this passage?*

If the previous questions surface the *situational context*, this one attends to the *literary context*. With the exception of Proverbs,[50] we usually cannot understand a verse without first looking at the flow of thought presented by the larger passage. As much as we want to mine into a verse, or a word in a verse, we must first try to trace the *author's train of thought* in the entire passage. Here's a related analogy: a photo-editor may zoom in on one small section in a photograph of a situation, and frame it in such a way that a viewer, unaware of the large original picture, may conclude something untrue or peripheral about the situation. However, if the viewer first sees the original large-frame picture, they will be less likely to misinterpret or give exaggerated weight to what is in the zoomed-in picture.

This single interpretive principle, perhaps more than any other, is what separates those who wish to see what they want to see in the Bible from those who want to see what's there. As a second analogy, think how often in public discourse, one person may quote the exact words of another in order to undermine them. The other then responds by saying that, "Those were my words, but you took them out of context, and re-presented them in such a way to mean something I was not saying." If it is unfair to take another's words out of context, it is especially unwise to do the same with Scripture.

We might read Paul saying, "As for those agitators, I wish they would go the whole way and emasculate themselves!"[51] and conclude that when people irritate us, we should wish upon them the removal of their genitals. Only as we understand that these agitators are trying to get all the boys and men in a Gentile church to be circumcised in order to properly be accepted by God into his family, can we understand his

---

[50] That said, even the Proverbs are arranged in groups and sections, in such a way that the grouping itself sometimes casts light on each proverb in that group.

[51] Galatians 5:12

sentiment and level of frustration.

"The most important contextual question you will ever ask—and it must be asked over and over of every sentence and every paragraph—is, 'What's the point?'"[52]

Since each book of the Bible has a structure, usually evident in several sections, and is not just a mass of unrelated verses, we must learn to identify new sections or *units of thought* as we read. Most modern translations try to "help us along" by adding headings and using line breaks, though these are not in the original manuscripts and are not always helpful.

The original writers did not use chapter numbers and headings. Instead they provide clues to help us identify new sections. For example, narrative sections, such as the story of Joseph, advance by moving from one scene to the next, each new scene signaled by a new location, time or set of characters. The authors may break up teachings into sections using other devices too. For example, Jesus' Beatitudes in the Sermon on the Mount start and end with "theirs is the kingdom of heaven."[53] Then verses later, Jesus begins a new section in his message by saying, "Do not think that I have come to abolish the Law or the Prophets…"[54] and this section evidently comes to an end with similar wording later, "For this sums up the Law and the Prophets."[55] So doing, Matthew helps us to see these as sections within his Gospel. Straight after that Matthew then recounts many of Jesus' healings—these are evidently a section too.

Paul does the same. In 1 Corinthians 7:1 he writes, "Now for the matters you wrote about…" meaning he will speak to the many questions they put forward in a letter to him. As we read on we find the words "now about" recurring many times[56]—each time a new subject is dealt with—sex and marriage, virgins, food sacrificed to idols, head-

[52] Gordon Fee and Douglas Stuart: 2013, How to read the Bible for all its worth, 4th Edition, Zondervan, Kindle location 469.
[53] Matthew 5:3, 10
[54] Matthew 5:17
[55] Matthew 7:12
[56] 1 Corinthians 7:25; 8:1; 12:1; 16:1; 16:12

coverings in worship, spiritual gifts, the collection and the return of Apollos.

This list of strange situations leads into the next question...

QUESTION 5: THE CULTURAL BACKGROUND

Next we must ask: *Are there any ancient cultural assumptions, situations or practices referred to that are different than our own?*

Allow me to labour the point: only once we discover the ancient meaning to the readers in their ancient situation can we begin to discern the timeless message which we then can, with the help of the Spirit, *re-apply* into the very different situations and contexts we find ourselves in.

In many if not most texts, the situation behind the text is something we can easily enough grasp and to which we can relate. Nonetheless, in many passages the social, historical and cultural world is a universe away from our own, thus making it far more difficult to comprehend and apply. When we fail to acknowledge the distance between their cultural situation and our own, we are more likely to misunderstand and misapply the passage.

Consider as an example the subjects, which we just listed, that Paul deals with in 1 Corinthians: The Corinthian church had particular marriage customs, very different to ours. They were being invited to eat at the temple-restaurants by their pagan friends. A woman's head covering signified basic respectfulness. They were hyper-charismatic, everyone rattling off in tongues at the same time in church meetings. They were busy collecting money for the Jerusalem church, and so on. But see, very few modern churches can relate to any of these situational realities. What is evident from this is how very different their world was to ours.

As much as we may want God to speak to us through Paul's words, we must not bypass the effort needed first to enter into the social, historical, and cultural world of the original readers.

"Ultimately, everything in the Bible was written in particular times and cultures. So even though everything in it is for all time, not everything in it is for all circumstances. The better we understand the circumstances a passage originally addressed, the more confidently we can reapply its message to appropriate circumstances today."[57]

As we are swept up into a story Jesus tells in which neither of two Jewish religious leaders are the hero, but a Samaritan is, it helps to know that the Jews of the time despised Samaritans, disregarding them as contaminated, lost "half-breeds". In so doing, Jesus teaches that not only will some of the most despised people, in our warped view, be included, but they will be instrumental in his kingdom.

When we wonder why the Jewish authorities did not merely privately assassinate Jesus, but sought to bring him to public humiliation on a cross, it helps to understand the *shame-and-honour* culture of the Middle East—they wanted to balance out the many public embarrassments Jesus had brought on them in the course of their many attempts to show him up in public.[58]

As we read of an early internal problem in the first church in which the Grecian Jewish widows were being overlooked in the daily distribution of food while the Hebrew ones were not,[59] it helps to realize the long history of hierarchy in the Jewish world, in which Judean Jews saw themselves as superior to the Jews of other lands. In fact, even Jesus experienced something like this—his and the apostles' Galilean accents were counted against them in Jerusalem.[60]

As we struggle to make sense of Paul's instructions to husbands-wives, parents-children, and master-slaves in the Ephesian households,[61] it helps to know that Greco-Roman culture had elevated Aristotle's household codes in which the father of a house was to rule his wife, his children and his slaves, in that order. Paul draws on the re-

---

[57] Craig Keener: 2016, *The NIV Cultural Background Study Bible*, Zondervan, introductory chapter.
[58] Mark 12:1–7 and Matthew 21:23–22:46 for example.
[59] Acts 6:1
[60] John 7:41–43, Matthew 26:73
[61] Ephesians 5:22–6:9

sources of the gospel and, the good missionary he is, applies them to the Greco-Roman cultural codes in such a way as to redeem those roles, as well as innovatively reframing them within a radical call to joyful, mutual submission.[62]

There's plenty of geographical insights that help us to make sense of the Bible. For example, as we read that, "A man was going *down* from Jerusalem to Jericho"[63] it helps to know that Jerusalem is 2500 feet above sea level while Jericho is 800 feet below sea level. The height of Jerusalem also helps us make sense of why 15 of the Psalms[64] are called "songs of the ascent"—which pilgrims sung while they climbed one of the many uphill paths to the city.

You might ask how an ordinary Bible reader can lay hold of these bits of crucial background information? Where do we get help? Most Study Bibles provide it, though none better in my opinion than the *NIV Cultural Background Study Bible*.

QUESTION 6: WORD AND SENTENCE STUDY

Next we ask: *What do the words, phrases, and their grammatical relationship to each other mean?*

This is where many of us start—analyzing the words and sentence we're studying. But I hope by now you can see that the previous five questions set us up to do this well.

To give you a grasp of how you might analyze a sentence, let us try out a case study of a single verse. Let's look at Romans 8:13:

> *"For if you live according to the flesh, you will die; but if by the Spirit you put to death the misdeeds of the body, you will live."*[65]

Here are some questions we might ask of any verse that might help

---

[62] Ephesians 5:18–21. Additionally, instead of echoing the household code's emphasis of a husband's "lordship" or "rule" over his wife, he calls the husband to love and sacrifice for his wife like Jesus does for his bride, the church (Ephesians 5:25–30).
[63] Luke 10:30
[64] Psalms 120–134
[65] Romans 8:13

us to tease out its meaning:

- *Ask about the words themselves, always in the light of the sentence.* As we compare various translations of the verse,[66] we find the word "live" literally means, "walk"—Paul is referring to our daily choices and lifestyle here, not to our philosophical approach to life. We also learn that the Greek word for "flesh" (*sarx*) means body in other places in the New Testament, but in this sentence, Paul obviously means "sinful nature". The word "die" can be literal or figurative, but in this context, it is more likely figurative, implying we will experience the negative consequences of the misdeeds of our body.

- *Ask about phrases.* A phrase is a group of words that describe some action or person or thing. The phrase "by the Spirit" adds so much to this verse—we do not try to kill our sin on our own, rather we do it in the power of the Spirit.

- *Ask about verbs.* An active verb is something you do. A passive verb is something that is done to you. "Live" in live by the Spirit and "put" in put to death are active verbs, whereas "will live" and "will die" are passive. There are two things we must and can actively do—live by the Spirit and put some things to death.

- *Ask about cause and effect.* Cause and effect occurs in a sentence when the format is, "If this, then that." If we walk by the Spirit, then we will live. If we do not, we die. These are conditional.

- *Ask about connecting words.* The conjunction "for" means that this sentence supports the one preceding it—it is the reason "we do not have an obligation to the sinful nature" (v12). The word "but" means Paul is making his point by using a contrast—either we let sin live and we die, or we kill sin and live.[67]

---

[66] This is such an important point, we return to it in the chapter 12, and Appendix 4.

[67] This is such an important point, we will return to it in the chapter 12 section titled, "Because" and "therefore".

After all those questions, we pull all the threads together. The end of a sentence study, as in a word study, is to re-write the passage in our own words. How would you go about paraphrasing this verse?[68]

To summarize the big idea of this chapter: to find the author's intended meaning, we start off surveying the whole forest then zoom in on a particular tree and then look closer still at its branches. The whole determines the part. Context determines the meaning. The whole Bible is the context for each of its books. Each book is the context for each of its sections. Each section is the context for each of its paragraphs. Each paragraph is the context for each of its sentences. Each sentence is the context for each of its words. Take any text out of its context and you just might be left with a con.

---

[68] Mine is: "If, in your habitual everyday choices, you comply with the desires of your sinful nature, you will suffer the consequences, but if, as you delight in, rely on and keep in step with the Holy Spirit, you learn to deny your sinful desires, you will know the liveliness and peace that only the Holy Spirit can give."

8

THE TIMELESS MESSAGE

The devil took Jesus to... the highest point of the temple. "If you are the Son of God," he said, "throw yourself down. For it is written: 'He will command his angels concerning you, and they will lift you up in their hands.'"... Jesus answered him, "It is also written: 'Do not put the Lord your God to the test.'"

Matthew 4:5-7

In the last chapter we learnt how to plumb into the earthly author's intended meaning to his original recipients. But the best is yet to come: now we learn how to draw out the Heavenly Author's timeless message to us now. To recap, with every text, we are to answer two questions:

1.   What did the human author say to the original audience? That's the ancient meaning, what it meant for them.

2.   What is God saying to us here and now? That's the timeless message, what it means for us.

Having answered the first question, let's move on to the second to discover God's Word for us today.[1]

---

[1] The writer to the Hebrews says God spoke in many ways in the past days via many prophets (Hebrews 1:1). Scot McKnight, in his book *The Blue Parakeet*, rephrases this as God speaking in "those days" in "those ways." So God spoke in Moses' days in Moses' ways. He also spoke in David's days in David's ways, in Jeremiah's days in Jeremiah's ways, in Jesus' days in Jesus' ways, in John's days in John's ways. The task before us then is to hear God speak once again, this time to us in our days and in our ways, through the very words that he once spoke to others in their days and their ways.

The six questions in the previous chapter bring us to the seventh question and perhaps most important to ask of any passage.

QUESTION 7: ITS TIMELESS MESSAGE

What is the timeless message in this text that we must re-apply to our situation? To a person longing to hear God speak to them, this is the prize question. It may deliver such a sweet reply, that we will be tempted to bypass the previous six questions. We must not jump over the first six questions for the reason that:

> *"The Christian today is separated from the biblical audience by a "river" of differences (e.g., language, culture, circumstances, stage in the redemptive story). This river hinders us from moving straight from meaning in their context to meaning in ours. We are certainly part of the same great story, but our place in the story is often different from that of our spiritual ancestors. Sometimes the river is wide, requiring a long bridge for crossing. At other times, it is a narrow creek, which we can cross easily. We need to know just how wide the river is before we start trying to construct a principalizing bridge across it."[2]*

Don't be intimidated by the big words in this quote. Call it what you will, the goal is to get to the "principalizing bridge" or "theologising principle" or (my preference) "timeless message" which we can apply to our lives, our church and our world. Depending on the particular passage, this timeless message tends to come in one of the following forms. There might be some...

- principle to apply
- example to follow
- warning to heed
- promise to believe

---

[2] Duvall and Hays: 2012, *Grasping God's Word*, Zondervan, ch 13.

- doctrine to grasp[3]

- wisdom to learn

- instruction to obey

These are the seven forms timeless truth usually takes. In case this is too abstract for you, let me provide some examples of the articulations of the first five forms in the list above that I noticed as I was recently reading the book of Esther...

In 2:11-20, I found this *principle to apply* as I read about Esther's year long preparation to become queen in Persia: *patience, humility and wise mentors may help us prepare for our future work for God.*

In 4:15-17, I noted this *example to follow* as Esther, heeding God's nudge through her uncle Mordecai, takes the life-threatening risk of approaching the king uninvited: *true obedience leaves the outcome to God.*

In 5:9-13, I spotted this *warning to heed* as I read about a man called Haman letting his social position and affluence go to his head and eventually lead to his death: *prosperity can make us dangerously proud.*

In 8:14-17, I identified this *promise to believe* as I read of a genocidal plot to destroy God's people backfiring, and bringing them honour instead: *God works all things for the good of those who believe.*

Finally, since the author of Esther records dates so carefully all the way through, I discerned this *doctrine to grasp: our times are in God's hands.* (If you're curious, in *Appendix 1* at the back of this book, I show you more fully how I get to these articulations in each case in Esther.)

If you're brand new to identifying these timeless messages in the Bible's pages, you might be overly impressed by my ability to find them. I know what you feel, for I felt the same when I first started out in Bible study, but I assure you that you too will be able to find them as you start to practice.

---

[3] By "doctrine" I mean what the Bible teaches about those subjects that loom largest in Scripture, such as God, Jesus, the Holy Spirit, Scripture itself, humanity, creation, salvation, the church, the kingdom, and the future of all things. In this book, the word is used interchangeably with theology.

THE ART OF ARTICULATING TIMELESS TRUTHS

Putting the timeless message in words is not a science. It is an art. This morning my wife and I enjoyed a rare moment of reading and discussing a Bible chapter together. Having established that Psalm 127 is a wisdom Psalm, we sought to identify its teaching. We found two principles to apply:

- *Trust-based rest is a form of spiritual warfare (v1-2)*

- *Joyfully raising children is a form of spiritual warfare (v3-5)*

Today is both our day of weekly rest and of extra time together as a family, so this insight is especially well timed. (It's amazing how God tends to do that by the way.) But the thing I stress here is that arriving at these two articulations of this Psalm's timeless message, took not only logic, but also a kind of creativity, which you too can learn. Here is a hodgepodge of four aspects to this art form that has helped me...

First, most times, putting the timeless message in a phrase or sentence is the heart of the art. The authors of the book, *Grasping God's Word*,[4] call these statements "the theologizing principle," the truth that bridges the biblical world and ours. The authors also give us litmus test questions to make sure that we have properly articulated it:

- Is this "truth" truly evident in the text?

- Is it relevant to both the original biblical audience and the contemporary audience?

- Is it stated in a timeless way, not tied to a particular culture or situation?

Second, some parts of the Bible seem to be more truth-intensive. All Scripture is equally inspired, but not all Scripture is equally rich in timeless meaning. Especially, I have found that teaching sections of

---

[4] Duvall and Hays: 2012, *Grasping God's Word*, Zondervan, chapter 2. I have left out a fourth criteria they mentioned, "Does it correspond with the rest of Scripture?" because I deal with that point in the next section.

Scripture—Jesus' teachings and the New Testament epistles for example—are often far more "truth-intensive" than narrative or poetic portions of Scripture. By this I do not mean that they are truer or more important, just that there are more truths in the same amount of text. For instance, one might read and study an entire chapter or two from a narrative section in 1 or 2 Kings and identify three or four timeless messages that arise from it, whereas just one or two verses in the letter to the Ephesians or Romans may be embedded with the same number.[5]

Third, and this counterbalances the previous point, narrative truths are powered by the story itself. We must never merely extract or "nutshell" the truth from a biblical story, then forget the story itself. Especially in narrative sections, the truth and story are inseparable—a story has the power to settle on us in a way that an isolated pithy statement never could.

For example, a few days ago I pondered the story in which king David's son drives him from his home and throne in a *coup d'etat.* As he dejectedly marches out into the countryside, someone called Shimei walks alongside him for hours, calling him a scoundrel, saying he deserves this ejection from Jerusalem, and pelting him with stones. One of David's generals offers to cut off Shimei's head, but David opts to receive the shameful treatment instead because he does not feel this is a cause worth fighting.[6] To merely reduce this Scripture passage to a pithy "let the haters hate" or "criticism may humiliate," then toss out the story like an empty container drains those truths of much of their power. For me, with that story in my mind for the day—I could picture dirt being mercilessly flung at David's weeping face—I was able to find consolation from God as I gave over to him some painful memories of times when I, in a time of great vulnerability, have endured persistent and sometimes unfair criticism cast upon me like mud upon my tears.

---

[5] This becomes evident in the typical length of Bible commentaries or sermon series—as a preacher I have found it possible to preach through Nehemiah in seven messages, whereas it takes twice that amount of time at least to do so through Ephesians, a much shorter book.

[6] 2 Samuel 16:5-13

Fourth, as in all art forms, learn from better artists:

"If reading Scripture is an art, another conclusion follows: we learn the practice of an art through apprenticeship to those who have become masters. Learning to read Scripture well and imaginatively must be done at the feet of those who have gone before us and performed, in their lives of embodied faithfulness, beautiful interpretations of Scripture."[7]

Whose feet do *you* sit at? Who are the preachers, teachers, Bible Study leaders, authors or pastoral commentary writers that will guide you in this art? My advice here is that you have more rather than fewer artists that you learn from—if you fixate on one, there is the danger that you merely imitate their art. In fact, it is only as you are exposed to a plethora of artistic styles, that you are more likely to find your own.

EIGHT PRINCIPLES FOR FINDING THE TIMELESS MESSAGE

We're on sacred ground here. Correctly drawing out a passage's timeless truth for our lives is essential, for it shapes what we ought to believe and how we ought to live.

For a few of you our current exploration of interpretive principles is old hat and perhaps an easy read, but if you're a first-timer to the world of biblical interpretation, and you've been reading straight through from the previous chapter, I can imagine your brain being a little *tired*. So go ahead, put the book down, get a hot drink or take a walk and come back with a fresh brain, because there are still eight critically important things you need to know that will equip you to better understand and apply so much of the Bible. (The next chapter onwards will be a relatively easier read, so hang in there.)

Over and above the six questions we explored in the last chapter for discovering the ancient meaning, *here are eight interpretive principles to keep in mind as we seek to mine out the timeless message in a passage:*

---

[7] *The Art of Reading Scripture*, 2003, iBooks, introductory chapter.

The Old Shines On The New

The first principle is to let the Old Testament shine light on the New Testament. Since God reveals himself progressively across the time-span of Scripture, explore references to earlier Scriptures. About one in ten verses in the New Testament cite or allude to something in the Old Testament. The New Testament writers see Christ as the fulfillment, not the contradiction, of what went before. The earlier writings throw light on the later writings.

For example, when Jesus tells Nicodemus that he is to be born of water and the Spirit,[8] he can't be referring to Christian baptism which he only instates three years later. Rather, he is alluding to Ezekiel's prophecy about how God would one day sprinkle cleansing water and renew by the Spirit the hearts of people.[9]

Likewise, Jesus' preferred title "the Son of man" alludes to Daniel's prophecy about "someone like a son of man,"[10] a divine figure who would co-rule the nations with God and receive their worship. The Revelation's vision of the new Jerusalem in the shape of a cube[11] has deliberate links to the cubed Most Holy Place in the Jerusalem temple.[12] What comes before throws light on what comes after.

Across the span of the many stages of God's people in the Bible, God shines more and more light on subjects that slowly unveil. Theologians call this *progressive revelation.* One example of this is how, across the breadth of the Old Testament, there's only a few hints of the afterlife, growing in clarity over time, starting with Moses' writing, then that of David, Isaiah, and Daniel.[13] Jesus and the apostles finally add much more detail to this teaching.

The same is true of almost every doctrine of Scripture. As new au-

---

[8] John 3:5
[9] Ezekiel 36:25–27
[10] Daniel 7:13–14
[11] Revelation 21:16
[12] 2 Chronicles 3:8
[13] First Moses' writings in Genesis 5:25; 25:8 and Exodus 3:6, then David in Psalms 16:0–11; 49:9,15; 73:24–26, then Isaiah in Isaiah 25:8; 26:19 and Daniel in Daniel 12:2,13..

thors write their books, God gives us more and more to help us understand, for example, the work of Satan, the person of Jesus, the nature of God, and the destiny of humankind. Evidently, across the Bible's time span, from Genesis 1 to Revelation 22, God adds new hues of meaning and revelation to almost every doctrine, topic, or theme.[14]

In all this, the later bits don't contradict the earlier bits, any more than later brush strokes on a canvas contradict the artist's layers of colour underneath. Every brush-stroke matters, but it's only after the final layer is added, so enriched by the deeper strokes, that we understand the whole picture.

The New Shines On The Old

The second principle is to let the New Testament shine light on the Old. Not only do we interpret the newer parts in light of the older, we do so the other way around too. Let us consider how the New Testament helps us interpret and apply Moses' law and the Old Testament stories:

First, the New Testament shines light on the Old Testament law. To a modern Western reader of non-Jewish descent, the strangest part of the Bible are the 613 laws of Moses, most of which are ceremonial or civil, but also some of which are moral in nature. How do we interpret and apply these laws in Exodus through Deuteronomy that make up the bulk of the Bible's first quarter and take up some 2,000 verses? I will try to answer concisely:

The ceremonial laws have to do with the tabernacle structure, the priests' responsibilities, the sorts of animals to be sacrificed and how to make such offerings. Hebrews teaches us that these ceremonial laws are all fulfilled, made obsolete, in Jesus' high-priestly ministry and once-for-all sacrifice on the cross.

The civil laws detail penalties for various crimes, some major and some minor, for which one might be arrested and tried in Israel. Since the people of God are no longer an ethnic tribe, these civil laws no longer apply to God's people.

---

[14] We will especially make this point in chapter 16.

Civil laws and ceremonial laws no longer binding, what about the moral laws? Many argue that overtly *moral laws* like the 10 commands apply to believers.[15] Many of the 10 commands are repeated in other words in the New Testament. But even here Jesus claims to lead us into a new command of Christ-like love that not only incorporates but also *outstrips* what Moses called for. Jesus would say about these preceding moral laws, "You have heard it said... but I tell you..."[16] Being under Jesus' leadership is something higher and more dynamic than being under Moses' law. The apostle Paul likewise calls followers of Jesus to live *intentionally* in step with the Spirit as he daily leads us into a life of radical love for God, neighbour and enemy. As we do so, we find that we will *incidentally* fulfill the moral requirements of Moses' law.[17]

When it comes to these laws of Moses, keep in mind that the Bible is a multi-staged story, one that is for all people, yet instructions given in one part or one level (to return to our analogy of a building) of the story do not necessarily apply to those in other stages of it.[18] So that's what to do with the laws of Moses, but what about the stories of God's people before Jesus came? Glad you asked...

Second, the New Testament shines light on the Old Testament stories. The first pastor I sat under Sunday after Sunday used to love preaching Old Testament narrative parts of the Bible. He used to say, "Many of the Old Testament stories are picture-forms of New Testament truths." For example, as he preached about Esther being beautified in preparation for her role as the queen, he would jump to Ephesians 5 and speak of the church being beautified in godliness as part of what it means to be Christ's bride. When Esther boldly approaches the king in his throne room to make a request, he would bounce to the passage in Hebrews where we are instructed to approach God's throne of mercy with

---

[15] One exception is that the application of the Sabbath is revised from a stringent law to a principle of work-rest rhythm, and also depicts the salvation-rest Jesus has purchased for his people (see Hebrews 4:1–11).
[16] For example, Matthew 5:21–22.
[17] Galatians 5:13–25
[18] Another example of this is that the way David structured his political kingdom is hardly the basis for how church leaders should organize their churches.

confidence. When the plan of Haman, Esther's enemy backfires and leaves the people of God in a better place, he would delight in the way Satan's efforts to crucify Jesus backfired and put the world in a much better place. Then near the end of Esther, when she sends out the news of a potentially life-saving decree to the Jews across the vast Persian Empire, he would remind us of the urgency of the "life-saving" gospel message to go to the ends of the world.

Was this pastor violating Scripture by using Old Testament stories as analogies of New Testament truths?

There are two schools of thought: The one is to limit ourselves only to what is evidently being communicated by the original author to the original readers, and only draw out any additional analogies if a New Testament author does so with that very story at hand. So when we come to Jacob and Esau, we may consider how Paul uses that part of Genesis to teach on God's sovereign, unmerited choice of people to do his work.[19] Or when we come to Hagar/Ishmael and Sarah/Isaac, we may use their rivalry as an analogy of the difference between the old and new covenants only because Paul does so.[20] So, by this school of thought, my pastor had gone too far, because no New Testament texts made those particular connections to Esther.

The second school of thought takes everything the first says as true but denies the use of the word "only". This view *also accepts, even encourages, an appreciation for the ways many an Old Testament story depicts or illustrates certain New Testament truths, even if no New Testament writer articulated this connection.*

My own feeling is that it would be a mistake to forbid this way of preaching Scripture and reading it devotionally in the name of "good interpretation." As we said, Paul did it and we may follow his example. In one place[21] he waxes lyrically about the ancient Israelites passing through the sea "of baptism," then spiritually drinking from the "rock of Christ" "which accompanied them" in the wilderness journey, then

---

[19] Romans 9:6–18
[20] Galatians 4:21–31
[21] 1 Corinthians 10:1–11

sinning (or "testing Christ") and having their bodies scattered in the desert as a result, an analogy of future judgment. In this sermonic flourish he liberally draws analogies between the Israelites in the wilderness and our present experience of Christ. He even calls these connections *typoi*—a Greek word meaning "types" or "patterns." Following on Paul's heels, some of the most famous Christian preachers in history have done the same. Bishop Ambrose in the fourth century converted Augustine with this kind of preaching[22] and Charles Spurgeon, the famed prince of preachers, used the same approach in almost every message.[23]

This approach to reading the Old Testament has particularly helped me when it comes to the numerous stories of God's people, sometimes disturbingly violent, involved in bloody wars or combat of some kind with human enemies. These Old Testament stories, as well as the Psalm-writers' many prayers directed *against* some enemy shed old light on the ways God now enables us to recognize, withstand and defeat "the spiritual forces of darkness" that wage war against us still. After all, in the new covenant and in the age of the church we find ourselves in, our true enemies are not "flesh and blood," but "spiritual forces" like unbelief, compromise, disunity, heresy, injustice, intimidation, sin, Satan and death.[24] Through these ancient stories "God trains our hands for war."[25]

All that to say, I propose that we feel the same liberty as Paul, Ambrose and Spurgeon did to look for New Testament truths which may

---

[22] Of interest, Augustine rejected the Bible because he struggled to believe that some of the Old Testament stories were historically true, but when he heard Ambrose preaching from those stories, and experienced the power of the gospel-illuminating points Ambrose made, he was able, in his mind, to accept the Bible as the Word of God. I suspect many a skeptic has taken a similar path to faith in the Bible. For the sake of skeptics present, in my own preaching on the flood for example, I spend less time trying to persuade my hearers that "the flood really happened", and more time declaring the gospel truths it so vividly portrays.

[23] Spurgeon would counsel other preachers, when preaching New Testament truths, to try to find an illustration in the Bible itself before reaching for one in their own life experience.

[24] See 2 Corinthians 10:3-5, Ephesians 6:10-18.

[25] Psalm 114:1

be illustrated in Old Testament stories.

Having said that, three warnings must be issued. Firstly, do not side-step finding the author's intended meaning. The danger is that if we are particularly imaginative and good at making connections, we might too quickly jump to the New Testament truths and fail to see just how much God intends to say to us in the Old Testament text, even without the "aid" of the New Testament.

Secondly, be careful not to see connections that are almost definitely *not* there. I heard of a Bible teacher enthusiastically "explaining" how the tent pegs in the Old Testament tabernacle pointed to Christ: he noted that they were made of bronze to depict how Christ's work for us on the cross would not corrode; also the tent pegs were half in the ground *and* half protruded, which, the preacher said with certainty, referred to the death *and* resurrection of Jesus.

Finally, do not assume that all of God's people are *meant* to see each connection. Very possibly, God's Spirit never intended that connection as he inspired the Bible, even if the parallel is quite compelling to you, and perhaps you are spiritually encouraged by it.

For example I once preached through Esther and, just seven verses in, I was struck by a detail of the king's banquet: he liberally supplied wine to each person in their own golden goblet, and as much as they wished. I saw a connection between it and John chapter two, when king Jesus revealed his glory at a wedding feast by supplying abundant wine to all, and also Ephesians chapter five which says that instead of getting drunk on wine we should be filled with God's Spirit. Though I was quite excited by the connections, I knew it was wise to introduce my point with a disclaimer: "*I am not saying God meant for us all to see this*, but this wine-saturated banquet reminds me of…"

Scripture Interprets Scripture

The third principle is to read Scripture in the light of all other Scripture. As we read at the start of this chapter, Jesus used this same principle when Satan quoted Psalm 91 to pressure Jesus to jump off a cliff and claim God's promise to be caught by angels. He shot back, correcting the evil one's misinterpretation, by quoting another passage that forbids testing God.[26] According to Jesus, *Scripture is the best interpreter of Scripture.*

Especially when a passage's meaning is unclear, read it in light of other things said by the same author, as well as the rest of Scripture on the same topic. Simpler passages are those that are easier to interpret, while more difficult passages are called so precisely because they can be interpreted in several ways.

Very practically this means that we list all the ways a difficult passage could be plausibly interpreted, then narrow that list down by eliminating those ways which are incompatible with the teaching of clearer passages on the same subject elsewhere.

For example, does Paul mean for women to remain silent in all the Corinthian worship meetings, and indeed all churches everywhere, for all time?[27] In a small frame, looking at only these verses, that might seem to be what Paul is saying. But zooming out to see the bigger frame shows otherwise. In this case, it contradicts Paul's many instructions *in the same letter* for women to share teachings, prayers and prophecies in their meetings.[28]

Does Paul really instruct that women may never, in any church setting, lead or teach where a man is present?[29] A small frame may cause us to accept this interpretation. But when we read this Scripture in light of other Scripture on the same subject, we are led to ask why Paul then co-planted the very church he is now addressing with a married couple, Priscilla and Aquila, who both taught doctrine to a man.[30] Paul also later commended Priscilla and several other women, apparently all part of the leadership core of the Roman church, for their high-impact kingdom contributions.[31]

---

[26] Deuteronomy 6:16
[27] 1 Corinthians 14:34–35
[28] 1 Corinthians 11:5, 14:6
[29] 1 Timothy 2:12
[30] Acts 18:18–26
[31] In Romans 16:1–16, Paul greets 27 people by name, people he has had a history of serving God alongside. He marks out ten of them in particular with the terms "those

Figurative vs Literal

The fourth principle is to distinguish between figurative and literal elements. Even outside the poetic books of the Bible, figurative elements and figures of speech abound. These parts should not be taken literally, any more than I do if my wife says to me, "I've asked you a thousand times," or if I tell my oldest kid, "You are a night owl."

Does the ground literally "open its mouth to receive" Abel's blood, which then "cries out"?[32] Does Jesus literally hand us "the keys of the kingdom"? [33] Is Jesus' blood "real drink" and his flesh "real food" in a literal sense?[34] No, on all counts something *real but not literal* is being described.

And when the Bible speaks about the prospect of facing God's final judgment without Jesus by our side, it describes it in various places as a second death, a desolate graveyard called *Sheol* or *Hades*, a lake of fire, worms that do not die, weeping and gnashing of teeth, rising smoke, outer darkness, *Tartarus*[35] (where the Titans were chained for their punishment in the Greek literary work of the Odyssey) and *Gehenna*[36] (the cursed valley of Hinnom near Jerusalem where Jewish kings once sacrificed their children). Though these speak of something real and clearly terrible, we must remember they are not actual descriptions (unless one can imagine fire *and* darkness being the same thing, and Tartarus *and* Gehenna being the same place).

Jesus employed figures of speech all the time. One of his favourite was using *hyperbole* (overstatement) to make a point vividly. For example, he tells us to remove our offending limb or eye; to not let our left hand know what our right hand is doing; not to call any man on

---

who work hard in the Lord" and "fellow-workers." Elsewhere Paul uses these terms to describe not only his own ministry (1 Corinthians 4:12; Galatians 4:11) but also the ministry of the most senior leaders who worked alongside him, such as Timothy (Rom 16:21), Apollos (1 Corinthians 3:9), Titus (2 Corinthians 8:23) and Luke (Philemon 24). Yet in this chapter, of the ten people described by these terms, seven are women.
[32] Genesis 4:10
[33] Matthew 16:19
[34] John 6:55
[35] 2 Peter 2:4
[36] Luke 12:5

earth father; and to hate our family in comparison to our love for him. We should take him seriously but not literally, in each case there is some pressing truth he wants us to get: avoid sin; give without trying to draw praise for your giving; recognize God as your ultimate father; and find your primary identity in God not your family.

Jesus' parables are the most prominent example of his figurative teaching. When he tells a story of a scolding woman wearing down the patience of a judge, or a king plunging into an ill-planned war, or a group of children quarreling in the street, or a man mugged and left for dead by robbers, or a single woman who loses a penny and acts as if she has lost everything[37] he communicates a surprising truth about his kingdom on the back of an everyday scenario. In each story he starts with what we know, our field of lived experience, and then takes us to what we do not know, his field of spiritual reality. By using pictures and stories his message bypasses our intellectual defenses and goes straight to our hearts. For example, instead of merely saying, "God loves you no matter what," he tells a story of a heartsick father who scans the horizon every night for some sign of his wayward son.

A vital thing to remember about parables is that, though one or two of them are analogies with many points (such as the parable of the sower who sows seed in four places, each representing a different state of heart), in almost all cases *each parable makes only a single point.* So when we read Jesus' parable of the mustard seed[38] we pick up on Jesus' recurring idea about the reversal of fortunes—in the same way a tiny seed becomes the largest tree, so the small, obscure kingdom revolution he was starting would eventually take over history. With that main point in mind, we should *not* additionally try to find a meaning in his references to the many branches and the birds in the branches. These are side-details that merely fill out the picture and story.

Also be on the look out for *picture words* in the Bible. When we find them, *we should not import our modern or personal associations onto*

---

[37] Credit to Philip Yancey in *The Jesus I Never knew* for this way of describing some of Jesus' parables.
[38] Mark 4:30–32

them, but try to understand what ancient readers might have "seen" in them. For example, when we read in Ephesians that Jesus is the *head* of the church his body, or the husband is the *head* of the wife, we moderns tend to read it only as a synonym for chief, ruler, governor or leader (think "head waiter" or "head of state" for example). The first readers however would likely have visualized something far more nuanced: a head intricately connected to the body it responsively partners with as it cares for, nourishes, serves and guides it.

Or when we read that God is *our Father*, we must make sure that we mentally populate this pivotal metaphor not with our personal experiences of earthly fathers who may have been absent, apathetic, aloof, authoritarian or abusive. Rather we are to think *only of those associations the New Testament writers pack into the metaphor*—a God who gives us spiritual life, a royal identity and a place in his family: a God who is unconditionally loving and all-wise, showing the deepest imaginable interest in us, our situation and our development; and a God who is ready to encourage, protect, provide for, deliver, guide, instruct, correct, praise, and heap lavish affection upon us.

Particular vs Universal

The fifth principle is to distinguish between particular and universal commands. Since we are not part of the old covenant but the new one, every Scripture-recorded command to the ancient nation of Israel should be assumed to be commands *particular to people in that stage of the story of redemption.* Whether commands not to eat shellfish, to offer animal sacrifices, or to march around a city seven times, there may (or may not) be some timeless principle encoded into that particular command that applies to us—but we must not assume God wants us to obey the command in the same way they received it.

Likewise, every Scripture-recorded command to an individual should be taken as a particular, not universal, command. When Jesus tells a blind man to receive his healing by washing in the pool of Siloam, he is not saying that all blind people should wash in some designated pool. When Paul tells Timothy to take some wine for his stomach troubles, he is not suggesting that pharmaceutical companies will not find even better medicines. When Jesus tells the rich man to sell everything and give it to the poor, he is not instructing all wealthy people to do the same.

Yet, even in these commands to particular people, there is often timeless truth for all: People who are trusting God for healing may be directed by the Spirit to take some action that requires faith. When a friend is sick, we do not only pray for their healing, but may encourage them to use medicine. All wealthy Christ-followers will need to lay their wealth on the altar, trust in God not money, be generous generally and be open to Spirit-guided promptings to give unusually large gifts.

Also, we must ask if this is a message for the church or a message for the entire world. So far we have not distinguished between what is the revealed will of God for all people everywhere as opposed to the will of God for followers of Jesus and the church.

An interesting exercise is to ask, "What commands or principles in the Bible are applicable to non-believers and all of society?" What we discover is how little there is in Scripture in terms of ethics that speak directly to those outside of the faith community. In the Old Testament, even the ten commands are given specifically to those who have been "brought out of Egypt."[39] Even the Proverbs, which offer nuggets of wisdom, insist that they only make sense upon the foundation of "the fear of the Lord."[40] Paul did not take it upon himself to hold the whole of society to account for their sins, only the church. He says, "What business is it of mine to judge those outside the church?"[41] Unlike the Islamic Quran that focuses on the reformation of society under Allah, the New Testament's focus is on the people of Jesus living as a redemptive, countercultural community within a largely unbelieving world.

As much as believers in the past and now have tried to offer society a *watertight* code of morality that they claim is explicitly revealed from

---

[39] Exodus 20:2
[40] Proverbs 9:10
[41] 1 Corinthians 5:21

God to the whole world, they have often merely projected the teaching and standards of Jesus onto a non-believing people. Yet the Sermon on the Mount was given to Jesus' disciples and those who wanted to learn about life in his kingdom. In the New Testament, every letter and the Revelation are written for believers. The Gospels, however, address both believers and non-believers. John's Gospel, for example, was "written that you may believe that Jesus is the Messiah, the Son of God, and that by believing you may have life in his name."[42]

So what message is the church meant to take to the world? John's Gospel sets us on course—the primary application of Scripture *to a non-believing world* is the life-giving message of the Son of God, it is not a call to morality. Only once we believe do we receive the spiritual resources needed to live a morally renewed life.[43]

Transcultural vs Cultural

The sixth principle is to distinguish between transcultural (and timeless) truth and the ancient cultural application of it. Our earlier question about cultural background will prove immensely helpful at this point. When we fail to acknowledge the wide river between the cultural world of the ancients and that of our own, we run the risk of naïvely trying to export not only the transcultural, timeless message but also bits of that culture into our own.[44] Said another way, we must keep the "kernel"

---

[42] John 20:30

[43] In the same vein, in the many evangelistic messages recorded in the book of Acts, it is evident that the early church apparently did not try to impose its God-revealed standards of godliness on society, but rather used what limited airtime they had to communicate the gospel of Jesus. Although there are many lists in the New Testament of the kinds of sins present in non-believing people (Romans 1:21–32), these lists are not checklists of things that society and sinners should "try to avoid from now on." If anything, they can be applied as a means of persuading people not of their need for moral reformation by their own strength, but of their need for a personal salvation from sin's penalty and power that will then, as a byproduct, begin to renew them morally (Philippians 2:12).

[44] The fact that God was willing to incarnate his gospel into a particular culture in history, as recorded in Scripture, does not mean he wants to export that culture to all cultures in the future. Disentangling what is transcultural from what is cultural is a crucial task of the Bible reader. The same can be said of Jesus incarnating into Jewish culture. As the Jerusalem Council in Acts 15 would later conclude, this does not mean

but discard the "husk."

Some examples. When Jesus tells his disciples to wash the weary traveller's feet, we may apply the transcultural principle of humble service differently in our particular culture—finding ways to get out of our comfort zones, and serving people of seemingly lower position practically.

When Paul advocates short hair in men, and women covering their heads in the Corinthian church,[45] he likely appeals to local, cultural norms that will send out a message of credibility for the fledgling church in the eyes of a suspicious culture. The likely "kernel" principle is a mutually honouring relationship between genders and the avoidance of sexual allure in one's presentation. The culture-specific "husk" of wearing headscarves can be left behind.

When Paul tells a church to greet each other with a holy kiss, we may apply the principle of familial warmth *appropriate in our particular culture*—a fist bump, high five, elbow tap, or a hug perhaps.[46] And when he tells women in one church not to wear braided hair, ornate jewelry and expensive clothing in church meetings, but rather adorn themselves with godly deeds,[47] he is countering the ways some wealthy Ephesian women would ostentatiously flaunt their wealth and/or beautification in that society. The timeless principles are humility and sensitivity to people with less in the church, something not only women but all believers must remember. Indeed, in other cultures it may be appropriate to wear jewelry and do up one's hair while still holding to these values.

Clear vs Cloudy

The seventh principle is to distinguish between what is clear/central and

---

that his followers outside of Israel would have to take on Jewish culture.

[45] 1 Corinthians 11:4–5

[46] It's important to isolate the timeless principle correctly. For example, when Paul tells the Corinthians not to eat idol-meat in the temples, he is not saying we should avoid restaurants—rather we should avoid gatherings where witchcraft and the occult are on show.

[47] 1 Timothy 2:9

what is cloudy or peripheral. Most texts are clear, but some are cloudy.[48] A cloudy text is one which has an unusual number of obscure terms, or does not make sense according to a "straight-forward" reading, or that is particularly difficult to apply in concrete situations. Its most obvious indicator is that it gives rise to many diverse interpretations, and is thus heavily debated by scholars.[49]

The general rule is that cloudy texts must be interpreted in light of clearer ones.[50] Central and clear texts are those with content that is attested in multiple verses—salvation by grace through faith, Jesus' deity, Jesus' promised return, the Spirit's power and so on.[51] Peripheral texts, usually with a solitary mention of what they seem to say, such as wearing head-coverings "because of the angels"[52] or being "baptized for the dead"[53] or Christ's preaching to the "imprisoned spirits"[54] or "women being saved through childbearing,"[55] must not be given as much weight as the clear, central ones. Instead of being dogmatic or building substantial doctrines or practices on these cloudier passages, churches should hold their interpretations of them more lightly.

Prescriptive vs Descriptive

The eighth principle is to distinguish between what the Bible merely de-

---

[48] For example, Peter acknowledged things that were "hard to understand" in Paul's writings (2 Peter 3:16). Peter's term was also used in the ancient world of oracles, which were notoriously capable of more than one interpretation.

[49] For example, Hebrews 6:4-6 has at least 18 lines of interpretation, and 1 Timothy 2:12 has 12.

[50] For example, Tertullian, the second-century church father, wrote that "uncertain statements should be determined by certain ones, and obscure ones by such as are clear and plain." (*On the Resurrection of the Flesh*, 21, in *ANF* 3:569, cited in Gregg Allison: 2011, *Historical Theology*, Zondervan, 122).

[51] Section 1.7 in *the Westminster Confession of Faith* says, "All things in Scripture are not alike plain in themselves, nor alike clear unto all; yet those things which are necessary to be known, believed, and observed for salvation, are so clearly propounded, and opened in some place of Scripture or other, that not only the learned, but the unlearned, in a due use of the ordinary means, may attain unto a sufficient understanding of them."

[52] 1 Corinthians 11:10

[53] 1 Corinthians 15:29

[54] 1 Peter 3:19

[55] 1 Timothy 2:15

scribes and what it prescribes. Jesus went to Jerusalem two or three times a year. Should we do the same? No, because he never instructed us to do so. Gideon put out a fleece to confirm God's will.[56] Do we do the same? Not at all, especially because the narrator shows God using Gideon, not because of his faith, but despite his lack of it.

The Roman and Ephesian church were told to obey and pray for their emperor and king.[57] Does this mean that God's preferred form of government in every nation is a monarchy? No, because these verses describe the form of government of that time, they don't prescribe it for all nations at all times.

Bible characters, such as Abraham and Sarah, Moses and Joshua, king Saul and king David, Esther and Mordecai, and Peter and John, are sometimes good and wise, sometimes evil or foolish, sometimes an example to follow and others times a warning to heed. We are not always told whether their characteristics and actions are universally prescribed or forbidden or neither. Here especially we must confirm our insights with parts of the Bible where instructions and commands *are* clearly given on the matter.[58]

Said another way, the teaching portions of the Bible, when correctly interpreted, help us to interpret and apply correctly the narrated portions of the Bible. In other words, Joseph's fleeing adultery is something all of us should do, we know for sure, because of the many biblical texts that expressly forbid adultery and esteem sexually faithful, monogamous marriages.

WHAT ALL CHURCHES MUST DO

Can you see by now why the obedience of Christians and churches to God's Word must be married to study? The longing to obey God is

---

[56] Judges 6:36–40

[57] Romans 13:1, 1 Timothy 2:1–2

[58] Common sense comes in handy too—it's obvious enough that we should follow David's example of trusting God in a tight spot, but not follow his example of sleeping with his friend's wife.

good, but can be misguided if we fail in the task of good interpretation. Eugene Peterson in "Eat this book," tells of a Jewish rabbi he once studied the Old Testament with who would say, "For us Jews, studying Scripture is more important than obeying it because if you don't understand it rightly you will obey it wrongly and your obedience will be disobedience."

This is very wise. As a preacher, I have become more aware of the possibility that I will use Scripture to call God's people to do something that, if only I understood the Bible better, God does not in fact expect from them. How do we discern from Scripture what specific practices all churches in all cultures *must* do? My advice is to be sure, not doubly but triply—the clearest indication is a positive answer to three questions:

- Did Jesus do it and command it in the Gospels?
- Did the first churches practice it in Acts and the epistles?
- Did the apostles command it of all churches in Acts and the epistles?

Texts that fulfill these criteria offer us, in terms of interpretation, "a narrow creek, which we can cross easily." When we ask these three questions about whether we should give our allegiance to Jesus as Lord, take communion, be baptized in water, make disciples, reach out to people far from God, preach the gospel, study and teach the Scriptures, serve and uplift the poor, pursue justice for others, include the outsider, care for new believers, raise up leaders, pray fervently, sing praises to God, humble ourselves, repent of our sins, forgive our enemies, endure hardships with unswerving faith, give generously to God's work, treat fellow-believers like family, and pursue the Spirit's empowering—the answer comes back each and every time with an unequivocal YES! YES! And YES! That's enough certainty to keep us, as individuals and churches, busy doing very meaningful things, in Jesus' words, "until the very end."[59]

---

[59] Matthew 28:20

9

CLEAN YOUR LENSES

*The time will come when people will not put up with sound doctrine.
Instead, to suit their own desires, they will gather around them a great
number of teachers to say what their itching ears want to hear.*

2 Timothy 4:3

I have this in common with you: neither of us is neutral when we come
to the Scriptures. We both tend to hear what we *want to hear*. This is
why Paul warns Timothy about people's tendency to read and hear
what they already believe or would rather believe. Likewise, Jesus
warns us all, "You have a fine way of setting aside the commands of
God in order to observe your own traditions!"[1]

Bible scholars speak of the difference between *exegesis* and *eisegesis*.
Exegesis is trying to understand what *is* there in the text, uncovering its
ancient meaning, discovering its timeless truth. *Eisegesis* on the other
hand is reading into the text something that is *not* there. Like a person
with a spot on their glasses imagining there is a blotch on the wall they
are looking at, we see not what is there but what we assume is there,
because of the assumptions or preferences we've brought with us.

A common kind of *eisegesis* is *proof-texting* in which we find verses
to support our prior belief. A book as large as the Bible is vulnerable to
being twisted to support any number of these beliefs. I remember hearing a Bible teacher illustrating this point by saying, "Tell me what you

---

[1] Mark 7:9

believe about how society should be arranged—democracy, socialism, capitalism, patriarchy, hyper-feminism, slave-ownership, slave-abolition, political liberalism, political conservatism, war, pacifism—then give me ten minutes and I will provide five Scriptures from each Testament to support your view."

This is why, in the same way that praying sport supporters have appealed to God to back opposing teams, so Bible readers have tended to appeal to God's Word to legitimize opposing causes. For example, early last century, Afrikaners in my country, South Africa, used the Exodus story to endorse their political right to power, while Black liberation theologians used the same story to endorse taking up weapons in their fight for freedom. How easily we make Scripture our servant rather than our master.

May I warn strongly against subordinating Scripture to our preferences by quoting the biblical scholar, Ellen Davies:

> "Using the text to confirm our presuppositions is sinful; it is an act of resistance against God's fresh speaking to us, an effective denial that the Bible is the word of the living God. The only alternative to proof-texting is reading with a view to what the New Testament calls metanoia, repentance—literally, 'change of mind'."[2]

We need to read the Bible not to defend our prior views, but to evaluate them. We need to clean our lenses. Here are three ways to do that:

READ THE BIBLE WITH PEOPLE OF OTHER CULTURES AND CENTURIES

First, let's talk about reading it with people of other cultures. We tend to read the Scriptures through the lens of our culture, rather than read our culture through the lens of Scripture.

Think of how one's national identity might affect what we notice most as we read the story of Joseph. Americans might see it as a rags-to-riches story. Germans might notice Joseph's administrative excel-

---

[2] *The Art of Reading Scripture*, 2003, iBooks, ch 1.

lence. Africans might remark, "Wherever a man goes in the world, he never forgets his family." Indians may notice how powerful fate is in the story. Western people notice the sex he turns down, and the need to feed all nations from the storehouse. In the Middle East, they might identify with him when he is thrown into the pit, but might also see it as strange he doesn't equalize the scales when he gets the chance.[3]

Timothy Keller tells of a heated conversation in a Bible seminary with both Asians and Westerners present. The Westerners felt that the Asians were overly obedient to their pastors and governments, and quoted, "We must obey God rather than human beings!"[4] and Revelation 13, which conflates the government with Satan. The Asians in turn charged the Westerners for having an unbiblical disrespect for superiors, be it the aged or the government, citing "you who are younger, submit yourself to your elders"[5] and Romans 13, which describes the emperor as God's agent. Evidently, both cultures had a bias to notice and emphasize some texts, and miss or underplay others. *Only by reading the Bible together could they see all of what was there.*

Additionally, we might read Bible commentary written by people of other cultures—for example, as a person in Africa, I am so grateful for the 2017 *NLT Africa Study Bible,* which brings together 350 contributors from 50 countries to help us see Scripture through African eyes.[6]

Let's talk about reading it with people of other centuries. As important as it is to read Scripture alongside believers across many cultures, we also need to learn to read Scripture alongside believers across many centuries. Constrained to our brief moment in time, we are more easily taken captive by, not only cultural, but also chronological narrowness.

---

[3] I heard Andy McCullough run through this scenario, at an event that gathered church leaders from around the world, in a talk entitled *Global Humility: Attitudes for Mission.* He has since written a book by the same name.

[4] Acts 5:29

[5] 1 Peter 5:5

[6] A Congolese friend of mine recently lamented to me how Christianity reached Africa long before Europe, but now our reading of Scripture comes to us through European eyes. He tells me that Thomas Oden's 2010 book helps reclaim the long history of the African continent with Scripture: *How Africa shaped the Christian mind.*

I understand that this may be too much to ask of the average person, but at some point it is helpful to go back and see how the early church fathers, and the early teachers within Greek Orthodox, Roman Catholic, Coptic, Protestant and Pentecostal streams have read texts. And to find out more about famous church Councils, and also the formation of creeds and confessions. Perhaps a good place to start is to read a concise book on church history, and take it from there.[7]

This worthy pursuit promises three things: first, seeing our place in the long march of God's people through the ages brings much more richness to our own moment. I know many believers whose faith felt thin until they started tapping into its historical depth and breadth.

Second, reading the earlier church's take on Scripture helps us to see what is in the text, and perhaps more importantly it helps us to see what is probably *not* in the text:

"If upon reading a particular passage you have come up with an interpretation that has escaped the notice of every other Christian for two thousand years, or has been championed by universally recognized heretics, chances are pretty good that you had better abandon your interpretation."[8]

Third, by seeing how often the church in the past misread the Bible through the lens of *their* cultural framework and blind spots, we are warned of the danger of doing the same in ours. For example, some early church fathers, despite their wonderful contribution to Christian interpretation, replaced the Hebrew Bible with Greek philosophy, so popular at the time, as the main interpretative lens of the New Testament and its teaching. This led to many nonbiblical and philosophical assumptions filtering into Christian theology, which in turn blinded the church even more to the Old Testament root system of Jesus and the gospel. In addition some church fathers seem to have used proof-texts to affirm rather than challenge the denigration of women so rife in the Greco-Roman world.

---

[7] I recommend, *The Story of Christianity*, by David Bentley Hart.

[8] Michael Horton, editor, *The Agony of Deceit*, Moody Publishers, 34–35.

REVISIT YOUR PET VERSES

Even after being equipped to interpret the Bible, we still tend to hold on to some Bible verses as kinds of proof-texts. Somehow we imagine that because it exists in a verse, we are somehow authorized to snatch it from its chapter or context and treat it as a self-standing truth-capsule. To whet your appetite for revisiting the real meaning of our favourite Scriptures, here are seven examples of unexamined popular verses:[9]

"Do not judge, or you too will be judged."[10]
This is not our defense proof-text to be used against a person who lovingly confronts us. Neither does it mean we should not distinguish between wrong and right, nor that we should never hold others accountable for their actions. The very next verse deals with taking the plank out of our eye—revealing that Jesus speaks here about repenting of an ungracious, judgmental attitude. Yet moral and spiritual discernment is still crucial—verses later, we are told to evaluate the lives of prophets: "By their fruit you will recognize them…"[11]

"For I know the plans I have for you," declares the Lord, "plans to prosper you and not to harm you, plans to give you hope and a future."[12]
This should not be used as a proof-text that each of our lives will get better and better in the short-term. Read the verse before: "When seventy years are completed for Babylon, I will come to you and fulfill my gracious promise to bring you back to this place." It is a particular, not a universal promise, given to the exiles in Babylon, assuring them that their descendants in many decades time will be released from exile. Within this particular promise, there is nonetheless a timeless message, but to identify it we must read it through the lens of the gospel. When

---

[9] I draw most of these examples from Eric Bargerhuff: 2012, *The Most Misused Verses in the Bible*, Bethany House Publishers, chapters 2, 3, 4, 6, 9 and 12.
[10] Matthew 7:1
[11] Matthew 7:16
[12] Jeremiah 29:11

we do that, we find that it powerfully illustrates those promises for the church that "there are good works prepared in advance for us to do"[13] and that, whatever sufferings we may experience, God will ultimately use them for our highest good and eternal blessing.[14]

"For where two or three are gathered together in my name, there am I in the midst of them."[15]

This is not a proof-text for small prayer meetings, as important as those are. Read the verses before it. Jesus is in fact saying that whenever a church is pursuing and involved in a reconciliation process with someone who has refused to repent, they can rest assured that God's blessing is with them in their efforts.

"For the love of money is a root of all kinds of evils."[16]

This verse is often misquoted as, "Money is the root of all evil." But notice that money is not the problem, the *love* of it is. Also, notice that this love of money is *a* root (not *the* root)—sinful and serious as it is, greed is not the only cause of evil.

"I can do all things through Christ who strengthens me."[17]

Of course, we need all the encouragement we can get, and God's reassurances abound in Scripture, but this particular verse should not be used as a guarantee that we will achieve anything we prayerfully put our minds to. In the previous verses, the imprisoned Paul speaks about Christ's strength to be content in every circumstance we find ourselves, not achieving every goal to which we set our minds. Given enough life experience, we will find that some of our prayer-drenched initiatives may fail or be so strongly resisted that we are seemingly stopped in our tracks—as Paul was when he was jailed for his efforts to spread the gospel, only to discover new depths to God's power while in chains.

---

[13] Ephesians 2:10
[14] As Romans 8:28–29 says.
[15] Matthew 18:20
[16] 1 Timothy 6:10
[17] Philippians 4:13

"When I am lifted up from the earth, I will draw all people to myself."[18]

As important as lifting Jesus up in corporate praise is, the very next verse clarifies that Jesus is talking about his imminent crucifixion. Read rightly, we learn that what ultimately draws people to God is not our vibrant praises, but Jesus' sacrificial death.

"Whoever eats the bread or drinks the cup of the Lord in an unworthy manner will be guilty of sinning against the body and blood of the Lord. Everyone ought to examine themselves before... for those who eat and drink without discerning the body of Christ, eat and drink judgment on themselves."[19]

We commonly take this to mean we should weed out all sin from our lives, and focus on Jesus before taking communion. These are sometimes good things to do, but that's not what this passage is saying. Look at the verses before. Paul wants insensitive wealthy people to stop "despising the church of God by humiliating those who have nothing."

The unworthy and unexamined manner is not some hidden sin in our hearts or lives, but the obvious ways these people were mistreating poor people in their church. More likely, the "body of Christ" that some fail to discern, in this passage, is the presence of Christ not in the elements of communion themselves, but in the multi-socio-economic church-body. This brings us to our final point...

DON'T ASSUME YOU'RE INNOCENT

When we read a story in the Bible, we tend to identify with the under-dog or the innocent. We're David, not Goliath, nor Saul. We're Mary and Joseph, not Herod. But should we be so quick to see ourselves in the position of the innocent?

After all, Psalm 14 speaks of the mass of godless rebellious people

---

[18] John 12:32
[19] 1 Corinthians 11:27–29

who devour the people of God, yet when Paul quotes Psalm 14 in the third chapter of Romans, he does not place the readers in the category of the oppressed people of God, but rather in the category of the godless people whose hearts are turned away from God.

Or think about those passages that warn the powerful and the rich to humble themselves, and to serve others. Why is it that we tend to assume that this is addressed to people we see as *more* socially powerful or materially wealthy than ourselves? Luke quotes Jesus as saying, "Blessed are the poor." Yet most Westerners only quote Matthew's version, "Blessed are the poor *in spirit*." Of course both are true, but why is it that so few people with social and political power quote Luke's words? In fact, not just a few specific passages here and there, but the vantage point of the entire Bible seems to bias towards crushed and overlooked people in the world.

Ancient historical accounts are written by the victors, those in power. The Bible stands alone as an account of history written primarily by those who were the defeated and dominated, the occupied and the oppressed. It is not a top-down perspective but a bottom-up one.

As author Brian Zahnd writes,

> *"It's the story of Egypt told not by Pharaoh but by the slaves. The story of Babylon told not by Nebuchadnezzar but by the exiles. The story of Rome told not by Caesar but by the occupied. Even the brief moments when Israel appeared on top, the prophets who spoke for God assumed the view of the peasant poor as a critique of the royal elite."*[20]

But what happens if we lose sight of the prophetically subversive vantage point of the Bible? What happens if those on top—ancient Egyptians, comfortable Babylonians, Romans in a villa, and many of us today, with our high levels of privilege and power—read *ourselves* into the story, not as the dominant but as the underdogs and victims?

That's when you get the bizarre phenomenon of the elite and entitled using the Bible to endorse their dominance as God's will. This is much of Roman Christianity after Constantine. This is Christendom

---

[20] Adapted from: "My problem with the Bible." www.bit.ly/3moocv3 (accessed 06/20).

on crusade. This is the European colonist seeing Africa or the Americas or Australia as the Promised Land and the native inhabitants as Canaanites to be conquered and kept in place. This is doctrinally elitist, mono-racial, only-men-on-the-stage, no-heart-for-the-poor, wealthy church communities being ready to preach on and repent of everything *except* proud separatism, ethnocentricity and prejudice, sexism, ageism, heartless self-preservation, or greed.[21]

---

[21] I don't have one church in mind. I write this as a warning to all churches—if every church does the important, never-ending work of whole-Bible self-critique, the problem of selective interpretation will be kept at bay.

10

TRUE AND TRUSTWORTHY

We also thank God continually because, when you received the word of God, which you heard from us, you accepted it not as a human word, but as it actually is, the word of God, which is indeed at work in you who believe.

1 Thessalonians 2:13

"How can you trust a book with so many mistakes in it? And if you can't trust the book then how can you trust its message about Jesus?" I first heard these words from a friend as I tried to explain to him my newfound faith. I answered with a question: "What mistakes?"

Lucky for me, he couldn't think of any. But as the years ticked on, I have encountered all kinds of claims about mistakes in the Bible—clashes with science, contradictions, factual and historical errors and more. I even have an uncle who stopped believing in Jesus because of some of them.

Having grappled with each of these claims myself, I have found that merely asserting that the Bible has no mistakes has not helped sincere seekers or doubting believers (of which I have been one). This chapter's contents shows how I have remained convinced that the Bible is trustworthy *by thinking more carefully about exactly what it means and what it does not mean when we say that it is "true" and "without error."*

WHO SAYS IT'S TRUSTWORTHY?

Can we really trust God's Word? If we are going to receive its gospel as the Thessalonians did (in the opening verse of this chapter), then the words in our Bible must be reliable, trustworthy and true. I believe they are, but don't merely take my word for it. How can we know they're true? Or, more to the point, who says they are?

First, Jesus declared God's Word to be trustworthy. As stated before, most people don't believe the Bible is inspired and true because the Bible itself says so, but because we believe Jesus is right about who he says he is, and therefore right about everything else, including what he said about the Word. In one place he says, "Scripture cannot be broken."[1] If Jesus is the Son of God, then the Bible is the Word of God.

Second, the Bible itself claims to be trustworthy. If God breathed out the words of Scripture, and if God tells no lies, then God's Word is true. "The grass withers, and the flower falls, but the word of the Lord remains forever."[2] What God says is "true and righteous altogether."[3] God's word is a firm foundation for life, according to Jesus and the Scriptures themselves. Listening to God and his Son is like building our house on a rock, not sand.[4] As succinctly put by theologian Michael Bird, "The testimony of God's Word to itself is that it is an authentic and authoritative account of everything it declares to have happened, to be, or will yet take place. God speaks to reality as it was, as it is, and as it yet will be."[5]

Third, person after person attests to its trustworthiness. Jesus said, "I praise you, Father, Lord of heaven and earth, because you have hidden these things from the wise and learned, and revealed them to little children."[6] According to Jesus, sophisticated people might come to the Scriptures with a jaded cynicism or an arrogant intellectualism that

---

[1] John 10:35
[2] 1 Peter 1:24–25
[3] Psalm 19:9
[4] Matthew 7:24
[5] Michael Bird 2013, *Evangelical Theology*, Zondervan, Kindle location 14587.
[6] Matthew 11:25

blinds them to the whisper of the Spirit, while even little children may discern its source and authority. Many people who come to trust in God, may start off not trusting in the words of the whole Bible, but as they are exposed to it bit by bit, each time a little more light comes in, and eventually they declare with the Psalmist, "The sum of your word is truth."[7]

Finally, God's Spirit witnesses to its trustworthiness. As one theologian puts it:

> "We know the Bible is God's Word not because we have evidence that demands a verdict or because any church council said so, but on account of the witness of the Holy Spirit to our own spirit that we are reading the words of a Holy God through Holy Scripture. All other evidence, from apologetics or historical theology, though having a valid place, is secondary to the work of the Holy Spirit in authoring and authenticating Scripture."[8]

If you are now wondering what "apologetics" is, the word refers to that field of Christian thought that attempts to provide a rational explanation and defense for whatever tenet of Christian belief is in question.

Charles Spurgeon, the famed "prince of preachers" understood so well the Spirit's readiness to rest mightily upon the preaching of the Bible that he preferred not to support the Bible's authority with apologetic defenses. His rationale: "You don't have to defend a lion. All you have to do is let the lion loose, and the lion will defend itself."

I get where Spurgeon is coming from, as I have seen many of the most skeptical people, even staunch atheists, coming to faith when they heard the Word of God being preached with self-attesting spiritual power. Nonetheless, with so much skepticism about the Bible in the air, there is nothing to lose and much to gain if we take a good and proper look at the lion itself. The Christian faith, and Scriptures upon which it is founded, *is* a rational faith—as so many excellent apologetic

---

[7] Psalm 119:160
[8] Michael Bird 2013, *Evangelical Theology*, Zondervan, Kindle location 14651.

works can show.[9] It is also the reason that I like to include what Timothy Keller calls "apologetic side-bars" into my messages. Times have changed since Spurgeon—more than before, we need to know to know *why* we believe *what* we believe.

IN WHAT SENSE IS GOD'S WORD TRUE?

The Bible is true in at least two main ways: it tells a true gospel, and it conveys true meaning. *First, God's Word is true in all it says about the gospel.* What is the message of the Bible? At the risk of oversimplification, it tells us the truth about:

- God, who is great yet good, just yet merciful, one yet three.

- the world, which is God-created yet sin-corrupted, God-magnifying yet redemption-longing.

- humanity, made in God's image yet fallen, beautiful yet broken.

- Jesus, who is divine yet human, king yet servant, crucified yet risen, ascended yet soon-to-return.

- salvation, which is costly yet free, faith-received yet works-effecting.

- the kingdom, which is future yet present, cosmic yet local, comprehensive yet personal.

- the church, which is universal yet local, organic yet organized, edifying yet evangelistic.

- how to live in a way that is confident yet humble, liberated yet surrendered, abandoned yet vigilant.

---

[9] Here is a reading list to get you started: Amy Orr-Ewing, *Why Trust the Bible?* (2005), Craig Blomberg, *Can We Still Believe the Bible?* (2014), Craig Blomberg, *The Historical Reliability of the New Testament* (2016), F. F. Bruce, *The Canon of Scripture* (1988), Kenneth Kitchen, *On the Reliability of the Old Testament* (2006), Lee Martin McDonald, *The Biblical Canon: Its Origin, Transmission and Authority* (2007), and Peter J. Williams, *Can We Trust the Gospels?* (2018).

If Scripture is primarily God's self-revelation, then this core message is mainly what the Bible affirms as true.[10]

Second, God's Word is true in all God means for it to say to us. This is why interpretation is so important. We should ask of each part of the Bible, "Why did the Spirit orchestrate that these words would be in the Bible, and what is its timeless truth?" God's Word may be infallible, but our interpretations most certainly can be fallible.

A shoddy interpretation of Scripture can hardly be proclaimed to be "God's true and authoritative word." A preacher might open up Colossians 2 and read, "Do not touch! Do not handle! Do not taste!" then advocate a list of legalistic rules, yet because the preacher fails to explain that Paul is actually quoting then refuting the words of the ascetic false teachers in Colossae, that sermon is not an expounding of, but a distortion of, God's Word.

In Christian circles, arguments often start with, "The Bible *clearly* says…" One reason I wrote this book is to encourage us all to be surer that the Bible *really* says what we *think* it says. Only what it *really* says is the truth that God *means* to say.

That's all easy enough to grasp I hope, now let's get to the more nuanced part of the conversation about the Bible's "infallibility"…

WHAT WE DO NOT MEAN BY THE BIBLE BEING TRUE

"Every word of God is flawless; he is a shield to those who take refuge in him."[11] Since the Scriptures are true, they are trustworthy. And since they are trustworthy, they are true. If we cannot trust them as true, then how can we take shield in the One whom they speak of?

Yet skeptics continue to challenge its truthfulness. However, I have found that most of the lines of "attack" are based on straw man argu-

---

[10] On this point, the Catholic Catechism rightly states, "We must acknowledge that the books of Scripture firmly, faithfully, and without error teach the truth which God, for the sake of our salvation, wished to see confided in them."

[11] Proverbs 30:5

ments. In other words, they misunderstand what the Bible's truthfulness means in the first place, and then refute their own misrepresentation.

This is why we need a proper understanding of the Bible's trustworthiness or "infallibility." With decades of pastoral experience, I have found that a non-nuanced understanding of the Bible's infallibility does not help sincere seekers or doubting believers. It is important to tell the difference between what is true and without error in the Bible and what conclusions or assumptions we have about the Bible's truthfulness that might not be true at all—there are five of them:

Faulty Copyists and Textual Critics

First, the Bible's truthfulness does not mean that ancient copyists and textual critics are without fault.

We can say that the original documents in their original language were the inspired Word of God. However there may be several mistakes along the way—copyists made mistakes, and textual critics, studying these variants in the multiple copies, may have reached wrong conclusions about which variant was correct.

This simple fact surely accounts for many of the apparent contradictions in the Old Testament that skeptics tend to point out. Did Baasha, the king of Israel die in the 26th year of king Asa's reign,[12] or was he still alive in the 36th year?[13] When did Ahazia become king? When he was 21?[14] Or when he was 42?[15] Evidently, copyists made a mistake.[16]

Limited Natural Knowledge

Second, the Bible's truthfulness does not mean that the authors were supernaturally given knowledge about all things.

---

[12] 1 Kings 15:33
[13] 2 Chronicles 16:1
[14] 2 Kings 8:26
[15] 2 Chronicles 22:2
[16] Reading the number 26 and writing down the number 36, or reading the number 21 and writing down the number 42 are plausible mistakes a weary copyists may make.

Like a kindergarten teacher teaching kids by starting where they are in their limited knowledge, so God *condescended*[17] again and again to reveal things to and through these ancient authors that started with their level of understanding, and prioritized the things of primary importance.

For instance, when God spoke to Moses about the origins of the universe, his priority message was not *how* all things were created but *why* they were created. Genesis 1 offers a theology of God, creation, and humanity—not a study in cosmology, geology or biology.[18] This is why, when God inspired Moses to write down, "God said let there be light and there was light," he did not also whisper in his ear, "By the way, the speed of light is almost 300 million metres per second."[19] These kinds of scientific truths were encoded into creation for enquirers to discover *eventually*.[20]

Theologians sometimes speak of God giving us two books: *the Book of Scripture*, unveiled by God's special revelation, and *the Book of Nature*, unveiled by the human race's ongoing scientific research. Since the same Author has written both books, we should not expect them, in the final analysis, to contradict.

God's concern with Scripture was and is to tell us things that *no* scientist could ever discover apart from God revealing it. An acclaimed Old Testament scholar and expert in the culture of the Ancient Near

---

[17] This is a theological term, roughly meaning, "God kindly stooped down to reach into the minds of people limited by their finite perspectives, intelligence levels, and cultural assumptions."

[18] For an example of Genesis 1 being primarily concerned with theology not cosmology, consider that in the ancient world the sun and moon were worshipped as gods, yet it says that "God made the two great lights, the greater light to govern the day, and the lesser light to govern the night; He made the stars also" (Genesis 1:16)—the sun and moon are not even named! So doing, Genesis 1 defies the gods by de-deifying them.

[19] One way we misread Scripture is to assume that the people it was written to were asking the same questions we ask, or that the writers of Scripture were trying to answer the questions we assume they would try to answer. In our scientific age, we long to know precisely how creation was made, whereas the ancients wanted to know why it was made. Genesis answers their questions, not ours.

[20] Proverbs 25:2

East[21] says that Moses, along with his entire prescientific society, did not know that the stars were suns, the earth was spherical, the high sky was vaporous (not a solid layer which was thought to hold back the waters), and that the sun was further away than the moon. And yet God did not correct this faulty understanding, but rather accommodated[22] to it as he revealed to them *theological* truths about his role in nature's existence and his disclosure in the world's meaning.

The same is true of the Bible's botany and geography. Jesus refers to the mustard seed "as the smallest of all seeds"[23] yet there are in fact smaller seeds. Paul speaks of the gospel reaching "the whole world"[24] yet we now know that it had not gone to Australia or the Americas yet. But see, both of these are examples of speaking to *the actual lived experience of the original readers.* Even in a scientific age, we still speak like this—think how we talk about the nonscientific ideas of sunset and sunrise (and who knows what antiquated ideas we still hold that may one day be scientifically refuted).

What matters is that God spoke to them (as he now does to us) by sowing the seeds of revelation into their (and our) field of present understanding and lived experience.

Imprecise Reporting

Third, the Bible's truthfulness does not mean that the authors had a modern-day journalistic devotion to precision reporting.

We simply cannot impose onto the Bible's historical narratives the precisionist notion of truth, which is rooted in our modernistic period of history. For example, when we read that Jesus was in the tomb for three days, we assume he was there for 72 hours. Yet if we follow the account carefully he was in the tomb for half of that time, not for three

---

[21] John Walton: 2009, *The Lost World of Genesis 1*, IVPress.

[22] Another word for "condescended." John Walton, in *The Lost World of Scripture*, says, "Every successful act of communication is accomplished by various degrees of accommodation on the part of the communicator for the sake of the audience. (There is the need to) tailor the communication to the needs and circumstances of the audience. Without this, effective communication could not take place."

[23] Matthew 13:32

[24] Colossians 1:6

full days, but over three subsequent days—Friday sunset to Sunday sunrise.

Based on Luke's commitment to excellence, eyewitness interviews[25] and his archeologically confirmed comments (like the names of six religious and political authorities and the exact years of their public roles[26]) we can assume he reported as best he could.

John Calvin admires Luke's diligence but nonetheless concludes, "We know that the Evangelists were not very exact as to the order of dates, or even in detailing minutely everything that Jesus did or said."[27] A cross-check of Old Testament citations shows that the Gospel writers did not always quote them *exactly*. Also, the sayings, stories, and sermons of Jesus are not likely all word for word either, but are condensed, faithful reporting of what Jesus meant. Take the Sermon on the Mount as an example.[28] It takes ten minutes to read, but surely the original message that warranted Jesus getting out of town, and gathering a crowd on a hillside, took much longer.

As is expected of all ancient historical narrators, the Gospel authors were *selective* and did not feel any obligation to report *all the facts*. Take for example a skeptic's common line of attack on the Gospels' accuracy: *Both* the thieves crucified with Jesus either did, as Mark[29] says, or did not, as Luke[30] says, mock Jesus. Was it both who mocked (according to Mark) or only one (according to Luke)? Yet all this question proves is Mark's and Luke's *selective* account. Besides, even a little bit of thought can reconcile the two. Both thieves mocked Jesus initially, and thus Mark is right. However after Jesus had said, "Father, forgive them, for they do not know what they are doing," one of the thieves has a change of heart and repents on the cross, while the other continues to mock, thus Luke is right too.

Another common criticism against the historic reliability of the

---

[25] Luke 1:1–3

[26] Luke 3:1–2

[27] John Calvin: 1989 edition, *Commentary on a Harmony of the Evangelists,* 216.

[28] Matthew 5–7

[29] Mark 15:32

[30] Luke 23:43

Gospels, at the scene of Jesus' resurrection, is to highlight the differences between the women's number and names, the exact time of the morning, and the number of angels. But critics fail to see is that this proves multiple, independent affirmations of the story with no collusion, thereby making what they agree on *more credible not less.* In the field of law, there is a distinction between material and immaterial discrepancies. The former refer to an actual contradiction between witnesses, while the latter are simply different accounts that nevertheless cohere, like pieces in a jigsaw puzzle.

As it turns out the differences in the resurrection accounts are *immaterial.* For example, what time did the women arrive? Was it "still dark" (as John writes[31]), or "very early in the morning" (as Luke says[32]), or "just after sunrise" (as Mark indicates[33]). Well, if the visit was "at dawn" (as Matthew says[34]) then they were likely describing approximately *the same time with different words.*

As for the number and names of the women, none of the Gospels pretend to give a complete list. They all include Mary Magdalene, while Matthew, Mark, and Luke cite other women. Perhaps Mary Magdalene arrived first and that's why only John mentions her. That's hardly a contradiction.

How many angels were there? Was it one (according to Matthew) or two (according to John)? What is not up for discussion is an angelic presence, and yet perhaps some eyewitnesses saw only one, whilst another saw two.

Most significantly, each of the authors emphatically agrees on the same salient point, the one skeptics should be hesitant to try to ignore: the tomb that once held Jesus' body is now empty.[35]

---

[31] John 20:1
[32] Luke 24:1
[33] Mark 16:2
[34] Matthew 28:1
[35] I adapted an interview with Dr. William Lane Craig and Dr. Norman Geisler to write this section on dealing with claimed contradictions about the resurrection.

Missing Tools and Insights

Fourth, the Bible's truthfulness does not assume that we currently have the tools and insights to see what some texts are saying.

Like the biblical authors, we are not omniscient. I am sure that it is obvious that ordinary folk like you and me do not understand all that the authors were intending to say, but the same is true even of top biblical scholars.

How long ago did Adam and Eve live? Do the Scriptures tell us? Genesis 5, for example, is a father-son-father-son genealogy from Adam to Noah that lists 10 generations of people who lived mind-bogglingly long: 930, 912, 905, 840, 895, 962, 365, 969, 777 and 950 years to be exact.

Some, like Bishop Ussher in the 1600s, worked out the overlapping years to calculate how long ago Adam lived. But is this the way God intended us to interpret this passage? Biblical scholars are divided. Some argue that only a few generations of pivotal importance are listed, throwing out the possibility of accurate date finding.

Others who argue for a less literal reading highlight that 10 additional ages are interspersed—how old they were when they each had their first son—and yet these 20 total ages all end in 0, 2, 5, 7 or 9. Mathematically, this has a chance probability of one in a billion! All that to say, we may not even (yet) have the interpretive keys to understand all that this passage is really saying. Perhaps we soon will make an archeological discovery that helps us. Until then we best not be too dogmatic in our conclusions.[36]

As we look to the future of biblical scholarship, we know that more light will probably come, because as we look back, we see that much more light has already come through the diligent efforts of biblical and historical scholars. Though we steadily march away from biblical times, these scholars get closer and closer to the original texts and their context in understanding. As N.T. Wright says,

---

[36] As someone who believes the earth likely began 4,5 billion years ago, I suggest we disregard Ussher's "calculation" in 1650 that it began on 23 October, 4004 BCE.

"Biblical scholarship is a great gift of God to the church, aiding it in its task of going ever deeper into the meaning of Scripture and so being refreshed and energized for the tasks to which we are called for the sake of the world."[37]

For example, in the last 80 years so much more light has come to our understanding of the Gospels. The historical church had severed from its Jewish roots after the destruction of Jerusalem in CE 70, but we now have tools to understand better the Jewish Jesus who, it turns out, was predominantly focused on the future age, which he had launched in the midst of the fallen age. This groundbreaking understanding about Jesus was only made possible and certain through a study of the Jewish literature written in the centuries before his coming, in which scholars came to understand what Jesus actually meant by "the kingdom of God." The finding of the Dead Sea Scrolls and the increased collaboration of Jewish and Christian scholars, both happening in the immediate wake of WW2, made the study of that literature, and thus the rediscovery of the times and focus of Jesus, come to the fore. This new ground in scholarship has wonderfully opened up our understanding of the Gospels and Scripture's storyline.[38]

I don't offer these two examples to make us insecure about what we don't yet understand, but rather to deepen our humility as we attempt to mine (using N.T. Wright's words) "ever deeper" into the meaning of biblical texts. Acknowledging we may misunderstand something has always been the right way to approach Scripture, a humble approach the church father Augustine encouraged:

"If in these writings I am perplexed by anything which appears to me opposed to truth, I do not hesitate to suppose that either the manuscript is faulty, or the translator has not caught the meaning of what was said, or I myself have failed to understand."[39]

Augustine brings us to a final point...

---

[37] From *Scripture and the Authority of God*, 2011, HarperCollins, ch 8.
[38] See for example Derek Morphew: 2020, *The Kingdom Reformation*, Vineyard Publishing.
[39] St Augustine in his Letter No. 82, addressed to St Jerome.

Flawed Interpretation and Translation

Fifth, the Bible's truthfulness does not mean that our interpretations and translations are without error.

Since translators are also interpreters, their translations may be incorrect or misleading. Let's consider two major examples of passages with disputed interpretations and translations:

The first is one of the most debated texts in the Bible: "I do not permit a women to teach nor to *authentein* (Greek word) a man."[40] All translators agree that the word is about *authority*, but does it refer to a *neutral or positive* use of authority (as in "lead") or a *negative or ungodly* kind (as in "usurp" or "domineer")? Some translations opt for the positive (ESV), some for the negative (NIV). This changes the meaning substantially: if it is a *neutral* kind of authority, then Paul is telling the Ephesian women not to do something that only certain men can do. However, if it is a *negative* authority, then Paul is telling them not to do something that even godly men should not do. In that case the command is more likely particular to the heresy-torn Ephesian church and not universal to all churches at all times.

The second example, showing how the meaning of just two words can affect major doctrinal conclusions, are the words "save him" in James 2:14: "What good is it, my brothers and sisters, if someone claims to have faith but has no deeds? Can such faith *save him?*"

Theologians have long asked of this verse: Are we saved by faith-and-works? Or by faith-in-grace-alone? And does saving faith automatically result in a life dedicated to social justice?

Traditionally, Catholic theologians have used this verse to articulate their belief that salvation is not by faith alone. It is by faith *and* works. On the other hand, traditionally Protestants, as a matter of belief, argue that salvation is by faith alone, though true faith will never stay alone—faith will inevitably express itself in works. The problem with the traditional Catholic view is that it does not hold with Paul's message else-

---

[40] 1 Timothy 2:12

where[41] that we are saved by faith in God's grace alone, not by works, in which case the principle of "Scripture interpreting Scripture" makes this view unlikely. The problem with the traditional Protestant view is that, if the text effectively means "faith without works cannot save one-self," then the Catholic reading seems more like what James *is* saying. (This is why the father of Protestantism, Martin Luther, even suggested James was not inspired.) Also, contra the traditional Protestant view, if saving faith *inevitably* results in compassionate action, then why does James even need to encourage us to do it? And what security of salvation is there for a professing believer who has not recently engaged in acts of service?

This impasse gives rise to the continued study of this text. Other questions can be asked: whose "good" is in mind—the person with the faith, or someone else's? And does "save" here refer to receiving salvation, or something else? And does "him" here refer to the one claiming to have faith, or someone else?

These questions lead to other views such as one compelling, albeit minority, interpretation[42] that asserts that both Catholic and Protestant scholars have been wrong all along. This third view claims the truth has been hidden in plain sight—the verses before and after provide the context to better guide our interpretation, and as for the phrase "save him," the word translated "save" can also be translated "rescue or help" and "him" refers not to the person with faith but to "the poor man," mentioned earlier in the chapter (in verses 3 and 6, though the NIV obscures the second reference by translating it as "the poor" rather than "the poor man"). By this view, this generic poor man is still in mind in the subsequent verse about people who have no food and clothing (v15) so that James in effect asks, "What good is it *for others* if someone claims to have faith but does not express their faith in practical love? Can such a faith *rescue the poor man?*"

---

[41] in Ephesians 2:8-9

[42] By biblical scholars like Michael Eaton and R.T. Kendal. I have heard these men, who were both mentored and shaped by the famous pastor-theologian Martin Lloyd Jones, say that in his final years he believed the same.

The result of our chosen interpretation of this passage is substantial. By the Catholic reading, we are saved in part by compassionate action to others. By the traditional Protestant reading, truly saved people automatically act compassionately. In contrast, this third way of reading this passage concludes it is possible to be saved and yet tragically we do not engage in compassionate action, but should be encouraged to do so—a view which, I think, sits much better with the Bible's larger teaching on social justice: all too often God's people leverage their faith to benefit themselves alone and fail to utilize it to make a positive difference in a suffering world. Indeed, what good is it for others who suffer if our faith does not overflow in acts of service to them?

You might notice from my wording that I have come to hold this third view, but of course I may be wrong. (If you're interested, I share my rationale in *Appendix 2* at the back of this book.)

WE MIGHT BE WRONG

Based on the previous two examples of possible fallibility in our interpretations and/or translations, I'd like to end this chapter by reminding us that we should cultivate the kind of humility that acknowledges we might be wrong as well as a generous spirit to those who interpret these passages differently—at the same time, continuing to converse with each other to discover more definitively the true meaning of the passages in question.

God is always right, and his word is always true, but we can and do mistranslate or misinterpret it at times. His word is infallible, but our interpretations are not.

Only by holding our current interpretations more lightly and humbly, will we be able to dialogue with, learn from and teach others who also believe in the truthfulness and authority of Scripture, yet see things differently. Certainly, the primary doctrines, such as those articulated in *the Apostle's Creed* should not be up for challenge, even if we need to find fresh ways of articulating them. But an inflexible, dogmatic approach to secondary and tertiary doctrines[43] may cause us to criticize or denounce those who, though equally loving God and Scripture, land elsewhere on these Scriptures. It may also lock us into an incorrect reading of Scripture, beyond the reach and help of those who in fact might see things more clearly.

This quest for truth requires an objectivity few of us have. In the fields of behavioural and neurological science, much has been recently discovered about *confirmation bias*: our unconscious tendency to latch onto evidence that supports our prior views, while ignoring or minimizing evidence that challenges it. This subjectivity is compounded by *belonging bias*: the way we unconsciously and immediately reject anything that the particular group in which we belong might not agree with. This explains why almost all people in all churches assume they "just happen" to be in the one that believes rightly. With these two biases unchecked, we will likely find ourselves in an echo chamber that seals us off from coming any closer to what God's Word really says on many matters.

Is there any hope? Certainly there is—we can pray, "God, show me my blind spots and biases. And teach me to genuinely listen to others in the body of Christ, even if I cannot finally agree with them." Deep biblical humility and security in our place in the universal church of Jesus goes a long way in helping dismantle these biases, which may be blocking us from discovering better, though probably not perfect interpretations of many Scriptural passages, and along with them better, yet still imperfect, doctrine.

At the same time, we must accept that every church and denomination, ours included, does not and may never have perfect theology. Trying to find the church with perfect theology may be a fool's errand, and even a church with one may fail at times in living those teachings out. So help us God.

---

[43] See this article in www.bit.ly/2XymPPH that masterfully distinguishes between three "levels" of doctrine—what he calls those written in blood (primary), ink (secondary) and pencil (tertiary).

11

DOUBT YOUR DOUBTS

Consult God's teaching and testimony. If (people) do not speak according to this word, it is because they have no light of dawn.

Isaiah 8:20

There is much, much more we could explore to reinforce our confidence in the Bible's truthfulness, and why it is worthy of being called "the light of dawn." Consider first *the prophecies* written in earlier parts that are fulfilled in later parts. In centuries past, many argued that Christians had long ago changed the words of Isaiah 53 in the existing scrolls to make it look like Jesus fulfilled so many of its descriptions of his death and resurrection. But, when in 1947 the Dead Sea Scrolls yielded a scroll of Isaiah, the oldest copy we have by a thousand years, copied some 250 years before Jesus' time, the charge was dropped.

Also, there are hundreds of *archeological finds and extra-biblical ancient documents* that corroborate all kinds of facts in the Bible's historical narratives. One small example: the Hittites were long thought to be a biblical legend, until their capital and records were discovered in Bogazkoy, Turkey in 1834. Likewise, scholars doubted the accuracy of a verse[1] that mentions a king called Sargon who captured Ashdod, then his palace was discovered in Khorsabad, Iraq. Remarkably, the same event described in the Bible is recorded on the ancient palace walls.[2]

---

[1] Isaiah 20:1
[2] Visit www.biblicalarcheology.org for more examples.

Most importantly, *the life, death and resurrection of Jesus* as described in the gospels is all well attested from a historical point of view.[3] Since most of us come to believe in the Bible only after we believe in Jesus, confidence in our historical knowledge about him is paramount. In particular, the case for the fact that on an actual day in history Jesus bodily rose from the dead to begin appearing to his flabbergasted disciples is formidable.[4]

Yet, as faith-igniting as all this may be, many thoughtful readers still have questions that make them doubt the Bible's truthfulness. The Bible itself says, "Be merciful to those who doubt."[5] We might need to extend that same mercy to ourselves. It's important to be honest about our doubts and questions. Since they can either snuff out or strengthen faith (like resistance training does for a muscle), my experience is that it's better to acknowledge each of them as they arise. Thankfully, many believing thinkers have devoted themselves to addressing them, so we need not wrestle with them all on our own.[6]

On that note, let's now explore four common objections or doubts *related to Scripture*. In each case, I will briefly articulate why this understandably causes doubt, and then suggest why we should perhaps doubt the doubt itself. To be fair, each of these objections deserves a more thorough treatment, but given the short space I have in the rest of this chapter, I will risk oversimplification rather than say nothing...

CANAANITES WIPED OUT

Sensitive readers wonder, *if the Bible is true, why are there commands to kill Canaanites?* When Joshua led the Israelites into the promised

---

[3] See John Dickson: 2019, *Is Jesus history?* and Craig Keener: 2012, *The Historical Jesus of the Gospels.*
[4] Apart from this event, we have no explanation either for the radical psychological change in his disciples, once intrepid cowards now willing martyrs, or for the explosive "arrival" of the church in human history, and that against all odds. For more evidence, see N.T. Wright: 2003, *The Resurrection of the Son of the God.*
[5] Jude 1:22
[6] See www.reasonablefaith.org and www.johnlennox.org/resources as starting points.

land they acted on divine orders: "In the cities of these peoples that your God is giving you as an inheritance, you shall not leave alive anything that breathes. But you shall utterly destroy them."[7]

How do we make sense of this supposedly divine instruction? With difficulty of course, but we can say a few things: first, consider the reason for the command. According to Scripture, the Canaanites were extremely corrupt, even offering child sacrifices to their gods. God did not want them to influence Israel.

Second, consider the overstatement. The command, "totally destroy them," may sound like genocide to a cursory reader, but a closer reading shows it is more likely a deliberately exaggerated, not literal, way of saying, "thoroughly conquer."[8] For example, in one chapter[9] they are told to drive them out and destroy them, but then told not to intermarry or do business with them. How do you do that with people you have utterly destroyed? The same applies to a later chapter[10] in which we're told they "left no survivors" in Hebron or Debir, yet chapters later these towns are still populated with Canaanites. In fact, the Bible tells of many Canaanites who turn to the God of Israel.

Third, and most importantly, consider the limit of the command. This instruction only came to those in stage four of the Old Testament story. This was God's dealing with people at a very particular moment in their story, bringing his justice on human evil and giving previously enslaved Israel a place in the world. Neither before nor in later stages does God ever command it. Later, for example, God deems David unworthy to build a temple because of the blood of war on his hands. Jesus has the final and lasting say on the matter: "Love your enemies."[11] God's people are no longer a geopolitical nation, we are servants of the gospel and the common good in every nation. Like Jesus, we should rather pray and die for, than prey upon and kill our enemies.

---

[7] Deuteronomy 20:16–20
[8] "It is the language of conventional warfare rhetoric." (Paul Copan: 2011, *Is God a Moral Monster? Making Sense of the Old Testament God*, Baker Books, 172).
[9] Deuteronomy 7
[10] Joshua 10
[11] Matthew 5:44

SLAVERY SUPPORTED

If the Bible is true, why does it endorse slavery? This accusation is not entirely based on fact: the New Testament does not encourage slave keeping, and in one place, it condemns slave-traders.[12] At the same time, it does not *outrightly* denounce slave keeping, but rather encourages Christian slaves to obey their masters, and Christian masters to treat their slaves "as a fellow man and as a brother in the Lord."[13]

Though I wish there were some more emphatically clear condemnations of slavery as an institution, I ask why did the apostles, as they planted churches into the Roman empire where a third or more of all people were slaves, not condemn this practice? One answer that holds water is that it would not have been strategic for a tiny movement to confront this unjust practice head on. Had they told slaves and masters to unbundle their relationships, not only would many of the slaves have lost their livelihoods, homes and indeed their lives, but the Roman empire would almost certainly have turned on the Christians for disrupting the order of society.

Rather than calling for an instant revolution, it seems that Scripture's approach was to sow the "seeds" of an eventual equalizing revolution. For example, God in creation etches intrinsic worth and freedom into every person; God in the Exodus delivers multitudes from slavery as his crowning achievement in Israel's history; God in Jesus announces that his great kingdom work will be modeled on the Jubilee in Moses' law, a recurring fifty year event that enabled economic justice and the end of slavery;[14] and God through the church declares a gospel in which "there is neither slave nor free."[15]

Given enough time, those "seeds" would germinate in churches and in wider society. In the early churches, some Christians literally sold

---

[12] 1 Timothy 1:10
[13] Philemon 16
[14] In Luke 4:18–19, Jesus adapts Isaiah 61, which in turn prophetically applies the Jubilee explained in Leviticus 25.
[15] Galatians 3:18

themselves into slavery to purchase the freedom of others, while others collected money to buy slaves' freedom.[16] As for society, later Christians, appealing to these "seeds," now having taken root in public consciousness, successfully overthrew the sinful structure itself: most famously, the stubborn William Wilberforce gave his life to leading the English government to abolish slave keeping and slave trade altogether.

AN OUTDATED SEX ETHIC

People often ask, *if the Bible is true, why is its sex ethic so outdated and oppressive?* A vein of teaching runs from the Bible's first chapter all the way to Jesus' and Paul's teaching: "A man will leave his mother and father and be united to his wife."[17] This is the basis of the church's historical interpretation on abstinence outside of marriage, and one man and one woman in a permanent covenant of marriage, which is to be celebrated and sealed by sex. While more traditional cultures may see some wisdom in this, secular ones now see it as archaic and repressive.[18] How should we respond?

Certainly, we must make sure that our interpretations are correct. But at the same time, we must never bend our interpretations to harmonize with our culture's or society's current convictions. God's

---

[16] 1 Clement 54:4-5; Ignatius to Polycarp 4:8-10; Shepherd of Hermas 38.10; 50.8
[17] Genesis 2:24, Matthew 19:5, Ephesians 5:31
[18] In our self-deifying culture, the new definition of sin is not disobedience to the will of God but disobedience to the "authentic" self. Our preferences and freedom to choose our own path and identity without restriction from an external voice, is our most prized pursuit. To tell a person who they may and may not have sex with is something akin to, in the Western mind, putting chains on them. This is not the first time culture has responded with shock to the Judeo-Christian understandings of sex. As Christianity first spread into the Greco-Roman world, the surrounding culture was perplexed by it too. One ancient observer commented with amazement: "Here is a strange group of people who are financially generous and sexually stingy. They do the exact opposite of everyone else: they share their money with all, and their bed with none." Many a believer has found from a lifetime of experience that following Jesus' sex ethic is not only *right*, but also *best*. One Psalmist writes, "I run in the path of your commands for you have set my heart free." (Ps 119:32) None of God's ethical imperatives related to money, sex or power are arbitrary. They are manifestations of his love and wisdom.

Word, if it is for all cultures, will inevitably cut across every culture in a different way, because each culture is fallen in its own particular way.[19]

For example, when individualistic Western societies read the Bible, they react to its teachings about sex, but tend to praise its teachings about forgiveness: "forgive your enemy," and "turn the other cheek." However more traditional cultures, such as those in the Middle East, tend to affirm the Bible's teaching about sex, perhaps even feeling it is not strict enough, but the Bible's talk of forgiving enemies does *not* sit well. Which culture is right?

To assume we just happen to live in the one and only culture and time period in history that has finally got everything right is the height of arrogance. Why is it that *our* cultural sensibilities, the one's we have absorbed in *our* time and place, should overrule everybody else's on every point? After all, one day our grandkids will surely shake their heads when they consider things our culture now believes and teaches. The fact that God's Word clashes with various parts of each and every culture, ours included, is not proof that it is not true. It is rather exactly what one would expect of any book that claimed to be God's Word for all people, in all places at all times.[20]

For all single people living in a sex-saturated world, the fact that the person at the epicenter of our faith is a single person, who never had sex and yet lived the fullest possible life, should be a huge encouragement. We can challenge the Bible's teachings about sex, or, we can let the Bible challenge our lifestyles and worldviews. We can butcher it— cutting out the bits we like and binning the rest. Or we can bow before it—affirming its accuracy in spite of the difficulties we have with it; allowing it to refine our view of God, the world, sexuality, and a myriad of other views too.[21]

Besides, surely we should never evaluate if something is true by

---

[19] I have reworded this argument from Timothy Keller: 2009, *The Reason for God*, Penguin Books, 100–110.

[20] In fact, if a book advocated a wide range of ethics that correlated perfectly with the aspirations of a particular culture, we could rightly assume that it is a product of that culture.

[21] I paraphrase Andrew Wilson in *Unbreakable*, 2012, Kindle location 468 and 474.

whether it suits us. Rejecting Jesus because we do not like his sex ethic is like walking away from the best doctor in town, because we do not like the taste of her medicine.

MIRACLES, MIRACLES EVERYWHERE

If the Bible is true why does it claim that so many miracles happened in history? You may not resonate with this objection personally, but if you are steeped in naturalistic assumptions about a universe that is purely material, then you certainly will. The Bible is a supernatural book about a supernatural God at work in his world, usually working within the natural laws of the natural world he created, but sometimes bypassing them in the form of miracles.

Since the "enlightenment" large portions of the academic elite have rejected the supernatural realm as a pre-scientific and un-scientific idea, and along with it the idea of miracles. When they then read about fire falling from heaven as Elijah prays, or Jesus healing a blind man or reviving a dead girl, they shake their heads and conclude, "We all know miracles are not real, so this book cannot be trusted." When pressed for why miracles are not real, such people may admit their atheistic assumptions, or merely say that miracles cannot be proven in science.

But hang on! This anti-supernatural bias is not itself scientific either. Perhaps no one does a better job of revisiting Jesus' miracles and miraculous power than leading New Testament scholar, Craig Keener in his 2011 tome, *Miracles: The Credibility of the New Testament Accounts*. In his two-volume work, he deconstructs anti-supernaturalism itself as an improvable starting assumption about reality. The scientific discipline is limited to the empirical, material realm and so cannot even identify, never mind reject, a cause beyond nature.

After exploring Jesus' miracles, Keener then spends hundreds of pages carefully investigating medically verified accounts of healings that have been reported in the name of Jesus across the world, including ten remarkable resuscitations that have happened in answer to prayer. Especially with the spread of Pentecostalism, millions of people now claim to have experienced miracles in Jesus' name. It is not an openness to the supernatural that should be rejected, Keener argues, but rather a biased, ungrounded assumption that there is not a God who is competent and caring enough to perform such miracles.[22]

Of course there are fake claims of miracles, for charlatans abound. But surely a God who can say, "Let there be light!" and a billion suns are born, is also the God who can say the words "See!", "Hear!", "Walk!", "Live!" and wonders unfold—not only in the biblical narratives, but in our own world today.

Sadly, though many believers will guard their quality of godliness from the influence of the world's impurity, we may fail to guard our quality of faith from the influence of modern academia's skepticism.

By biblical critique, the West's so-called "enlightened" claims about a material-only world should be disregarded. This is why much of Africa, Asia and Latin America have been so receptive to the gospel. Unlike the material secularism the West has tried to export, the gospel does not patronize nor belittle their supernatural openness but rather gives them a Christ who is powerfully present by his Spirit, and is willing and able to answer their prayers.

Mind you, not just in the Majority World, but also in the First World, miracles continue to happen in Jesus' name. For example, a church leader whom I know in the UK shares his favourite story of a healing he witnessed, in which a wheelchair bound lady was prayed for and completely healed.[23] This was medically verified, and even made the national press. Humorously, the government continued paying disability benefits. When she rang to say she no longer needed the money because she could walk again, the government bureaucrat refused: "Sorry, we haven't got a button to push that says 'miracle.'"

---

[22] The rejection of miracles relies on circular thinking, evident in its first proponent, "the great Scottish enlightenment philosopher David Hume who more or less declared that miracles *don't* happen because (wait for it...) they *can't* happen." (Marlin Watling, 2016: *The Marriage of Heaven and Earth*, Kindle Location 763).
[23] Andrew Wilson: 2019, *"A response to Tom Schreiner"* in Themelios volume 44, issue 1, p37, www.bit.ly/3efQl6h (accessed 03/21)

PART THREE

HOW TO TAP INTO ITS POWER

12

CONSIDER HOW YOU LISTEN

Jesus said, "Consider carefully how you listen. Whoever has will be given more; whoever does not have, even what they think they have will be taken from them."

Luke 8:18

Torrents of life-changing power course through the pages of Scripture. How practically to tap into that stream of life is what this, the third and final part of the book, is all about.

I plan to be as concrete and helpful as I possibly can, but before I suggest specific practices in the chapters that follow, in this one I want to start with something more *personal*. I want to invite you to take an honest look at your own *attitude* towards the Good Book.

Our attitude is always important: the way we approach someone determines the outcome of that interaction. For example, how we enter a job interview, or meet potential in-laws, or interact with a teacher, or even talk with a friend, makes a difference in the dynamism and engagement both parties have. It's the same when we come to the Bible.

According to the Bible, it's better to come to Scripture with a soft heart and an openness to hear the message that reverberates through its pages. Even if our hearts once received God's Word, we must all be aware of the possibility of a gradual hardening of our hearts. Most of the Old Testament prophets were not received in their day: Their audience "made their hearts as hard as flint and would not listen to the law or to the words that the Lord Almighty had sent by his Spirit through the earlier prophets. So the Lord Almighty was very angry."[1] Ezekiel, having preached until he was blue in the face, tried alternative ways of seizing the attention of God's people. First, he cooked barley cakes over a fire fed by excrement[2] then shaved off his hair and beard and used the hair to teach the people a lesson about the impending siege.[3] Tragically, nothing got through to them.

Jesus experienced something similar with the religious leaders of his day. He once asked, "Why do you not understand what I say? It is because you cannot bear to hear my words."[4]

Consider his parable of the sower. In it, God sows the seed of his word on different soils or states of the heart. Some seed lands on the hard ground of closed minds. These people, through pride or deception, think they have nothing to learn. Some seed lands on shallow soil. These people do not receive the word as God's Word, but rather as a little bit of inspiration, which soon enough fades. Some seed lands on thorny ground. These people receive God's Word, but simply place it alongside and not above all the other competing voices in their lives. Soon enough God's Word is crowded out and little to no fruit is born from it. Some seed, however, lands on fertile ground. These people humbly receive the words of God, and place them above all the other voices. As Jesus says, "The seed on good soil stands for those with a noble and good heart, who hear the word, retain it, and by persevering produce a crop."[5]

Jesus' point is that *what* God says is not the only important thing— *how* we listen plays a crucial part in how deeply it will impact our lives and transform our hearts. God's Word itself is a good seed, containing the catalytic power to change our lives, but it tends to need a receptive heart to produce a harvest. That's why Jesus says directly after this parable of the sower: "Consider carefully *how* you listen."[6]

---

[1] Zechariah 7:12
[2] Ezekiel 4:12–15
[3] Ezekiel 5:1–17
[4] John 8:43
[5] Luke 8:15
[6] Luke 8:18

HOW TO COME TO THE WORD

How then should we come to God's Word when we read it, study it, hear it read, or hear it preached? As I study multiple Scriptures that speak to this point, I am able to group them into four arterial attitudes...

COME WITH HUMILITY

Since God's Word is a life-giving seed, we should eagerly open up the fields of our life and heart to whatever the Sower might sow into them, "humbly accepting the word planted in us, which can save us."[7] We also prayerfully rely on the Spirit who inspired and uses the Word as rain to activate those seeds, "watering the earth and making it bud and flourish."[8]

Keep in mind that humility is not automatic. It is much like pulling weeds from a garden—just when we think we have attained a state of humility, a prideful attitude can easily spring up. The biblical imperative to "humble yourself" is not one to be applied monthly, but daily. A self-magnifying attitude is as old as the devil and as rife as his reach, and to make matters worse, it is also now entrenched in the prevailing mindset and spirit of our age—what might be called "self-sovereignty." This is the assumption that each of us is the rightful center of our own universe, with no one allowed to infringe on our freedom to determine who we are, what we should value and how we will live.

Yet the very opening words of Scripture dethrone us: *"In the beginning, God..."* We are not the center of the universe. God is. This affects not only our attitude but our interpretations of biblical passages too. For instance, we must be careful not to impose our preferred meaning upon them, but rather let them speak what they will.

In a vision, Isaiah sees God's ultimate plan, in which the "the word

---

[7] James 1:21
[8] Isaiah 55:10

of the Lord goes out to the nations" so that we all "may be taught God's way and walk in God's paths."[9] However, if because of pride we are unteachable, we will forfeit discovering God's ways and God's paths.

We are not *over* the Word. We are *under* it. We think of Ezra who read and preached the Word to the people from a "high wooden platform".[10] The reason for this was not to elevate the preacher or even the sermon, but to recognize the elevation of Scripture. We are under it, not the other way around. Similarly, through the ages, some Bible readers have adopted the practice of reading it on their knees—a postural reminder that humility keeps us in the range of God's voice.

COME WITH THIRST AND HUNGER

Our dependency on Scripture is a corollary to our dependency on God himself. Our soul's reliance on God is likened to our body's reliance on food and drink. According to Psalm 23, he is the heavenly Shepherd who feeds us on green pasture and leads us to refreshing, quiet waters. He also prepares a table of delights before us and fills our cup to overflowing. One of the ways God delivers this water and feast is by giving us his Word. According to Psalm 1, his Word is to us as life-giving liquid is to a riverside tree. Like Job we can say, "I treasure the words of his mouth more than my daily bread."[11]

Though we may not always be aware of our thirst and hunger, it is as we drink and eat that we discover both our appetite for God and his ability to satisfy us. George Muller, a Christian leader who centuries ago started many orphanages, used to say that the priority task of the Christ-follower is to "get one's soul happy in God every day" especially by praying and reading God's Word. Yet he knew that the practice did not always deliver immediate joy:

---

[9] Isaiah 2:3
[10] Nehemiah 8:4
[11] Job 23:12

"It is common for us to give up the reading of the Bible... when our en-joyment is gone; as if it were of no use to read the Scriptures when we do not enjoy them. The truth is that to enjoy the Word, we ought to contin-ue to read it. The less we read the Word of God, the less we desire to read it."

Joy awaits those who live in the Word. Those who ate the daily manna said it tasted like "wafers made with honey."[12] This food does not, all by itself, fall into our mouths. Like the Israelites, we must as-sume responsibility to get up out of bed, or at least sit up in bed, and to go, and get it, to take it in, to think it over, chew on it and digest it. As we do so, each and every day, God's Spirit will satisfy us with it and metabolize its nutrients into the energy of a changed life.

COME READY TO YIELD

By yielding to Scripture, I mean that we let the biblical text do in our lives what it will. It is true that the Bible "makes us participants in the world of God's being and action" but Eugene Peterson also stresses that we must realize that we do not "participate on our own. We don't get to make up the plot or decide what character we will be. This book has generative power; things happen to us as we let the text call forth, stimulate, rebuke, and prune us. We don't end up the same."[13]

This all starts with acknowledging whose word it is. Not the word of people, but the Word of God. Jesus said, "Anyone who chooses to do the will of God will find out whether my teaching comes from God or whether I speak on my own."[14] In other words, if we determine before-hand that our lives will not change, then we will most likely not discern the power of God in the Word. Hard hearts are unyielding and undis-cerning.

God calls us to yield with a prayer of surrender. *Then* we will see the light in God's Word and experience it as a sin-removing surgical blade

---

[12] Exodus 16:31
[13] Eugene Peterson. 2006: Eat This Book: Eerdmans, p66.
[14] John 7:17

and soul-healing medicine—first removing from us what impedes our spiritual health, then making us better than new. We should regularly pray, "God, show me in your Word the person you want me to become. God, search my heart, and remove what is offensive to you." That kind of prayer puts us in the place where God's Word can do its intended work in and through our lives.

COME WITH EXPECTANCY

When Jesus was walking on earth as *Immanuel*, God with us, everywhere he went the crowds would flock to him. Faith-filled expectancy seemed to unlock his wonder-working power. Conversely, a lack of it would tie his hands it seems. We're told in one place that, "he did not do many miracles there because of their unbelief."[15]

The highlight reel of the Gospels shows expectant people, time and again, receiving Jesus' life-changing word, his body-healing touch, his situation-invading light, and his direction-altering nudge. Since Jesus is the same yesterday, today and forever, each time we encounter him (now, not in the flesh, but by his Spirit and Word) we are asked the same question as those in the Gospels: "Do you believe?" "What do you expect?" Our heart's answers function like a tap—we either shut off some of God's power or we let it flow.

Now, I'm not saying that this kind of expectancy and power will flow each and every time we read the Bible, but overall our interaction with God in prayer and with his Word in reading will be marked by strangling familiarity or on-your-toes wonder, by jaded unbelief or childlike faith.

We do not merely come to a book. We come to its author. Unlike any other book, we read the Word *in the presence of its Author*, an Author who yearns to make himself known to us as we read his words.

This is why Scriptural engagement can never *merely* be a discipline or a duty. Although there may not be fireworks every time, a meeting

---

[15] Matthew 13:58

with the universe's Creator and Redeemer can never be just another meeting. Couples do not only go on dates because it's "the right thing to do" but because they long to know and enjoy each other more.

If the thought of approaching God terrifies you, then think of Jesus saying, "fear not" to calm your heart. If the prospect of drawing closer to God leaves you feeling condemned or unworthy, then remind yourself that you have confident access to God not because of your righteousness, but by his grace alone.[16]

Now, with pride, fears, and a sense of unworthiness cast away, come to the Word and be "careful how you listen," bringing a receptive heart, one that is humble, thirsty, hungry, yielded, and expectant. In the opening verse in this chapter, Jesus promises that if we do this, what we have from him will be multiplied. We will live in an ever-multiplying, life-changing revelation of God and from God.

No person better shows us how to receive the life-generating power of God's Word than Mary the soon-to-be mother of Jesus when Gabriel announces news of the conception of Jesus: "I am the Lord's servant. May everything you have said about me come true."[17]

I have hoped that this chapter will motivate you to come to God's Word with this highly receptive frame of mind and state of heart. If however, it has had the opposite effect, *demotivating* you with how little of this you have, despair not: like the little boy with few fishes and loaves, bring what you have, how ever meager it may seem. Bring your "little" hunger, your little faith, your small expectations to God and his Word. Do it again and again and again, every time you approach the Scriptures. And just watch what he does with it...

---

[16] Ephesians 2:18, 3:12
[17] Luke 1:38 (NLT)

13

HEAR, READ AND STUDY SCRIPTURE

Now the Berean Jews were of more noble character than those in Thessalonica, for they received the message with great eagerness and examined the Scriptures every day to see if what Paul said was true.

Acts 17:11

Luke, the author of Acts, drops into his narrative this description of some new believers who set a benchmark for us—these Berean Jews interacted with and examined the Scriptures every day of their lives, weighing every message they received from other sources against it. We learn from them the importance of regular, if not daily, reading and studying the Bible, and doing so both individually and communally.

In the previous chapter, I promised that this third part of the book would be enormously *practical.* In other words, I will guide you in exactly those practices that you, your family and your faith community can do to regularly and predictably unleash the transforming power of Scripture. Let's get to them right away. In this chapter, we will learn why and how to hear Scripture read, to hear it preached, to read it, and to study it. I will also show you how these spiritual practices can be done on your own and along with others:

LISTEN TO THE BIBLE BEING READ

Although our present individualistic age tends to skew our general approach to the Bible, Christianity is not a solitary faith, but a communal one. The Bible was and is first a book for the people of God, then only after that, for the person of God. In the mid-400s, a Syrian monk, Simeon Stylites experimented with the solitary faith. For decades he lived alone at the top of a 50-foot high pole. A strange experiment perhaps, but not much more strange than any follower of Jesus who tries to follow Jesus alone today. Outside of community, our biases, blind spots, and idiosyncrasies will remain unchallenged, and will easily take us off-track.

Paul counselled a church leader: "Devote yourself to the public reading of Scripture, and to preaching and teaching."[1] The word "public" refers to larger weekly gatherings. Still today, one of the key roles of pastors and ministers is to see to it that people, when gathered together, hear "the public reading" and the "preaching and teaching" of Scripture. One theologian writes,

> *"Reading the Bible silently to oneself was virtually unheard of until quite recent times. Private reading of Scripture may help one meditate on certain passages and truths, nevertheless it is subordinate to the public preaching that socializes individual readers into a covenant community. Only then is the private reading held in check and informed by the hearing of the wider communion of saints."*[2]

Though each message we hear in a church meeting might not be as Scripture-saturated as this theologian might assume, his point is taken: God's plan is that engaging God's Word together is meant to provide us with the riverbanks for engaging it alone.

Let's explore the public reading of Scripture. As we scan biblical history, we discover how God's people have, as a norm, sat under the Word of God being read aloud.

---

[1] 1 Timothy 4:3
[2] Michael Horton: 2013, *Pilgrim's Theology*, Zondervan, Kindle location 1981.

In 1300 BCE, the Israelites had come out of slavery and were asking the questions, "What is our story? Who are we? How do we live?" So Moses read the Word to thousands gathered.[3] The same thing happened again when they entered the Promised Land. Joshua read it aloud to the gathered people[4] who needed to know who they were, what story they were in, and how they were to live.

When the Israelites stopped reading God's Word for generations they became like a boat lost at sea. Anchorless, they forgot God's identity and their own, and the story of what God had done and how they were called to live in light of that. There was a brief arrest of this spiritual decay when a young king "accidentally" found some lost scrolls of Moses in the temple. As he read to the people, breathing life back into them, they hoisted their sails, awakened once again to their true call.[5]

Then later, when the exiled and dislocated people of God returned to their broken city of Jerusalem, Ezra gathered everyone and read the Scriptures to them for an entire week. The people were brought to weeping repentance and joyful renewal.[6] From then on the Jewish synagogues read the scrolls every Sabbath. Jesus grew up in this practice— recall how he launched his ministry by reading Isaiah's scroll in his home synagogue.[7]

Following in this long tradition, Paul commended the same practice to the young pastor Timothy. Then following on from the New Testament, the earliest churches did the same. The church father Tertullian in the 200s wrote, "We assemble to read our sacred writings. The sacred words nourish our faith, animate our hope, make our confidence more steadfast; and confirm our good habits."

Every believer can learn to read the Scriptures aloud to themselves, their children, in small groups and larger gatherings. Assuming you have advanced warning, here are four tips to excel in this ministry:

First, consider your pace. Project your voice. Choose some places to

---

[3] Exodus 24
[4] Joshua 8:34–35
[5] 2 Kings 23:1–3
[6] Nehemiah 8:1–12
[7] Luke 4:16–21

pause. Second, capture the emotion and energy of the passage. Identify its tone. Do not read a praise psalm with a bored or casual voice, but neither read a psalm of lament with a cheerful one. Third, vary your volume and inflection, paying attention to the final punctuation used—question marks and exclamation marks especially guide the way we should say things. Fourth, pray for God's power upon his Word to be evident to all.[8]

Hearing God's Word read together tends to lead to the next practice, which is hearing God's Word preached...

LISTEN TO THE BIBLE BEING PREACHED

Although all of us may teach bits and pieces of Scripture to each other informally and in smaller groups, God calls some to develop their God-given gifts of teaching and preaching so as to serve the church in a much broader capacity.

Some think that someone standing up and speaking for a period of time has become outdated in our information-saturated, image-driven, attention-deficit world. But God, the one who preached the universe into existence,[9] has ordained it as a primary means for working in and through a faith community.[10] In fact, preaching is a pivotal way that God *creates, sustains and sends* local churches. Consider first, how in the book of Acts, the apostles preach the gospel, and churches spring up in its wake—*the preached word created the church.* Second, Jesus told Peter to "feed his sheep" suggesting that a church with substance-less preaching is a malnourished one—*the preached word sustains the church.* Finally, as we sit under good preaching, we are inspired and equipped to pass the message of good news on to others—*the preached word sends the church.*

---

[8] We remember that faith communities once recognized the inspiration of the biblical books precisely because its words carried a power when they were read.

[9] Genesis 1:1–3

[10] Romans 10:8–17. This passage suggests that God's empowering Spirit rests not only on the word of Scripture or the gospel, but the word of the preacher.

HOW TO LISTEN TO A SERMON

Involvement in a church means that a large segment of your experience of spiritual community will include you listening to other people preaching and teaching God's Word. Here are four pieces of biblical advice to help you to get the most out of every message you hear…

Soften your heart. We have already spoken about the need to come to the Word with humility, hunger, yieldedness, and expectancy. When we do, we focus on the message, not the sermon or the preacher. God can use even a boring preacher or a confusing message to change our lives.

Don't compare preachers. Each preacher has their own unique flavour and grace and should be appreciated for what that grace is, not criticized for what that grace is not. Who in a church where there is more than one preacher can admit that they have a preferred preacher?

There is nothing wrong with this fact, but if it causes us to close off our hearts to God when a preacher whose style we do not enjoy as much stands up to address us, we might need to take it as an opportunity to grow in spiritual maturity. After all, Paul rebuked the Corinthian church for arguing about who their favourite preacher was, urging them to keep their hearts open to God regardless of the human conduit of truth he used:

"For when one says, "I follow Paul," and another, "I follow Apollos," are you not mere human beings? What, after all, is Apollos? And what is Paul? Only servants, through whom you came to believe—as the Lord has assigned to each his task. I planted the seed, Apollos watered it, but God has been making it grow. So neither the one who plants nor the one who waters is anything, but only God, who makes things grow."[11]

Listen to preachers who love you. With thousands of sermons available online, we must still give our ears primarily to those who care about us—our pastors and ministers. They know us and our context

---

[11] 1 Corinthians 6:3–6

better than any superstar preacher from another city can. Ever since Jesus told Peter, the first pastor in the first church, to "feed my sheep," preaching is meant to be, amongst other things, *pastoral*—the words of Jesus' under-shepherds to the sheep whom they know and have been entrusted to spiritually protect, lead and feed.

Write it down and share it with others. Note-taking during sermons helps many to take note of what God is saying to them. And expressing to others what God said to us through the message has a way of impressing even more deeply that message in us.

How will we survive if no one feeds us? Or, "how will (we) hear if no one preaches to (us)?"[12] I am forever grateful to every person called by God to preach and teach to me all these past years. All good food is God's love made visible. That includes people's messages to me.

To be honest, I cannot offhand remember most of what they said to me any more than I can bring to mind every meal that has been served to me. However, in the same way my present physical health is a result of all the plates of nutritious and delicious food dished up for me, so my present spiritual health is partly a result of all the messages lovingly served up to me.

Speaking of the joy of feeding on the preached word, let me say something to those fellow spiritual chefs and dieticians whom God has entrusted to nourish the rest of us…

HOW TO FEED A CHURCH

Here are four important things God's Word itself says about spiritually feeding people:

Cover all the basics. I suggest that at least every two or so years, tell the church everything they most need to know. Over two years, Paul claimed to have proclaimed to the Ephesian church "the whole will of God."[13] This does not necessarily mean he preached every verse in the

---

[12] Romans 10:14
[13] Acts 20:27

Bible to them, but it does suggest that he taught them on every major theme of the Bible, as well as every dimension of discipleship. Preachers must resist the temptation to teach only their pet themes and passages. Each must go over the Bible's main truths again and again, driving them deeper in each time.

Speak to the lives, challenges and questions of the people. Paul told the Ephesian church, "I have not hesitated to preach anything that would be helpful to you."[14] The role of the preacher is to plunge into the ancient texts, draw out their timeless truths and then apply them to the real worlds and actual lives of their hearers. This is why shepherding goes hand in hand with preaching. The preacher should not know and love only the Word. They should also do their best to know and love the people they are speaking to.

In this way, the preacher seeks to build a bridge between God's Word and our world, or as one theologian puts it:

> *"The church must be constantly retelling the story of Scripture, never losing sight of the landmark events, never losing touch with the main lines of meaning in Scripture, always remaining open to the never exhausted potential of the texts in their resonances with contemporary life."*[15]

Learn how to hold attention. Nearly as important as the content of our message is our delivery of it. How we say things is a close second to what we say. Think about Jesus' delivery in his preaching ministry. People would stay captivated by his teachings *for days.* In the same way, our delivery of the truths revealed in the Bible should at least try to hold our audience's attention too. Without going so far as to perpetuate the entertainment-fixation in our culture, we must do our honest best not to bore people with the Bible. How did Jesus do this? He taught the truth about the kingdom in a myriad of highly engaging ways—he used illustrations, object lessons, current events, stories, lecture format, dialogue, rhetorical questions, and proverbs.[16]

---

[14] Acts 20:20

[15] Ellen Davis, editor: 2003, *The Art of Reading Scripture*, iBooks, ch 4.

[16] Luke 7:31–32, Matthew 6:28, Luke 13:4–5, Mark 4:2, Matthew 24, John 3, Luke 18:8, Luke 7:45

Keep the main thing, the main thing. At the heart of Paul's preaching was always the gospel. He says to the Ephesian church that he also preached about faith in our Lord Jesus, the good news of God's grace and the kingdom.[17] Since the gospel is the nucleus of the Bible, it should be front and centre in our preaching, both for edifying believers and evangelizing the unconvinced. "Do the work of an evangelist,"[18] says Paul to Timothy, and to every aspiring preacher since.

READ SCRIPTURE ON YOUR OWN

Jesus invites us to remain in him and let his words remain in us[19]— literally to make ourselves at home in him even as his Word makes a home in us. As I shared in the introduction of this book, though the Bible started off as a strange land for me, over time it became my second home. Getting comfortable with God, I found, directly connects with getting comfortable with his Word.

God desires that the Word would be near us, in our mouths (as we read it aloud) and in our hearts (as we believe it).[20] To make ourselves at home with God and his Word, we must spend plenty of time in it. Old Testament kings were commanded to read the Bible every day. "When he takes his throne, the king is to write for himself on a scroll a copy of this law. It is to be with him, and he is to read it every day of his life so that he may learn to revere the LORD." [21] The king was, after all, one of the few people in Israel who could afford his own copy. For most of the church's history, only Catholic priests got personally to read the Bible. Written in Latin and more expensive than a house, the scrolls were out of reach for the common person. Add to that the fact that few could read.[22]

---

[17] Acts 20:21, 24, 25
[18] 2 Timothy 4:5
[19] John 15:7
[20] Romans 10:8
[21] Deuteronomy 17:18–19
[22] While only Old Testament kings and first millennium priests read the Bible, thanks to the gospel, we're all kings and priests in Christ.

Yet the average modern literate believer, with access to their own copy on the shelf and on their smartphone, is more faithful to news sites and social media feeds. Various studies in Western cities show that Millennials and Gen Z consume 4-10 hours of media per day, while other studies reveal that only 10% of church-going young people interact with the Bible on any given day, and if they do, it's generally just for a few minutes.

Perhaps part of the problem is a prevailing sense that reading the Bible just isn't do-able. Many try to approach it as they would any other book (starting at the beginning and working their way through from there), only eventually to give up somewhere between Leviticus and Judges—feeling a little defeated and far *less* sure of what they know about God and his Scriptures. Yet reading through the Bible is actually *very* do-able. If you allocate just 12 minutes a day, the entire Bible can be read through in 365 days.

Then again, reading the Bible over a single year may not work for you. After all, there's no need to sprint through it—whether you go through the whole Bible in five months or five years is not as important as whether the whole Bible goes through you.[23] Having said that, there are several possible methods used to read through the Bible:

Read Select Scriptures

To any first-time reader who decides to read the Bible from beginning to end, I suggest they skip over Leviticus and Deuteronomy. Some may express concern about that, but I have seen too many would-be Bible readers sprinting off excitedly into Genesis and Exodus, only to encounter the hundreds of laws of Moses and give up before they have reached the end of the first five books—called the Torah or Pentateuch. I also suggest that they skip 1 and 2 Chronicles (which duplicates so much of 1 and 2 Samuel and 1 and 2 Kings). Finally, I suggest as they

---

[3] Eugene Peterson reminds us that we read the Bible to absorb its words, something that does not usually happen if we merely speed through our reading: "Reading is an immense gift, but only if the words are assimilated, taken into the soul—eaten, chewed, gnawed, and received in unhurried delight." (Eugene Peterson. 2006: *Eat This Book*, Eerdmans, 66).

come to "The Prophets," the last two-fifths of the Old Testament, that they read only Isaiah and Daniel of the five long-book (or major) prophets, and only two of the 12 subsequent short-book (or minor) prophets, perhaps Joel and Jonah. Again, this advice is pastorally forged: many new readers who do manage to get through the Torah hurdle do not make it over the Prophets. Which is a pity, because the New Testament is just about to begin. Of course, I tell them to come back to the books they have skipped in the future, but in their first round of Scripture, these can be jumped over.

For new residents to this home we call the Bible, there are even more selective approaches. A 70-hour long book may still intimidate a beginner. Many have found it helpful to take a fly-over of the Bible by reading through a selection of 100–250 passages which those who created the lists deemed to be the most essential for the Bible's storyline and its core doctrinal content.[24]

Listen to an Audio Bible or Read it Aloud Yourself

The portal *www.biblegateway.com* offers a selection of excellent readings for free. You can listen to the Bible while you commute, exercise, or lie in bed. Perhaps you'd even like to go to sleep each night after listening for a while.

One notch higher than listening to someone else read the Bible to you, is hearing yourself read the Bible. The *silent* reading of books and the Bible is a recent trend in history. God's words were written to be read and heard aloud.[25] There's a rhythm and energy to them that makes them go deeper in when heard or declared aloud. So don't just read the words with your eyes and in your head, read them with your mouth and hear them with your ears.

Have a Bible Reading Plan

Instead of randomly reading the Bible, adopt a plan. Decide on how

---

[24] For example, see Scripture Union's Essential 100 list: www.bit.ly/3qevFz6.
[25] We remember that all the New Testament epistles addressed to churches were meant to be read to a gathered church, most likely all the way through.

much you want to read or listen to each day.

One idea is to read a book of the Old Testament, then a book of the New, and so on. Another idea is the *Three Bookmarks* method. Put one bookmark in Genesis 1, one in Psalms 1, and one in Matthew 1, then read a chapter of each and move the bookmarks along. If you are trying to go through the whole Bible in a year, you can read all three chapters in one go (per day).

Do whatever works for you, although I'd personally discourage just flipping the book open each time and seeing where you land. Some think that this is a more "spiritual" approach because it gives God a chance each time to lead you to the right passage. Yet this wrongly assumes that the Spirit is better able to orchestrate what we read when we *don't* have a plan. But think of Jesus in the synagogue in Luke 4. According to the synagogue roster, it was Jesus son of Joseph's turn to read. The next scroll to be read was Isaiah, for it was handed to him. He then read from what is now chapter 61 in Isaiah. My point is that Isaiah "just happened" to be the next scroll, and yet it was exactly what was needed to announce the inception of his ministry: "The Spirit of the Sovereign Lord is upon me…" It's my experience that when we have a plan to read Scriptures, we will find ourselves, again and again, reading words that speak directly into our current situation.

Having said that, there is no harm in flipping the Bible open *sometimes* and seeing where it lands. Or even being "led" to somewhere outside your plan. Just this morning, as I was about to turn to the next chapter in the book of the Bible I am currently in, the words, "Isaiah 2" popped into my mind, so I had a rich time reflecting on that passage. Tomorrow morning I will return to my plan.

Binge Read

There's something special about a daily habit, but there's also the example of Ezra reading the Hebrew Bible to the Israelites every day for a week. Imagine that! A whole week! You might want to try it some time. If reading the Bible everyday can be likened to a daily shower, then prolonged exposure to God's Word is like swimming far out into the open ocean, basking in its size, feel and depth.

Find a Time and a Place

One pastor and author tells of his daily practice with Scripture; notice especially his reference to time and place:

> *"Here's to tomorrow morning, six o'clock. Coffee in hand, on the chair by the window. Time to breathe. A psalm and a story from the Gospels. Hearing the Father's voice. Pouring out my own. Some sitting, resting. Maybe I'll hear a word from God that will alter my destiny ... Maybe I'll feel my mind settle like untouched water; maybe my mind will ricochet from thought to thought, and never come to rest. If so, that's fine. I'll be back, same time tomorrow. Starting my day in the quiet place."[26]*

As I look back on my decades of attempting to do this, I can recall numerous places and times that have worked for me at different stages. For example, I remember as a teenager, sitting at my desk from 6:55—7:15 am, Monday to Friday, before getting ready for school, reading through the Bible, and making marks on the pages with a blue pen. Then there are memories of listening to Scripture as I walked to work. At other times, I'd read Scripture on the train, and so on.

As for the time in the day, find what works for you. But I must say that there's something about mornings that's special. Though they have not always worked for me (especially during the heart of winter and when my kids were very small) my reflection is that there is something unmatched about letting God's Word be *the first word* we listen to every day. C.S. Lewis masterfully makes the point:

> *"The real problem of the Christian life comes where people do not usually look. It comes the very moment you wake up each morning. All your wishes and hopes for the day rush at you like wild animals. The very moment you wake up each morning (your) first job consists simply in shoving them all back; in listening to that other voice, taking that other point of view, letting that larger, stronger, quieter life come flowing in."[27]*

Writing in the 1950s, he knew nothing of the ferocious wild animals

---

[26] John Mark Comer: 2019, *The Ruthless Elimination of Hurry*, iBooks, Part 3.
[27] C.S. Lewis: 1952, *Mere Christianity*

that howl at us from the Smartphone at our bedside. May I suggest you refuse to open any news site, social media feed, or inbox before opening the Bible. In fact, I doubt I can give more life-changing advice than this: unless your season of life forbids it, put God's Word first by making it the first word you listen to every day. Perhaps, over time, you will begin to resonate with Isaiah who said, "Every morning God wakens my ear and teaches me to listen like one being taught."[28]

STUDY SCRIPTURE

Martin Luther distinguishes between reading and studying the Bible with this metaphor:

> *"I study my Bible like I gather apples. First, I shake the whole tree that the ripest may fall. Then I shake each limb, and when I have shaken each limb, I shake each branch and every twig. In the same way, I search the whole Bible, shaking the whole tree. Then I shake every limb, studying it book by book. Then I shake every branch, giving attention to the chapters. Then I shake every twig, examining the paragraphs, sentences, words, and their meanings."*

Luther's point is valid—a *quicker reading* of a large chunk shakes the tree, yielding the easy-to-get apples. But a *slower study* of a shorter passage is how to find the harder-to-reach apples, which are sometimes even sweeter. The question is, how do we shake those branches and twigs? Try these five ways:

Slow Down

I used to wish that I could read more *quickly*, but over the years I have come to wish that I could read more *slowly*. Perhaps spend days or weeks on one or several chapters. There is a time to read through an entire book of the Bible in one sitting, but there is also a time to wade very slowly through its verses and words.

---

[28] Isaiah 50:4

Study a Variety of Things

I suggest studying whole books of the Bible, or major sections of whole books. Start with something from the Old Testament for a month or however long it takes, perhaps Abraham or Daniel. Then something in the New Testament, such as Hebrews or the Sermon on the Mount. Then continue back and forth between the Testaments.

You might prefer to study a theme that runs *across* the Testaments, such as the gospel, God, humanity, Jesus, salvation, the kingdom, God's people, God's Spirit, final things, discipleship and God's Word (you're on that last theme right now).

We can mine down into other concepts that run through the Bible too, and especially trace how they "evolve" through the Bible's plotline of creation, the fall, Israel, Jesus, the church, and the consummation of all things. For example, you could study Sabbath-rest, prophecy, miracles, temple, redemption, covenant, the law of Moses, mission, judgment, mercy, and so on. Each of these themes tends to thread through tens or hundreds of individual texts. As you study those texts, you will pull on whichever thread you are studying and see how it connects to both earlier and later passages in the Bible's storyline.

Outside of these major themes, you can also study whatever topic of interest you find in the Bible. According to the search memory of *www.biblegateway.com*[29] some of the more popular topics are love, faith, peace, hope, marriage, joy, prayer, strength, grace, children, forgiveness, healing, fear, trust, the heart, comfort, worship, friendship, and generosity.[30] If I can make a personal plea: first start with the major themes, for they are foundational to understanding every other topic you might be interested in.

So much to study! So many journeys! Start somewhere, and then keep walking.

---

[29] www.bit.ly/37pnYxg (accessed 11/20)

[30] Try out www.openbible.info/topics. It's the site I use when I want a quick list of Bible verses on whatever topic. But remember that all of these verses are "snatched" out from their context. To understand what they are really saying you must read them in context.

Ask the Right Questions

Earlier in Part 2, we explored how to read the Bible right and unpacked the most important questions to ask to uncover the text's ancient meaning and to discover its timeless truth - do you remember them? Here is a quick refresher:

- Its place in the story: Where does the book that this text is in fit within the 14 stages in the Bible's larger story?

- Its genre type: What genre of literature is this text?

- Its author's purpose: Why was this particular book even written and what situation does it address?

- The flow of thought: Based on the section before and after, what is the author trying to say in this passage?

- The cultural background: Are there any ancient cultural assumptions, situations, or practices referred to that are different than our own?

- Word and sentence study: What do the words, phrases, and their grammatical relationship to each other mean?

- Its timeless message: In this passage is there some wisdom to learn, instruction to obey, an example to follow, warning to heed, a principle to apply, promise to believe, or doctrine to grasp?

As you may recall, in this final question, we may also need to explore references to earlier Scriptures, read the Old Testament in light of Christ and, especially when a passage's meaning is unclear, read it in light of other things said by the same author, as well as the rest of Scripture. In all of this remember to *distinguish* between God's particular and universal commands, the timeless principles and the ancient cultural application of them, what is literal and what is figurative, what is clear or central and what is cloudy or peripheral, and what the Bible merely *describes* versus what it *prescribes*.

Paraphrase the Passage

The litmus test of understanding a passage is whether you can restate the passage in your own words or not. Why is this so important? Dawson Trotman articulates a key principle of study: "Our many and varied thoughts disentangle themselves and take shape when they pass through our finger tips or our lips." So, either write it down, or voice record it, or share what you have learnt with someone else.

Study in Community

As we study passages together with others in small groups, they will help us to see many things we may have missed. By looking at the same text collectively, we will notice many more things than we could ever find on our own. We will discover more of God in the text, but also more of each other—people tucked deep into the trenches of Scripture together often bond in profound ways.[31] Also, the very act of studying the Bible together has a way of motivating and equipping us to study it on our own. See *Appendix 3* at the back of this book for a method of small group Bible Study that requires very little preparation and tends to work on most biblical passages.

Even on our own, we can study in community. We do so as we lean on skilled and trusted teachers and scholars who expound these passages in books or online. I have already mentioned two books[32] that are worthy of purchase, but there are more resources that may help you:

If possible, download a biblical commentary when studying a book of the Bible. See *www.bestcommentaries.com* for guidance on the top-rated ones for each book of the Bible. Unless you are an academic, be sure to select the more accessible, pastoral ones not the technical ones. You will find that there are entire series of commentaries: as a general rule, I recommend the *NIV Application Commentary* series.

---

[31] "The Bible creates community, by providing space for community to happen. It offers storied worlds and theological vocabularies around which people can come together in conversation about abiding questions. It calls for creative, collaborative participation." (Timothy Beal: 2012: *The Rise and Fall of the Bible*, Mariner Books, 188.)

[32] These are *The NIV Cultural Background Study Bible* and Fee and Stuart's *How to Read the Bible Book by Book.*

You can also use Bible study websites like:
www.biblehub.com
www.blueletterbible.com
www.biblegateway.com
www.terranwilliams.com[33]

FIVE MORE TIPS

I promised you I would provide you with as much practical advice as I could. So, here are five more tried-and-tested guidelines to help you engage the Good Book as you read and study it:

Ignore the Numbers

None of the biblical writers included headings, chapters, or verses in their manuscripts. The system of chapters was only introduced in CE 1238 by Cardinal Hugo de S. Caro for monks who read and meditated a manageable portion each day. Verse notations were only added in 1551 by Robertus Stephanus, after the advent of printing. In much the same way our physical addresses help people to find our home, universally accepted chapter and verse markings help people to locate and find specific texts portions of Scripture. However, there are two major downsides to these additions:

The first downside is that verse allocations create the impression that a verse or a chapter can stand on their own. *Yet few can.* None of us would pick up a novel and read the fourteenth sentence on page 228 and hope to really understand that sentence. As we learned earlier, words gain their meaning in sentences. Sentences gain their meaning in paragraphs. Paragraphs gain their meaning within a bigger more expansive story.

The second downside is that neither Hugo nor Robertus did a fantastic job of identifying sections. Perhaps if a more scholarly team had

---

[33] Dedicated to producing a growing collection of resources for individuals, groups and churches, I've snuck my humble offering into this list of much bigger and more established online biblical resources.

decided on the chapters and verses they may have served us better. Most English translation teams do help us by adding headings within the text. This helps us to identify new lines of thought in the book. Yet Robertus sometimes selected a chapter break right in the middle of a line of thought. Take 2 Corinthians 5-7 for example. Chapter 5 ends with Paul claiming to be Christ's ambassador, imploring people to be reconciled to God by trusting in the sin-bearing, saving work of Jesus. Then, for no apparent reason, Hugo starts chapter 6 even though Paul is still carrying on his line of thought: "As God's co-workers we urge you not to receive God's grace in vain..." The same thing happens again at the end of chapter 6 where Paul lists some wonderful promises. But Hugo cuts the tail-end off of this section once again, just before Paul says, "Therefore since we have these promises, dear friends, let us purify ourselves." (7:1)

My point: unless you are looking for a reference, ignore the numbers. Especially as you read through entire books of the Bible, it is best to try not to the chapter and verse numbers at all.

Feel the Author

Notice evocative language that is meant to arouse a specific emotion, often without naming that emotion.

C.S. Lewis once instructed other writers to make us feel something without naming the feeling for us. He said, "Instead of telling us something is terrible, describe it so we will be terrified. Don't say 'it was a delight.' Make us feel delighted when we read the description." Indeed, writing is an artform. At its best, it conveys more than information—it evokes imagination and stirs emotion. Similarly, many biblical authors hoped to communicate something more than concepts or ideas to their readers.

Ezekiel says much more than, "Beware God's judgment is coming" when he declares:

"Disaster! Unheard-of disaster! See, it comes! The end has come! See, it comes! Doom has come upon you. The time has come! The day is near! Doom has burst forth, the rod has budded, arrogance has blossomed, a

rod to punish the wicked. Let not the buyer rejoice, nor the seller grieve, for my wrath is on the whole crowd."[34]

He does not use the word, yet we feel it: terror. Moses says much more than, "God comforts you" when he writes:

"There is no one like the God of Jeshurun, who rides across the heavens to help you and on the clouds in his majesty. The eternal God is your refuge, and underneath are the everlasting arms."[35]

He does not use the word, but we feel it: comforted. John the Seer says more than, "God is worthy of worship" when he writes:

"And all the angels stood around the throne and around the elders and the four living creatures. And they fell facedown before the throne and worshipped God, saying, "Amen! Blessing and glory and wisdom and thanks and honour and power and strength be to our God forever and ever"."[36]

He does not use the word, but we feel it: awe. If we read these kinds of passages analytically, with our intellects alone, we end up being tone-deaf to so much of what the author is trying to convey.

Revel in Repetition

Notice repeating words and ideas, which emphasize the main idea.

Sometimes an author will try to emphasize something through repetition. For example, as we read in the opening verses of Daniel 3 about king Nebuchadnezzar commanding everyone to worship the huge image of himself, the author refers five times in these few verses to "the image the king had set up." Simply calling it "the image" would have sufficed, but the author repeatedly adds "the king had set up." As we reflect on why, we realize he is poking holes at the absurdity of people worshipping something that someone has made and has to set up himself. If we miss that, we miss the author's main idea and intent.

Or, can you spot Isaiah's repetition as he speaks of the coming Mes-

[34] Ezekiel 7:5–12
[35] Deuteronomy 33:26–27
[36] Revelation 7:11–12

siah in Isaiah 53:4-6?

> *"Surely he took up our pain and he bore our suffering... he was pierced for our transgressions, he was crushed for our iniquities; the punishment that brought us peace was on him, and by his wounds, we are healed. We all, like sheep, have gone astray... and the LORD has laid on him the iniquity of us all."*

In this passage, Isaiah flips back and forth between "he, our, he, our, he, our, us, him, his, we, we, him," each time putting this mysterious figure (the coming Messiah) in our place. The main idea in Isaiah's prophecy is that the Messiah's suffering and death is *emphatically* a death in our place. We must not miss the fact that God took our sin, put it on sinless Jesus, and punished it there.

Numerous New Testament passages also use repetition for emphasis. For example, count how many times the words "blessed," "comfort," and "remain" are used, respectively, in Matthew 5:1–12, 2 Corinthians 1:3–7, and John 15:1–11 and you will find they are used nine, nine, and ten times. That is repetition to revel in, for we discover that the God who *emphatically* wants to bless and comfort us is the one who invites us *emphatically* to remain in him, too.

"Because" and "Therefore"

Notice the connecting words that clarify the author's line of logic. Small as they are, these connecting words are crucial because they reveal *the author's train of thought.*

If I say, "I am sick, *therefore* I can't sing" the word "therefore" is the connecting word. The fact that I am sick explains *why* I can't sing. The reason precedes the connecting word, while the result follows. Then again, I can *reverse the order* and use a different connecting word: "I can't sing, *for* I am sick." In that case, the result precedes and the reason follows.

With this in mind, take note that there are two categories of connecting words that are important to keep an eye out for: *reason-then-result* ones and *result-then-reason* ones. The most common reason-then-result words include "therefore" and "so." The common result-then-reason ones are "for," "since," and "because."

How could this possibly help your Bible reading? Well, consider this: in 2 Corinthians 5 alone, Paul uses 14 connecting words: "for we" (four times), "because we" (three times), "therefore we" (three times), "since we" (twice), and "so we" (twice).

Yet very often our eyes simply skip over these connecting words. The result is that we hear a bunch of jumbled thoughts, when actually the author is revealing a clear line of logic.

Now look at this passage: "Thanks be to God, who delivers me through Jesus Christ our Lord! ... Therefore, there is now no condemnation for those who are in Christ Jesus, because... the Spirit... has set you free."[37]

We're told that there is no condemnation in Christ, but in this sentence, we are told much more. The fact of our no-condemnation in Christ is attached to not one but two connecting words—the words "therefore" on the front and "because" on the end. The word "therefore" (think reason-then-result) points us *back* to the reason for this result—namely, God has delivered us through Jesus Christ. The "because" (think result-then-reason) points us *forward* to another reason—the Spirit has set you free.

So to lay out Paul's line of thought, we can be so sure there is truly no condemnation for two reasons: Christ has delivered us *and* the Spirit is liberating us.

But see what we have realized here? Connecting words, which show how a reason leads to a result, may also help us to identify *the theology behind a command.*

Let me explain. Biblical authors often give a command or ethical instruction, while providing a theological reason for it. Consider this example: "Since we have these promises, dear friends, let us purify ourselves."[38] The theology (the great promises we have) is the reason that results in the command (to purify ourselves).

---

[37] Romans 7:25; 8:1–2. Unfortunately these verses are split apart by Hugo's section cutting referenced earlier in the chapter.
[38] 2 Corinthians 7:1

Or here's another example: "Do you not know that your bodies are temples of the Holy Spirit, who is in you, whom you have received from God? You are not your own; you were bought at a price. Therefore honour God with your bodies."[39] The word "therefore" is a reason-then-result connecting word. He does not only tell us that we must honour God with our bodies. He tells us why first. Too often we only notice the command instruction, but we fail to notice the reason. In fact, there are three theological truths given in the preceding verse: The Spirit lives in our body, the Father owns our body, and Jesus paid for our body.

Said another way, whenever you read in the New Testament a command with the word "therefore" in front of it, always ask what it's there for. It often points back to the wonderful theology that motivates and enables us to live in a certain way. However, when we only focus on the command and forget to steep ourselves in the theological reasons for them, we can be easily crushed under their weight, rather than empowered to obey them.[40]

Study Select Words

Earlier I mentioned topical studies—studying what the Bible has to say about love or marriage, for example. In this section, I refer to something far more specific: delving deeply into a Hebrew or Greek word so as to tease out its fuller meaning as it applies to its particular passage.

Of course, the English translation of the word in your Bible may have perfectly captured its meaning. But perhaps it has not got the meaning quite right, or got all of the meaning. The English word may say less than the original word or perhaps more.

As we study the meaning of an original Greek or Hebrew word, it

---

[39] 1 Corinthians 6:10–20

[40] The Puritan preachers used to warn against preaching "naked commands". What they meant was that a preacher might pluck a command out of the New Testament and press it upon his hearers, but fail to "clothe that command with the gospel." By this they meant the aspect of the gospel that is usually mentioned before or after the commands, and is the very reason for the command and the means with which to fulfill it. When gospel-clothed commands are preached, they tend to come with more power and we are enabled to obey them with greater levels of joy.

often reveals a greater depth and richness to our understanding of the text. Often enough, we find that the Greek or Hebrew word we are examining has a landscape of meaning that the English translation has not, or could not capture.

Take for example the word *compassion*. In English, it is derived from *com* (with) and *passio* (suffer). As rich a word as that is, it hardly does justice to the Hebrew word *rakhum*. The Hebrew word is closely related to the word for womb—suggesting the depth of God's compassion for us, as well as his ability to carry us in his tender, nurturing care. Likewise, the Greek word *splagchnizomai*, translated as compassion, means the stirring of one's inmost parts, literally the twisting of the intestines. My point is that there is no English word that can seize upon *the depth* of emotion conveyed in the original words. When we consider that 80% of all biblical uses of the word compassion are about God's or Jesus' compassion, we realize how a simple word study can lead us into a greater understanding of God.

Just to be clear, I am not saying you have to study every word in the language it was originally written in to begin to uncover the deeper truths in a passage. What I suggest is that, from time to time, select one or two words that seem to be significant within the context of the text and take those words and explore them a little more.

All very well, you might say, but what good is it if we do not have knowledge of Greek and Hebrew? Well, you might want to take out a few years of your life and learn those original languages of the Bible. Or you can read *Appendix 4*, in which I tell you exactly how I study any biblical word that I want to, using free online tools. I even give you a case study to make sure you grasp the process properly.

That brings us to the end of this chapter. I have shared with you a truckload of ways to engage Scripture in it, but there are far more. Had I stopped exploring ways to engage God's Word at this point, you would likely assume that the primary, or perhaps exclusive, way to tap into the power of God's Word is with your analytical faculty, for most of the practices in this chapter have been intellectual in character. Yet, that's only half the picture—as I will show you in the next chapter…

14

EXPERIENCE SCRIPTURE

Your words were found, and I ate them, and your words became to me a joy and the delight of my heart.

Jeremiah 15:16

According to Jeremiah, Scripture is food to savour. As stimulating and important as it is to study and analyze the words of Scripture, it is also important to *experience* them as "a joy."

Another experiential metaphor is of Scripture as a plunge pool—we're told that Jesus "cleanses (us) by the washing with water through the word."[1] Yes, we are intellectually to immerse ourselves in the Bible, but we are also to find ways to baptize ourselves experientially into Scripture, letting the biblical text bypass or penetrate through our analytical approach to things, and *letting it cleanse, refresh, touch and delight our hearts.*

How to do that is the subject of this chapter. Let's discover how to enjoy Scripture as we memorize, reflect on, pray, sing, journal and imaginatively enter it.

MEMORIZE SCRIPTURE

Listen to an earthly parent's plea to their child: "My son, keep my words and store up my commands within you. Keep my commands

---

[1] Ephesians 5:26

and you will live; guard my teachings as the apple of your eye. Bind them on your fingers; write them on the tablet of your heart."[2]

How much more should we do the same with our heavenly Father's words to us? We are to cherish God's Word, storing it up within and keeping it as the apple of our eye. Memorizing passages in the Bible is the way we can do this.

There are three benefits to memorizing Scripture:

First, it enables you to feed on God's Word anytime, anywhere. Jesus as a boy, like all Jewish boys, most likely memorized the entire first five books of the Bible and much of the rest of the Old Testament. Throughout his life and ministry, these Scriptures were his soul's food. He carried his Bible around with him—not on his phone or in the form of a book, but in his head and heart. In this way, he could feed on it all day long. In the same way, we are told to "let the Word of Christ dwell in (us) richly."[3] Memorizing select verses or passages makes this possible. In the words of Dallas Willard, a leading guide in spiritual practices: "Bible memorization is absolutely fundamental to spiritual formation. If I had to choose between all the disciplines of the spiritual life, I would choose Bible memorization, because it is a fundamental way of filling our minds with what it needs."[4]

Second, memorizing biblical passages means that God can speak to and through you more readily. Jesus teaches us that the Holy Spirit will "remind us of the things he has previously said to us."[5] Ask people who have memorized Scripture and they will tell of many times when, while they were praying, or when they were having a spiritual conversation with someone, or when they were trying to make a decision, or sometimes while they were merely day-dreaming, suddenly a Scripture long ago memorized pops into their mind, and they realize that God has just communicated with them

The other day, I was listening with one ear to someone who was

---

[2] Proverbs 7:1–3
[3] Colossians 3:16
[4] Dallas Willard says this in an article, "Spiritual Formation in Christ for the Whole Life and Whole Person" in *Vocatio*, Vol. 12, no 2, 2001, 7.
[5] John 14:26

overwhelmed by life's difficulties and by what appeared to be spiritual opposition. My other ear was attentive to the whisper of the Spirit, which came in the form of a memorized verse: "Greater is he who is in you than he who is in the world."[6] I knew just how to encourage my friend. Says one biblical teacher about remembering Scripture:

> *"No other single exercise pays greater spiritual dividends! Your prayer life will be strengthened. Your witnessing will be sharper and much more effective. Your attitudes and outlook will begin to change. Your mind will become alert and observant. Your confidence and assurance will be enhanced. Your faith will be solidified."[7]*

Third, committing Scripture to memory arms you for battle. When Satan tempted Jesus in the desert, he resisted it by quoting Scriptures he had memorized. He quoted three passages, all from the early chapters of Deuteronomy. Perhaps while he was walking through the desert, he'd been reflecting on that section of Scripture. When the battle started, he could deftly wield those Scriptures like a sword—piercing the darkness and slaying the lies of Satan.

Likewise, the Psalmist says, "I have hidden your word in my heart so that I might not sin against you."[8] Paul affirms this sentiment in his letter to the Ephesians too: when he says, "Take up the sword of the Spirit, which is the Word of God."[9]

When temptations and Satan's lies come our way, if we can recall and reaffirm a relevant Scripture as truth, we will find we have a life- and sanity-saving ally in the heat of spiritual battle.

While many of us claim to have poor memories, we all have thousands of ideas, facts, stories, and figures stored in our memory bank. A good memory is not measured by how easily you recall data, but by how good the data is that you have chosen to store in the first place. In the final analysis, we remember what is important to us. Our failure to commit any Scripture to memory may indicate the insufficient value

---

[6] 1 John 4:4
[7] Charles Swindoll: 1983, *Growing Strong in the Seasons of Life*, Zondervan.
[8] Psalms 119:11
[9] Ephesians 6:17

we place on it. But we can fix that.

I am sure you are motivated to learn passages off by heart, but you might be wondering where to start, and how.

As for what verses to memorize, in *Appendix 5* I recommend 40 verses to start with. The 40 Scriptures I've selected will help you in particular to: celebrate and communicate the gospel of salvation, grasp the basics of new life in Christ, follow Jesus more effectively, become more like Jesus, and finally trust God in difficult times.

As for how to memorize passages, here are seven keys I've found to be most helpful in my own journey of hiding more and more of God's Word in my heart:

- *Keep it accessible.* Write it down or store it on your phone so you can carry it with you and read it throughout the day.

- *Learn a verse at a time.* The more you verbally repeat it, the more it will stick.

- *Memorize the first few words especially well* and you will find the rest of the verse easier to call to mind.

- *Regularly review previously learnt verses.* Go back to them and reflect on them your whole life through! I find it helpful to keep a record of these verses in a single document or journal.

- *Use it or lose it.* The more you use memorized Scripture in your prayers and in ministry to others, the more it becomes internalized in you.

- *Try to memorize lengthier passages too.* The more you remember, the more spiritual arsenal you will have at your disposal.[10]

So we are to hide Scripture in the recesses of our minds, which brings us to our next experiential practice—we also need to let it penetrate the recesses of our hearts...

---

[10] To help you memorize entire chapters and books of the Bible, read Andrew Davis' book, *An approach to extended memorization of Scripture.*

REFLECT ON SCRIPTURE

In order to draw strength from food, we need to chew on it. We can't swallow a piece of bread whole. In the same way, to draw spiritual strength from a portion of Scripture, we must "chew" on it for a while, savouring its taste, breaking down its components, and absorbing its goodness into our inner being.

Paul writes, "Reflect on what I am saying, and the Lord will give you insight into it."[11] That's the goal of reflection—not just gleaning information but also *gaining insight* with the help of God.

But don't hear what Paul is not saying. He is not suggesting our intellectual functionality should be switched off. It is true that God wants to give us deeper insight into whatever passage is at hand, but according to Paul's word "reflect" we need to apply our minds for this to happen. The mind is to be in full gear, even as the Spirit draws near.

The common term for this practice is *biblical meditation*. We prayerfully focus our mind on some aspect of God or on a particular portion of Scripture for a period of time.

You may be glad to know that biblical meditation is not only for advanced believers. It is for every believer who wishes to make progress spiritually. And here's some even better news: if you know how to worry, you're already an expert in meditation. While worry focuses your thoughts on something negative, meditation sets your thoughts on the reality of God.

How exactly do we reflect on Scripture? To start, here is a simple four-step way to meditate on Scripture:

- *Step one: Choose a verse or a portion of a verse*, usually one that sticks out to you in the passage you have just read or studied.

- *Step two: Read it repeatedly and slowly to yourself.* Before you swallow actual foods, you're meant to chew close on 40 times. Similarly, to draw out spiritual energy and insight from this verse, you might need to read it again and again and again. A

---

[11] 2 Timothy 2:7

useful method is, each time you repeat it, to emphasize a different word, from the first to the last. So you might say to yourself, in your head, but even better aloud, "*I* am a new creation in Christ," then "I *am* a new creation in Christ," then "I am a *new* creation in Christ." And so on. Each repetition potentially releases something new into your mind and spirit.

- *Step three: Rely on the Holy Spirit* to give you ears to hear what the Spirit is saying. Ask him to give you insight into truth as well as to guide and empower your application of it to your life and your current situation. Then pray in response to what he shows you.

- *Step four: Optionally, write it out or memorize it so you can continue to ponder it in the hours ahead.* Instead of merely pondering it for a few minutes, why not take it with you (like a packed lunch), praying it over your life or others, for the rest of the day? My own experience is that this is the best way to carry the word I have received from God in my Bible reading time into the rest of my day.

That's one simple method—my preferred one—but it is not the *only* way to reflect and meditate on biblical texts…

Lectio Divina

Many Scripture meditators like to use another spiritual practice going back to the Benedictine monks of the 6th century called *Lectio Divina*.

Literally meaning *divine reading*, it is built around the need to encounter God regularly through prayerful, Scriptural meditation. It consists of five components: *silencio, lectio, meditatio, oratio, and contemplatio*. You can learn more about it in the first half of *Appendix 6*.

I have often used a *communal form of Lectio Divina*, in which a group of people reflect on a Scripture passage together, then share with each other what they have sensed God showing them. I discovered it as a twenty-something youth leader who had started to wonder if there was a way of, when gathered, ministering God's Word to young people outside of a sermon or a group Bible Study. When I tried this simple method, I was blown away by the way young people seemed personally to hear what God was saying to them through a simple passage of Scripture, a way that did not require my sermonizing nor facilitating an in-depth Bible Study (both of which still have their place). I have also used it as a way of helping ministry and leadership teams connect with God and his Word. You can learn more about this communal form of *Lectio Divina* in the second half of *Appendix 6*.

HEARING GOD IN SCRIPTURE

Talking about "hearing God" as we reflect on Scripture understandably raises some questions: Are we not meant to find out the ancient meaning and timeless message then call it quits—the intellectual exercise is the way we hear God? Surely God will say the same thing to all people through whatever text as long as they understand it rightly? Shouldn't we be wary of seeking out some additional personal meaning that God wants to communicate to us as individuals or as a community?

I appreciate these cautions. My chapter on committing to find the author's intended meaning is proof of that. And certainly, God's Spirit would not, through the same passage, say something to us now that *contradicts* what he said to the first readers back then.

However, I can only partially agree with the objections they raise. We'll speak more about the Spirit's role in the next chapter, but for now let me assert that we must not underplay the Spirit's work in our encounter with Scripture. Engaging our minds and hearts in Scriptural reflection is crucial, but it is nonetheless insufficient—*we also need to depend on the Holy Spirit to give us personal insight into the truth he vested into the passage, as well as to give us a nudge in the ways we might personally apply this insight to our particular situation.*[12]

---

[12] This is not only true for those of us who read God's Word. It is true for those of us who bring a message from God's Word to others. "If anyone speaks, they should do so as one who speaks the very words of God."[12] When I have had the privilege of training

In *Appendix 7,* I present an interesting way of thinking about this that shows how the Spirit will seek to re-apply a text's timeless message to each of us in our unique situation in a fresh, timeous and often unique way. This is part of what makes it so *exciting* to read and reflect on the Living Word in the presence of the Living God. Suffice to say, God's Spirit really does want to speak to each of us through God's Word.

PRAY SCRIPTURE

As entwined as hearing God and speaking to God is, so Scripture and prayer should never be separated. There are at least four ways to "pray Scripture"…

For starters, read prayerfully. In your heart pray while you read—asking God to give you eyes to see what is in his Word.

Pray the Bible's prayers. Besides the 150 Psalms, there are another 72 prayers recorded in the Bible, written by a multiplicity of people facing the full range of human emotions over the course of multiple centuries. You're free to take what prayers apply to you and pray them back to God, perhaps putting them in your own words.

Pray in response to what you have read. Reading the Bible first, and then praying allows the Scriptures to guide or even provide a template for our praying. This is Bible-and-prayer as a two-way conversation. God speaks to us in the Bible, and we speak back to him in prayer about what he has just said. Of course, we may talk to him about something unrelated that is pressing on our minds and hearts, but we should more often allow the passage at hand to determine the topic of conversation between us and God. We might start our prayer with words like, "God, thank you for showing me that…" then tell him what

---

preachers, I remind them that a *good* message is totally within their reach if they do the hard yards of excellent preparation, but that a *great* message additionally requires that it comes with the power of the Spirit, who uses the message to cut people to their hearts, to communicate insight to their minds, to convert people to Christ, and to convey a prophetic sense of the Spirit's current word to the church in its current season.

the verses we have read today have meant for us, and what we might still need from him related to what he has just shown us.[13]

Pray Scripture with others. In the book of Acts, in the only church prayer meeting where we're told what they prayed about, we find that they used a Scripture passage as a template for prayer.[14] Group prayer and prayer meetings are often richer and more powerful when Scripture is read aloud and prayed through.

SING SCRIPTURE

This morning I read Psalm 121 with my children. I explained that all the Psalms are prayer-songs, and in fact pilgrims sung this particular one as they ascended to Jerusalem for their annual feast. My one son who is in the choir at his school volunteered to sing it for us. We laughed but then let him have a go. The giggling faded as he sang with the most enchanting voice and tune, tears finally streaming down his face as he imagined himself among those pilgrims. After the holy hush, we all erupted in laughter again when his sister opted to have a go, now rapping the words.

Giggles aside, what we did was something close to God's heart. As we sing Scriptural truths, we're obeying Scripture: "Sing to the LORD a new song; proclaim his salvation day after day."[15]

In fact, Paul envisions followers of Jesus singing Scripture alongside and to each other: "Let the word of Christ dwell in you richly as you teach and admonish one another with all wisdom through psalms,

---

[3] Timothy Keller in his 2016 book, *Prayer* offers four questions we can ask of each passage that very naturally lead into four kinds of prayer: 1) Praise: What does it show me about God for which I should praise him? 2) Confess: What does it show me about my sin that I should confess and repent of, or what false attitudes, behaviour, emotions, or idols come alive in me whenever I forget this truth? 3) Ask: What does it show me about a need that I have, or what I need to do or become in light of this? 4) Rejoice: How is Jesus Christ or the grace that I have in him crucial to helping me overcome the sin I have confessed or to answering the need I have? (*iBooks, ch 15*.)
[4] In Acts 4, the church quotes Psalm 2 in their prayers, and prays along the themes of that Psalm.
[5] Psalm 96

hymns, and songs from the Spirit, singing to God with gratitude in your hearts."[16] The word "dwell" means to be at home. Scripture makes its home deep in our lives, says Paul, as we sing it. He also says here that singing truth is an excellent and central teaching device. Songs make words stick in our memory.

This is why worship leaders and songwriters in churches should give priority to songs that are infused with Scripture or articulate the main themes of Scripture.

We can also make up songs on the go, suggests Paul. We can sing "songs from the Spirit"—which likely refers to something more impromptu, like putting a melody to the verse we're busy reflecting on, and simply singing the words rather than merely thinking or reading them. As we do so, we let the melody take the words deeper and deeper still.

JOURNAL SCRIPTURE

Journal writing involves the jotting down of personal insights into a notebook, app or word document on your computer. The simple practice of regularly writing what's happening in your life; your thoughts and feelings, hopes and fears, has proven benefits for your overall mental health.

A *Scripture-centered* journal aims not only at mental health but spiritual health too. Nehemiah and David seem to have kept a journal, writing out their daily Scriptural meditations and prayers.[17]

Journaling what you have learned forces you to crystalize your insights, allows you to come back to them in the future, and enables you to articulate them to others. Here is a simple guideline for what to write. I call it the VIP method for Scripture-centred journaling, in which VIP stands for *Verse, Insight, Prayer*. After reading a passage,

---

[16] Colossians 3:16

[17] The book of Nehemiah is interlaced with fourteen of his prayers, which seem to read as cut-and-pasted journal entries. David too wrote down many of his psalms of prayer in response to specific situations he was facing or had recently faced.

simply write down a:

- *Verse* (or part of a verse) that most sticks out to you,

- *Insight* that comes to you as you ponder this verse, and

- *Prayer* related to the verse or insight.

This practice forces us to not skim merely over a chunk of Scripture and be on our way, but also to hear something God may be saying in it to us, as well as carrying that insight with us into the day as something to reflect on. It also provides a record of our daily interaction with God.

As for writing down Scripture, there's something powerful about writing the Bible's words down that helps us to take it in, slowly and deeply, not missing a single word. From time to time, we might want to write out an entire chapter or book of the Bible. After all, God commanded the kings of Israel personally, to write out a copy of the Hebrew Bible.[18]

IMAGINE SCRIPTURE

Imagine yourself into the Bible's stories. A half-millennium ago, St Ignatius pioneered the method of experiencing Jesus afresh by placing ourselves in any of the Gospel stories about him. This is not a good way to draw doctrine accurately out of a passage, but it is an effective way to experience the story, perhaps allowing the Spirit to open up the story and its insight to you in a fresh way.

Most of the Bible's 600 or more stories offer scant detail, and so they invite us to fill in the gaps with our imagination. Here is an example of how to do that...

Let's imagine you have chosen the story about Jesus in the boat calming the storm that had terrified the disciples.[19]

Read it one verse at a time...

---

[18] Deuteronomy 17:18
[19] Mark 4:35–41

"When evening came, he said to his disciples, "Let us go over to the other side." Leaving the crowd behind, they took him along, just as he was, in the boat."

Picture yourself as a disciple. It's evening on a lake. What scenery surrounds you? What sounds can you hear? What smells can you smell? What colour is the sky above and the water below? What is Jesus doing? What are you doing? What are you feeling?

Now read on…

"A furious squall came up, and the waves broke over the boat."

What's happening now? Can you feel the wind whipping your face as the waves begin to crest right over the boat? Are you soaked through yet? What else do you see? What can you hear? And how do you feel?

Next line…

"Jesus was in the stern, sleeping on a cushion."

Can you see him? What does he look like?

"The disciples woke him. 'Teacher, don't you care if we drown?'"

You get the idea—carry on imagining the scene as long as you'd like.

You can follow the same principles and kinds of questions for most stories in the Bible. Put yourself into one or more of the characters' shoes, either a main character, like Zacchaeus or the bleeding woman, or a bystander like Zacchaeus' neighbour or the women beside the fire who asks Peter if he knows Jesus.[20] As you do, ask the Spirit to speak to you.

---

[20] The extremely popular TV series that commenced in 2020, *The Chosen*, is an example of seeing Jesus through the eyes of characters in the Gospels—we too may fill in the gaps and attempt to vicariously feel what the characters felt as they saw, heard and interacted with Jesus.

15

THE SPIRIT AND THE WORD

They asked each other, "Were not our hearts burning within us as he opened the Scriptures to us?" They got up and returned at once to Jerusalem.

Luke 24:32-33

I'd been a Christian for about a year when my youth leader asked me to share a message one Friday night at the youth group. I'd been reading through Ephesians at that time, and so decided that I would speak on spiritual warfare and the spiritual armour God provides for us. I knew nothing about structuring a message, so I relied entirely on saying something from the text. The few hours before I spoke, I prayed like crazy, and read and re-read Ephesians 6:10-20.

As I did so, I vividly recall "seeing" not just the words in the text, *but through the words to the reality they spoke of:* a real authority we have in Jesus, a real enemy we have on earth. My eyes were opened and my spiritual pulse quickened—I felt gratitude for my rescuer Jesus, and urgency to take my stand against darkness, and to set other captives free. As I delivered the message, my expectations were exceeded: ten young people responded to the gospel, eager to walk in the path of light. Besides discovering my calling to public evangelism that night, I and those I preached to experienced the Spirit using the Word to open our eyes, to ignite our hearts and to redirect our paths.

At first I thought this was something exceptional in Christian experience, but when I later read Luke 24, I understood that this is something to be expected, ever since the day Jesus rose from the dead.

On that fateful day, two oblivious, heart-broken believers fled Jerusalem in fear and disappointment. Then Jesus approached them. They were unable to recognize him at first. He taught them the Word. One thing led to another and they were given eyes to see. Jesus then disappeared, and they asked each other: "Were not our hearts burning within us as he opened the Scriptures to us?" We're told that they then got up and returned at once to Jerusalem.[1]

Notice how *their eyes were opened, their hearts were burning and, after that, their feet got moving*—they immediately changed direction and headed back to Jerusalem. Observe how Jesus opens eyes to God's Word, ignites a flame in hearts and can redirect entire lives too. We should ask the Spirit of Jesus to do the same as we read and hear, reflect on and study God's Word...

EYES THAT SEE

As you read, ask the Spirit to open your eyes.

Jesus opened three things to the pair of disciples on route to Emmaus: their eyes to see Jesus (v31), the Scriptures about Jesus (v32) and their mind to understand Scripture (v45).

Imagine a blindfolded child being given a wrapped present. First they unwrap the present. Yet, until they remove the blindfold they cannot perceive what it is. In the same way, God has revealed truth to us in Scripture—the gift of reality is unwrapped. But still more is needed—our eyes and mind must be opened to the Word that is in front of us.

As important as intellectual knowledge of the Bible is, it is not enough. In order to see and savour the word of truth, we need the Spirit internally and supernaturally to confirm and reverberate it to us.[2]

---

[1] Luke 24:13–25

[2] I am aware that talking of the confirming, internal work of the Spirit may sound like an endorsement of the current cultural emphasis on "listening to your own heart". Yes,

We are all in desperate need of the Spirit who inspired Scripture in the first place to illuminate this same Scripture and open the eyes of our hearts to it.[3] Paul wrote, "The god of this age has blinded the minds of unbelievers, so that they cannot see the light. (But the) God, who said, "Let light shine out of darkness," has made his light shine in our hearts to give us the light of God's glory."[4]

Even a genius like Paul, deeply versed in Scripture, could not find God by his own cleverness. God's Spirit has to do for us what he did for Paul—remove the veil that covers the truth and blankets our mind. Unbelief so clouds our minds that we miss what God is saying even when the words are right in front of us. God's truth may shine brightly in itself, but apart from the Spirit's light, *we* are too dull to see it. So we ask the Spirit to open our eyes to see not only the words, but through the words to the spiritual reality they speak of.

HEARTS AFLAME

As you read, ask the Spirit to ignite a flame in your heart.

When the Spirit of God opens up your eyes to his Word, he also tends to spark a flame in your heart. Jeremiah the prophet once said, "His word is in my heart like a fire, a fire shut up in my bones. I am weary of holding it in; indeed, I cannot."[5]

Fire here is a symbol of energy and life. The God who spoke the universe into being by his Spirit is the same God who can make things come alive in us by his Spirit-energized words. Think of Ezekiel's vi-

---

there's something to be said of being true to one's self. Having said that however, the light we need within is the light of God's Spirit, not the light of our own spirit. Rene Descartes, the philosophical father of modern inward-looking individualism, isolated himself from all outside voices and trusted only his inner thoughts. A more biblical, and wiser, approach is to listen to God-ordained voices outside of us, that are not our own—the voices of Moses, Paul and Peter (and to a lesser degree, the voice of trusted pastors and godly friends) and especially the voice of the Spirit who witnesses to our hearts his agreement with those who speak the truth.

[4] Ephesians 1:18
[*] 2 Corinthians 4:4, 6
Jeremiah 20:9

sion[6] of preaching to a valley of lifeless skeletons. By the end of his sermon, a living army stands before him. Still today, the Word of God brings more than just light. It brings *fire* and *life*. His Word is still able to do in our lives what it did in Sarah's barren womb, "to give life to the dead and call into being things that were not."[7]

Indeed, the God the Bible speaks of is not far away and removed but rather poised to reach supernaturally into our lives. To experience his power, we must shake off our disbelief and approach his Word expectant to meet with the God who authored it. As Jesus said, "The Spirit gives life; the flesh counts for nothing. The words I have spoken to you—they are full of the Spirit and life."[8] Let's ask the Spirit to set our hearts alight and make us fully alive.

FEET THAT TURN

As you read, ask the Spirit to redirect your life in obedience.

Those two disciples who meet the risen Jesus don't only see new things and experience new life, they head in a new direction. With their mind learning, and their heart burning, their feet get turning. And so, the true goal of engaging Scripture is not more *in*formation, but more *trans*formation.

Its words are not to be sealed away in-between its covers, or in a quiet time, or only in our distant memories and Bible studies. They are to be carried into our workplaces, our playgrounds, our kitchens and our streets. "The Scriptures need to come to us in the power of the Holy Spirit. The voices of those who wrote long ago need to become living voices in our hearts by the Holy Spirit. What the Spirit said then, ready for them to obey in their days, we pray he will say to us now, ready for us to obey in our days."[9]

Certainly it's important we understand Scripture, for if we don't

---

[6] Ezekiel 37
[7] Romans 4:17
[8] John 6:63
[9] Michael Eaton: 2014, *The Plan and Purpose of God*, Africa Leadership School, p57

understand it we might think we are obeying him when we are potentially disobeying him. Still, exhaustive study is *not* the purpose. A changed life is the reason God speaks to us through his Word. He wants our eyes opened and our hearts burning *so that our feet will get moving along new paths of personal transformation and ministry impact.* This affects how we should come to Scripture…

Let the Bible Renew Your Mind

Scripture does more than help us live correctly. It helps us first *to see* correctly. "Be transformed by the renewing of your mind," says Paul, "then you will be able to discern God's will." As we immerse ourselves in Scripture, we are able to do more than hear specific commands God gives in Scripture. We start to live differently because we see differently. To paraphrase C.S. Lewis, when the sun rises, we are able to see more than just the sun, we are able to see the landscape it illuminates too. And so, Scriptural saturation attunes us first to the reality of God but then also to all of reality as God sees it.[10]

It's true that there are many commands in the Bible, but there are millions of situations we find ourselves in which those commands do not provide guidance for. However, if we are steeped in the story of the Bible—creation, fall, redemption, restoration—we have a four-point compass, a way of seeing the world, that guides us in almost every situation and every responsibility. This is a kind of obedience, but an obedience that is driven by insight as opposed to mere instruction and information. Then we can say with the Psalmist, "I run in the path of your commands, because you have broadened my understanding."[11]

---

[10] Immersing ourselves in Scripture is a key to the renewal of the mind. "Romans starts by saying, "their thinking became futile" (1:21), then tells the great story of Christ, Israel, and redemption, tying it all together with, "therefore, be transformed by the renewing of your mind" (12:2). Ephesians prays that, "the eyes of your understanding be enlightened" (1:18), calls non-believers, "darkened in their understanding" (4:18), and calls us to "be made new in the attitudes of your mind" (4:23). Philippians says, "Let the mind of Christ be in you" (2:5). Colossians urges us, "to set the mind on things above" (3:2). First Corinthians confirms, "we have the mind of Christ" (2:16).""
(Marlin Watling: 2016, *The Marriage of Heaven and Earth*, Kindle Locations 628–634).
[11] Psalm 119:32

Let the Bible Be Your Leader

Nowadays many people own a Bible. But our Bibles do not own enough of us. We are no more under God's authority than when we live in humble obedience to his Word and are under its searching eye. Jesus said, "Blessed are those who hear the word of God and obey it."[12] James, Jesus' brother says something similar: "Do not merely listen to the word, and so deceive yourselves. Do what it says."[13]

Paul amplifies the same point: "All Scripture... is useful for teaching, rebuking, correcting and training in righteousness."[14] Regarding this verse, correcting means, "That is what not to believe," whereas teaching means, "This is what to believe." In the same way, rebuking means, "That is how not to live," while training means, "This is how to live." In other words, God's Word tells us what and what not to believe, and how and how not to live. Paul continues: "... so that the servant of God will be thoroughly equipped for every good work." Notice the word thoroughly—if we do *not* thoroughly imbibe all of Scripture we are *not* as equipped to serve and enjoy God as we could be.

If God's Word is our leader, we will not only ask our questions of it, but also let it ask its questions of *us*. It's true that the Bible is full of answers. It tells us what creation is, who God is, who we are, why we are, and how to live. But we must not forget that it is also full of questions, questions that might expose darkness or ignorance in our lives and churches. It is true that the Bible is a comforting soul-balm, but it can also be a scorching laser beam. It's one thing reading the Bible, it's another letting the Bible read us. We should let its laser intersect with our lives in whatever way the Spirit empowers it to: perhaps guiding us, or spurring us on, or stopping us in our tracks, or helping us to see our situation in a brand new light.

I think of a Bible professor who every year paraphrases 2 Corinthians 8:13-15, then tells his students that these are the words of a French Marxist that they should critique. After they have thoroughly attacked

---

[12] Luke 11:28
[13] James 1:22
[14] 2 Timothy 3:16

it, he announces that they are in fact the words of Paul:

> *"Our desire is not that others might be relieved while you are hard pressed, but that there might be equality. At the present time your plenty will supply what they need, so that in turn their plenty will supply what you need. The goal is equality, as it is written: 'The one who gathered much did not have too much, and the one who gathered little did not have too little.'"*

The professor's point is amply made: let God's Word question you before you question it. In this case, the students wrongly assume the hyper-individualism, so popular in our culture, is superior to the radical communalism practiced in the first century churches, which brings us to the next point…

Let the Bible Fuse You Into Community

Jesus does not merely reveal himself through Scripture to one disciple on the road to Emmaus, but two—and the moment they see more clearly, they seek out the rest of God's people. Because God's Word is first a gift to God's people, not to individuals within God's people, it becomes much more clear and vivid as we read it and interpret it together. Says Ellen Davis, "Scripture is like a musical score that must be played or sung in order to be understood; therefore, the church interprets Scripture by forming communities of prayer, service, and faithful witness."[15] Richard Hays concurs: "Faithful interpretation of Scripture invites and presupposes participation in the community."[16]

We can hear sermon after sermon, and get puffed up in knowledge,[17] but never translate what we are learning into the force of a changed life. Community helps us to apply Scripture. In smaller groups with others, we can discuss how to implement what we are learning together in God's Word. Smaller groups, providing insight, support and accountability, are a great way to close the gap between the message we hear on Sundays and the lives we live in between.[18]

---

[15] *The Art of Reading Scripture*, 2003, iBooks.
[16] *Echoes of Scripture in the Gospels*, iBooks.
[17] 1 Corinthians 8:1
[18] Another tip by Rick Warren is to write down exactly what 'action step' the Spirit and

Let the Bible Draw Out a Heart-level Obedience

As I emphasize obedience to Scripture, I hope that I do not convey the idea that you should treat the Bible's commands as an impersonal law-code. The commands of Jesus and the apostles are not a list of laws to live by as much as they are the leading of the Spirit of Jesus in written form to people who can supernaturally resonate with them by the same Spirit of Christ who now lives within them. Of course, the Word tells us how to live, but this leadership comes to us in the context of our eyes wide-open to who Jesus is and our hearts now ignited by the flame of God's Spirit. Discerning God's command best flows out of knowing God's character and doing God's will best flows out of knowing God's warmth.

God's Word has a way of enthusing and equipping us to demonstrate God's character to others in ministry. A tree that sends its roots *deep* into the river of the Word will send its fruit-bearing branches *wide* into the world. A burning heart leads to moving feet. As Eugene Peterson says,

> "Christians don't simply learn or study or use Scripture; we assimilate it, take it into our lives in such a way that it gets metabolized into acts of love, cups of cold water, missions into all the world, and healing, evangelism and justice in Jesus' name."[19]

To the person who suspects that Scripture is not transforming them, I urge you to continue to expect results *slowly as they might come.* Daily, consistent exposure to God's Word changes us more than erratic exposures to it. When the first century rabbi Akiva was shepherding his flocks, he noticed a tiny stream dripping over a ledge onto a massive boulder. Surprisingly, the rock bore a deep impression. The drip, drip, drip of water over the centuries had hollowed away the stone. "If mere water can do this to hard rock," commented Akiva,

---

the text are highlighting to you. Writing it down causes it to not slip from memory and focuses your obedience. This step should be personal (involving you), practical (something you can do), and provable (with a deadline). (2002, *The Purpose Driven Life,* Zondervan, 244)

[19] Eugene Peterson: 2006, *Eat this book*, Hodder and Stoughton

THE SPIRIT AND THE WORD

"how much more can God's Word carve a way into my heart of flesh?" Still today, nothing can so change our lives over the long haul like the daily trickle of God's Word.[20]

Lois Tverberg tells the story in *Walking in the Dust of the Rabbi Jesus*, Zondervan, 2012.

16

Glimpses of the King

And beginning with Moses and all the Prophets, Jesus explained to them what was said in all the Scriptures concerning himself.

Luke 24:27

In the previous chapter we read of Jesus' conversation with the dejected pair of disciples on the day he rose from the dead. They were kept from recognizing Jesus as he spent a few hours walking on the road with them, talking over the Hebrew Bible, and showing them how everything in it converged in a promised Messiah.

Only after this panoramic Bible study did they stop and suddenly realize that this enigmatic Bible expositor was none other than the risen Messiah; the marvelous Centerpiece of Scripture itself.

What is most striking in this story is what Jesus wanted them to see *first*. We would have expected him to highlight to them that he was alive. Yet he doesn't say this. Apparently, that critically important revelation can wait for the moment. As important as it is to know that Jesus *is alive*, it's just as important to know Jesus *in Scripture*.

In the previous chapter, we learnt that the Bible teaches us how to live and what to believe. But even that is a *secondary priority*. If we read every passage merely asking, "How do I obey this passage?" we will miss its primary intention, which is seeing Jesus in every part of it.

JESUS IN THE OLD TESTAMENT

In the New Testament, Jesus' centrality and presence is obvious in every part and on every page. For example, 23 out of the 27 books mention Jesus by name *in their very first verse.*[1] As we read through the New Testament, we would do well to keep this question front and centre: "What aspect of Jesus does the Spirit want me to see in this text?"[2]

What is less obvious to many readers and some preachers, is how much Jesus populates even the Hebrew Bible, the Bible Jesus read. God wants us to see what those two disciples saw. Finding Jesus on these pages, however, is *less obvious*—his name is not mentioned once in its 929 chapters and 23,145 verses.

Still, any passage that touches upon any theme related to Christ can be read on two levels—first, what its human author said to its original readers, and then, second, the way the Divine Author intended it to be a signpost pointing toward Jesus. In Christ we are those "upon whom the fulfillment of the ages has come"[3] and are therefore privileged in hindsight to see more in those passages than even their writers could have comprehended at the time.

We can only wonder what exactly Jesus showed those two disciples. For the rest of this chapter, we will speculate. In chapter 6, we did a fly-over of the Hebrew Bible. As we examined the seven stages of its story, you might remember that we noticed at least 24 emerging themes.

Remarkably, each of these threads *converge* in Jesus Christ. Let's

---

[1] For example: Mark 1:1, Acts 1:1, James 1:1, Revelation 1:1
[2] There's just so much to discover about Jesus in the New Testament. In another book, What's so amazing about Jesus? I tried to sum up its teaching about Jesus—what it says about his incarnational revelation of God, his fulfillment of prophecy, his historicity, his birth and childhood, his humanity, his central emphasis on the kingdom, his relation to the Spirit, his intimacy with the Father, his exorcisms and combat with Satan, his passion for people, his choice of disciples, his miracles, his teachings, his elevation of women and children, his pathway to the cross, his death, his resurrection, his ascension, his identity as Lord, Christ and Son of God, and his numerous other titles. There's lifetimes of wonderful insights into Jesus packed into the New Testament alone.
[3] 1 Corinthians 10:11

briefly look at these themes in each of the seven stages, and see how each finds its resolution and fullest meaning in Jesus:

In stage one, *Creation and Fall*, Jesus fulfills its main themes:

- *Creation*—Jesus is the one through whom creation was made, is sustained and will be cosmically renewed; he even walked in the midst of it as one of us.[4]

- *Humanity*—Jesus is the true and better Adam, the true image of God who reflects the Father's good character perfectly and the ultimate enactor of God's good reign in the *Edenization* of the earth.[5]

- *Presence*—Though heaven and earth are rent asunder by humanity's sin, Jesus who is called Immanuel, God with us, brings about the remarriage of heaven and earth.[6]

- *Promise*—Jesus embodies God's faithfulness as the long-awaited seed of Eve who, though wounded by Satan on the cross, ultimately crushes the head of Satan in the same event.[7]

Jesus does the same in stage two, *the Patriarchs*:

- *Gracious calling*—Jesus is the new and better Abraham, the ultimate Chosen One, called by God.[8] The difference is that though Abraham once sinfully worshipped the moon, Jesus the Righteous One made the moon. As the author of our faith,[9] he responds to the One who calls him with perfect faith.[10]

- *International blessing*—Jesus is born in Abraham's bloodline and comes to fulfill Abraham's vision to bless the families of the

---

[4] John 1:1–3
[5] Colossians 1:15–20
[6] Matthew 1:23
[7] Genesis 3:15, Romans 16:20, Revelation 12:11–17
[8] John 1:33–34
[9] Hebrews 12:2
[10] Hebrews 2:13

whole world;[11] and he mediates the same promise to us—we are blessed to bless.[12]

- *Sovereignty*—Jesus is the new and better Joseph who forfeits his heavenly robe of glory, is rejected by his brothers, only to rise to the right hand of power, from which he intercedes and blesses the very brothers who cursed him, turning the tragedies and wickedness of their (and our) lives into something that blesses them (and us).[13]

Then there's stage three, *the Exodus and Desert Journey*:

- *Redemption*—Jesus is the Passover lamb that absorbs God's judgment, defeats our enemies and liberates us powerless sinners, turning us from slaves to free people.[14]

- *The temple*—Jesus walked this earth as the tabernacle-on-the-move, where God himself dwelt, heaven rejoined with earth, the meeting place of humanity and a Holy God.[15]

- *The sacrificial system*—Jesus is both the sinless sacrifice and the high priest who carries its blood into the Most Holy Place to cover the sins of the people.[16]

- *Law-code*—Jesus is the new and better Moses who inscribes the ways of godliness not on tablets of stone, but on human hearts by his Spirit.[17]

Stage four is *the Promised Land*:

- *Inheritance*—Jesus the new Joshua does more than save us from sin, he promises us a future inheritance in this life and beyond[18]

---

[11] Galatians 3:16
[12] Galatians 3:8
[13] Acts 2:23–24, Romans 8:28
[14] John 1:29
[15] John 1:14: the word "dwell" literally means "tabernacle."
[16] Hebrews 4:14–16, 10:1–21
[17] 2 Corinthians 3:7–18
[18] Acts 20:32

that is a subsection of his own,[19] drawing out of us a faith that obeys and perseveres.[20]

- *Faithful worship*—Though the Israelites bow to idols, Jesus models for us a love of his Father that involves all his heart, soul, mind and strength.[21]

- *Deliverance*—Jesus is the new and better Samson and Gideon who, through an act of supposed weakness, defeats the enemies of his people.[22]

The Monarchy is stage five:

- *Jerusalem*—One day Jesus will bring about a new Jerusalem, a new city and society, not our creation, but God's. Already now, his church is a city on a hill in the midst of every city.[23]

- *King*—Jesus is the new and better David, the king who turns hate-filled rebels into loving revolutionaries and who reigns over his people for their blessing and the world's good.[24]

- *Wisdom*—Paul declares Jesus has "become for us the wisdom of God."[25] Jesus is the artist, who utilizes not just rationality but imagination as he creates and communicates; he is the faithful sufferer who, like half the Psalms, gives voice to heartache even while he entrusts everything to his Father; he is the true and better Job who suffers though innocent; he is the wisest sage whose life embodies the full kaleidoscope of Proverb's wisdom; he is the true writer of Ecclesiastes who makes meaning of life's complexity and absurdity; he, like in Song of Songs, is the bride

---

[19] Psalm 2:8
[20] Romans 1:5, Hebrews 6:12
[21] John 14:31, Acts 20:32, Colossians 3:24, Hebrews 6:12
[22] 2 Corinthians 13:4
[23] Matthew 5:14, Revelation 21:2
[24] Revelation 1:5–6; 17:14
[25] 1 Corinthians 1:30

groom who passionately loves his bride (the church) and brings his blessing to every marriage that rests under his song.[26]

Stage six is *the Division and Captivity:*

- *Unity*—Unlike the dividing kingdom, Jesus is the only king who can pull together and hold together disparate groups, uniting them despite their difference in the family of God.[27]

- *Exile*—He is cast out of Jerusalem on our behalf so that we, who have been exiled from Eden by our sin, may be welcomed back in.[28]

- *Mission*—He is the true and better Daniel and Esther who enters into and transforms enemy-occupied territory so that we who live in fallen worlds may be in the world and for the world, but never of the world.[29]

- *Kingdom*—In him God reclaims his manifest, renewing and un-rivalled reign over creation. He launches a new exodus and a new creation, in part through his first coming, but fully in his second coming. As his kingdom comes, heaven invading earth, injustice and war are eclipsed by justice and peace; dark ignorance about God is driven out by the shining light of God being known; oppression succumbs to salvation; apathy and hatred are replaced by the divine love of neighbour; guilt by forgiveness; sickness and brokenness by healing and wholeness; and distress and despair by peace, comfort and joy.[30]

---

[26] Ephesians 5:22–32
[27] Ephesians 1:10; 2:14
[28] Hebrews 13:12
[29] John 17:16–18
[30] Mark 1:14–15, Luke 4:16–21

Finally, there's stage seven, *the Return*:

- *The Spirit*—Though the presence of God was lost by Israel, Jesus walks in the full power of the Spirit and lavishly pours out his Spirit on sons and daughters, and on the old and young.[31]

- *Disappointment*—Though the Old Testament ends anti-climatically as people return to rebuild a diminished nation whose hearts are as sinful as before, Jesus is the true Israel, the sun of righteousness rising with healing, who unlike the earlier Israel, fulfills God's mission to bless the entire planet.[32]

So what's the lesson? The New Testament, with its climax in Jesus, was always God's intended final chapter of the Old Testament. Or as Richard Bauckham puts it:

> "The long, ramshackle narrative of Israel with its promising starts and unexpected twists, with its ecstasies and its betrayals, its laws, its learning, its wisdom, its martyred prophets—this long narrative is retold and reevaluated in the light of the concluding chapter God has written in Jesus Christ."[33]

THE LIVING WORD

The purpose of the written Word is to allow us to discover the Living Word.

So pivotal is this previous sentence, you might want to read it again.

We know we have properly unlocked the Bible when we have unleashed its Saviour. Jesus once rebuked diligent Bible students: "You study the Scriptures diligently because you think that in them you have eternal life. These are the very Scriptures that testify about me ... If you believed Moses, you would believe me, for he wrote about me."[34] They

---

[31] Luke 4:14, Acts 1:8, Acts 2:1–18

[32] When the Apostles appeal to Joel 2:28–32 in Acts 2:16–21 and Amos 9:11–12 in Acts 15:16–17, this is what they have in view.

[33] Ellen Davis, editor: 2003, *The Art of Reading Scripture*, iBooks, ch 4.

[34] John 5:39, 46

were so enthralled by the deeds and words of Moses and David, they wrongly confused what were, in the final analysis, mere signposts with the destination they actually pointed to. As a result, they erroneously joined the dots to create a distorted image of God, and their reading of the Hebrew Bible was flat and two-dimensional.

To truly read the Bible correctly, we must ask the most critical question of every part of it: "Where is Jesus in this passage?" Only by seeing him rightly, can we begin to live rightly. For the Bible is not primarily a book about life-principles but a Living Person. *We* are not mainly what the Bible is about. *He* is.

Jesus is the centre of Scripture. He is the axle or hub onto which each of the 24 Old Testament themes I just revisited, like spokes, find their centre. The whole story rolls forward, holds together and gains momentum in Jesus.

Jesus is the screen on which the projector light falls. If, during a movie in a cinema, you were to face the back, you might be spellbound by the iridescent swirl of light shining from the projector. In the same way the Old Testament dazzles us with its variety of stories and themes. But it is only as that spiral of colour lands upon the screen of a particular first century Palestinian Jew that we finally see its true beauty.

Jesus is the hero of the story. We are not the hero of the story. In this story of heart-rending grace, Jesus is the protagonist and sacrificial hero who comes to defeat the antagonists of sin, Satan and death, and save us, the agonists.[35] This morning my children and I read Philippians 2: "God gave Jesus the name above every other name, so that at the name of Jesus, every knee … will bow, and every tongue will declare him as Lord."[36] As we prayed afterwards, I asked them what names might be *under* the name of Jesus. At first they rattled off their own names: *Eli, Fynn, Ivy, Charlie* and *Sam.* Then they got onto biblical names like *Mary, Joseph, Gabriel, the Magi* and *Herod.* Finally, they

---

[35] By agonists, I mean that the human race is in agony under the dark powers of death's tentacles, sin's guilt and enslavement, and Satan's accusation and deception. Jesus comes to rescue us from the misery and bondage of sin and share with us his eternal joy and freedom.

[36] Philippians 2:10-11

began to name those things that are a scourge to human existence—
Covid, Poverty, Racism, Crime and *Death.* So true! "God has exalted
above all things his name and his word"[37]—it is by his word that we
discover the authority and power of his name.

Jesus is the face on the puzzle box. Speaking of my children, Julie
and I are forever being called to help our younger ones complete a
puzzle that has them flummoxed. We give them this advice: "The cover
is your best clue." If each of the 66 books of the Bible are like puzzle
pieces, then when those pieces are rightly fitted together, one main image comes to view—a magnificent portrait of the Lord Jesus Christ:
who he is, what he has done, is doing and what he will still do.[38]

Jesus is the King in his palace. Ancient rabbis likened Scripture to a
palace, alive and bustling, full of grand halls, banquet rooms, secret
passages, and locked doors. Says one Rabbi: "The adventure lies in
learning the secrets of the palace, unlocking all the doors and perhaps
catching a glimpse of the King in all his splendour."[39]

For me, my friend Derek Morphew models this pursuit inspiringly.
He once shared, "When I'm discouraged or overwhelmed I have learnt
that what I need most is to drill down deeper into the Jesus mine of
Scripture—there is no end to the treasure there." Reflecting on his decades of theological research and writing about the historical and biblical Jesus, his voice softens and his eyes moisten. "I can honestly say
that over my half-century adventure in following Jesus, he has grown
on me more than ever and more than I knew was possible. The more of
Jesus I see in the whole Bible, the more of him I have to love."

---

[37] Psalm 138:2

[38] The unity of Scripture, especially evident in all its thematic strands gathering into
Jesus, is testament to the divine Authorship of Scripture. It is also why we not only try
to discern the intent of the many human authors, but the one divine Author's intent in
all of Scripture, which is to bring all things—even the themes, threads, characters and
events in the Hebrew Bible—under one head, Jesus Christ (Ephesians 1:10). Some
contemporary theologians rightly speak of the Bible's "multi-vocal" nature, and then
wrongly use this fact to argue against its unity. They try to portray it as a cacophony of
ideas that do not fit. Yet, its divine inspiration means that, though there are many human voices in the text, one Choir Master holds them together in a euphony that reaches its rapturous crescendo in Jesus and the world he opens up to us.

[39] Burton L. Visotzky: 2005, *Reading the Book*, Jewish Publication Society, p18 (as
quoted in Rachel Evans: 2016, *Inspired*, iBooks, Introduction chapter)

17

Spread the Word

Those who had been scattered preached the word wherever they went.

Acts 8:4

Over the course of your journey through this book, I have endeavoured to impart the tools you will need to take another thousand subsequent journeys through the many passages, books and themes of Scripture. I have hoped to impress upon you three main ways of engaging the Good Book:

Let Scripture Amaze You

No book has more positively impacted the world nor can infuse and impact your life (chapter one). Unique amongst all books, its authorship is fully human yet fully divine (chapter two)—this is why it is accessible yet authoritative, down-to-earth yet magnificent, diverse yet unified. The Bible is a quantum step in God's self-revelation to a people who otherwise would know very little about him (chapter three). Its big story is fascinating and millennia-long—though it consists of hundreds of stories, its larger story unfolds in stages, at least seven in the Hebrew Bible and seven in the New Testament (chapters four and five). It comes to us after passing through the dedicated care of people who recognized its divinity, copied it for others, textually analyzed it for certainty and translated it into hundreds of languages, ours included (chapter six).

Read It Right

Meant to be understood, the Bible itself provides us with the interpretive tools we need to uncover every passage's ancient meaning (chapter seven) as well as discover its timeless message (chapter eight). Even as we may wrestle with parts of the Bible, we rediscover that it is true and trustworthy (chapter ten) despite our biases (chapter nine) and doubts (chapter eleven).

Tap Into Its Life-changing Power

At a heart level, we must give attention to how we listen to the Word—we are to come to it with humility and expectancy (chapter twelve). More practically, God has designed its life to flow into our daily lives and communities through a myriad of rivulets. There are many different ways we are called to engage Scripture: as we listen to it read and preached in church, as we read it and study it ourselves (chapter thirteen), as we memorize it and reflect on it, as we pray it, sing it, enter its stories imaginatively, journal it (chapter fourteen), as we ask the Spirit to use it to ignite our hearts and redirect our paths (chapter fifteen), but especially to open our eyes to see the One whose name is whispered on every page (chapter sixteen).

If you resonate with any of this, then I am sure you agree that something this good should not be kept to ourselves. So—if you are game—let's consider how we can spread the Word to our near and dear, and far and wide.

TAKE IT TO THOSE NEAR TO YOU

Spread God's Word to the people in your everyday life. From the overflow of the heart, the mouth speaks, says Jesus.[1] As we daily read and ponder God's Word, his words will fall more naturally off our lips. "You shall talk of them when you sit in your house, and when you walk

---

[1] Matthew 12:34

by the way, and when you lie down, and when you rise."[2] Scripture-saturated people are more ready to mention something they have recently pondered in God's Word to their families, friends, neighbours, app-based groups, colleagues and connections—whether they are fellow-believers or not-yet-believers.

With this in mind, when appropriate, be confident to share Scripture in your conversations with Christian friends. Don't only talk about the latest news or what people are saying about this or that. Talk about the good news and what God has been saying to you through his Word lately.

When speaking to not-yet-believers, though it may not always be appropriate and it should never be forced into a conversation, it might be natural to say from time to time, "That reminds me of something I read in the Bible…" or "At church last week, I heard something that has stuck with me…" or "This reminds me of one my favourite Bible stories…" Don't hog the conversation or turn it into a sermon. You only need a little salt on your food to bring out the taste, so let your words from Scripture add seasoning to your conversations.[3]

Use social media wisely. If you share Scripture to your social media feed, be especially mindful how it will come across to people who don't yet believe. As a general rule share passages that will make sense, not sound judgmental or preachy, touch on a topic of interest and highlight the goodness of God to your unbelieving friends.

Encourage individuals with Scripture. When a friend is struggling with something or needs some encouragement, a piece of Scripture may be just what the Spirit wants to say to them. When you are giving them advice, you might have some pearls of wisdom, but make sure you share *God's* wisdom too. One simple way to minister powerfully to people in all stages of life and faith is, when you pray for them, ask the Holy Spirit to bring to mind a Scripture to share with them. Alternatively, when you have just read or heard something in the Word, ask the Spirit if there is anyone you can share it with. As he shows you,

---

[2] Deuteronomy 6:7
[3] Colossians 4:6

why not text or voice message them with it right away?

Tell stories. Most people love stories. It's why we watch series and movies, and get excited to tell others when something dramatic or exciting has happened to us. By some estimates 60% of the world's population can't, won't or prefer not to read. They would rather learn by hearing stories.[4] Jesus lived in an oral culture, which is partly why he mastered the art of packaging truth into stories and parables. Since the Bible has hundreds of these, we can learn to retell them in our conversations.[5]

TAKE IT TO THOSE DEAR TO YOU

The love of the Bible is always just one generation away from extinction. It is the privilege of those who have a love for the Scriptures to pass that baton on to the next generation. "Let the children come to me," said Jesus, "and let no one hinder them." Spread God's Word to our children is not an optional extra, it is a command: "Tell your children of it, and let your children tell their children, and their children to another generation."[6]

Parents, grandparents and those who one day might be parents: it is our great duty and privilege to invite every new generation to love, live on and live by the Scriptures. The baton of faith is to be passed on from seasoned disciples of Jesus to new ones, from parents to children. In recent decades however, there has been a growing trend of parents outsourcing the spiritual development of their children to the kids or youth ministry of their church, just as they might outsource soccer or swimming lessons.

This is a serious mistake. As wonderful and necessary as age-appropriate ministries and leaders may be, their influence on the kids in these ministries comes *nowhere* close to the time and influence par-

---

[4] www.bit.ly/33uClzv.
[5] We might even want to retell a modernized version of some stories. Here's two resources to get your creative juices going: www.bit.ly/37k32bc and www.bit.ly/3qfRdLx.
[6] Joel 1:3

ents have. As an example, every year, parents on average spend about 500 hours of focused time with their children,[7] while the same children connect to an age-related youth ministry for about one tenth of that time.

The primary and foundational disciple-making of our children cannot be outsourced. A command in the Hebrew Bible says this explicitly: "These words that I command you today are to be on your heart. You shall teach them diligently to your children."[8] A passage in the New Testament repeats this imperative: "Parents, bring your children up in the training and teaching of the Lord."[9]

One of the great leaders of the early church, young Timothy, was taught the faith as a child by his family. We know this because Paul his mentor writes to him and says, "I am reminded of your sincere faith, which first lived in your grandmother Lois and in your mother Eunice. Continue in what you have learned... because you know those from whom you learned it, and how from infancy you have known the Holy Scriptures, which are able to make you wise for salvation through faith in Christ Jesus."[10]

According to Scripture, a parent's job is not *primarily*, as in traditional parenting, to control their child's behaviour as disciplinarians of subordinates, Neither is it, as in modern parenting, to boost their child's self-esteem as a friend of equals,. Rather, it is to build their child's foundation of faith and wisdom as a disciple-maker of young disciples.

One of the joys of parenting is introducing our children to everything that we have come to prize over many decades—places, activities or ideas. As we do so, we ourselves see these things as though for the first time, and we come to appreciate them even more. Similarly, one

---

[7] I calculated this based on an average of 80 minutes per day that a modern parent might spend focused time with their kids. If all the time is included when we're in the presence of our kids, though doing different things, the number is much higher. See www.econ.st/2JxJLdR (accessed 09/20).

[8] Deuteronomy 6:6

[9] Ephesians 6:4

[10] 2 Timothy 1:5, 3:14–15

unexpected advantage of passing on a passion for and knowledge of Scripture to our kids is that doing so tends to reawaken our own passion for it and deepen our knowledge of it too. One verse teaches us that the more biblical truth we share with others, somehow the more of it we have as well: "I pray that as you share your faith you will more effectively grasp every good thing that is ours in Christ."[11]

How does one inculcate a love for Scripture in our children? I answer this as practically as I can in *Appendix 8.*

TAKE IT FAR

Play your part in spreading God's Word to people who are far from God. The book of Acts describes the powerful advance of God's kingdom into the world. Its name begs the question: Who does these "acts"? *Who is the doer that gets things done?*

As we read through Acts, most notice two different answers to that question: It is the apostles who are acting (first Peter, then Paul). But the Holy Spirit is also acting. He is both the flame that falls upon the praying church and the wind that blows that flame along. This is why the book is sometimes called "The Acts of the apostles" and other times "The Acts of the Holy Spirit."

Few people however spot a third "actor" and yet it is very evident in the story. In the book of Acts, the one major actor on the stage of redemption, the one pivotal doer that gets things done, is *God's Word itself.* In fact, Luke the author uses a simple device to break up the book into its key sections:

- "The word of God continued to increase, and the number of the disciples multiplied greatly in Jerusalem, and a great many of the priests became obedient to the faith."[12] This summarizes the spread of the kingdom in Jerusalem in the preceding section of Acts.

---

[11] Philemon 6
[12] Acts 6:7

- "But the word of God increased and multiplied."[13] This describes the spread of the church beyond Jerusalem into Judea, Samaria and Syria.

- Concerning Cyprus and Asia Minor we're told, "The word of the Lord was spreading throughout the whole region."[14]

- And about Europe, Luke says, "So the word of the Lord continued to increase and prevail mightily."[15]

In all these verses, "the word" is personified, and treated as one of the primary actors or agents in the story of God's kingdom coming.[16] Perhaps, the book can also be called "The Acts of The Word"? Jesus drives the church and its mission forward, not only by sending his Spirit and sending out apostles, but also by sending his Word—any by t bringing more and more people into his family, strengthening believers and churches, and equipping them for fruitful, world-changing ministry.

TAKE IT WIDE

Let me say something about the importance of Bible translation and distribution. Every family in every tribe and language group in the

---

[3] Acts 12:24

[4] Acts 13:49

[5] Acts 19:20

[6] "When the apostles speak of the "word of God" they mainly have the primary message of Scripture in mind, the gospel. For example, Peter and John proclaimed the word of the Lord" in Samaria, which is identical to "preaching the gospel" (Acts 8:25). Paul says to the Corinthians that "the word I preached to you" is the "gospel" by which they were saved (1 Corinthians 15:2). In Colossians and Ephesians there is a close correlation between the "word of truth" and the "gospel" (Ephesians 1:13; Colossians 1:5). To the Thessalonians, Paul wrote that the "gospel" that came to them and which they received was "the word of God" (1 Thessalonians 1:5; 2:13). Finally, in 2 Corinthians 4:1–6, Paul used a number of phrases to describe his ministry of apostolic instruction that includes "the word of God", "gospel", "what we preach" and "the knowledge of God's glory"." (Michael Bird 2013, *Evangelical Theology*, Zondervan, Kindle location 543.) Evidently knowledge of God begins with knowledge of the gospel, the central message encased in the Scriptures.

world needs the Bible in their own vernacular. Currently a billion people live in what is called *Bible poverty*, a term meaning they do not have access to a full Bible in their language,

In Revelation 4, John has a vision of a scroll from God that cannot be opened, and thus no one can know what is in it. He falls to pieces in grief. Then in his vision, all turns to joy when Jesus is able to open it. This is analogous of the grief we should feel that entire tribes precious to God might have the book in sight, yet sealed off from them because they cannot understand it.

I have tearfully (with happy tears) watched videos of a group of people jubilantly receiving, for the first time, the Bible in their own language. The moment they do, they are gifted with the realization that this book is God's gift not only to other cultures or nations but also to their own. They are, for the first time, truly able to hear God speak to them in their own heart language. Have you ever read a Bible in a second language? I have—even the passages that mean the most to me, seem to leave me cold. Or, I think of praying with friends whose second language is English and their first is Xhosa, German or Afrikaans. As they pour out their heart to God, they often slip into their home language. When we hear or read God's Word in our home language, our mother tongue—it speaks to our hearts.

Whatever ways we can find to get more Bibles, in more languages, into more people's hands or onto their smartphones, the better. Praise God that about half of the 7,361 languages in the world have the New Testament in their language, but we still have a way to go. An exciting collaboration, called *IllumiNations*[17] is working hard to end *Bible poverty*. It is a partnership of ten Bible translation agencies with the goal being to gift 95% of the world's population with a complete Bible in their home language by 2033, and 99.9% with a complete New Testament.

The Bible distribution ministry I carry closest to my heart is *Reach4Life*,[18] a New Testament with hundreds of interconnected in-

---

[17] www.illuminations.bible.
[18] www.biblica.com/reach4life/ – I had the joy of helping to create this resource.

serts that seek to introduce teenagers to Scripture, salvation, community, sexual purity and discipleship. Wonderfully, it has already been freely given to over two million teenagers in 30 languages. In my nation, entire high schools have adopted it as their religious curriculum, observing a marked increase in morale, grades, faith and a decrease in high-risk behaviours as they do.

We should also pray for the continued success of *the Bible App*, created by *Youversion*, which at the time of my writing, has been installed on over 400 million devices worldwide, enabling people to read a total of about 40 billion chapters per year.

Back behind the worldwide church's commitment to translate, print, digitalize and distribute Bibles is a passion that more men and women, girls and boys would come to know the Living Word through the written word. The same passion that drove the early translators should drive us. When William Tyndale, one of the first Bible translators to take advantage of the printing press, met a church leader who said that ordinary people should not read the Bible, he replied, "If God spares my life, before many years, I will cause a boy that drives the plough to know more of the Scripture than you do." Sadly, he was burnt to death before he could see the return of his labours, but the 1611 KJV would use three-quarters of his earlier translation, and reach millions, certainly including many boys who would no longer merely harvest the land, but now through their new knowledge of the gospel, be able to bring in God's "harvest" of people. More than that, in enough time, the influence of the Scriptures being read and understood by all would put an end to child labour altogether.

A BENEDICTION: DEEP AND WIDE

In this chapter I have spoken about spreading the Scriptures *wide*. And when we consider how many people, in their longing to help us have it and read it, were willing not only to pour out their ink, but their very blood—not least the blood Jesus shed—we have more than enough reason to feast on the Bible each and every day, and to invite others to the same feast. Knowing how delicious the Bible is, we can say to them, "Taste and see that the Lord is good."

Yet, even as we seek to spread the Word to others, let us never tire of spreading the Word *more deeply* into our own lives, families and churches.

Your first privilege and responsibility is *to cherish Scripture yourself.* The more you do, the more inevitable will be the success of your second privilege and responsibility: *to commend Scripture to others.* As you do, receive this final benediction:

"In the name of the God who uttered syllables
and everything that is came to be,
a God whose word holds all things together,
may the Holy Spirit inspire and equip you
to spend the rest of your life exploring
and experiencing the vast and intricate world
revealed in the Bible's pages.

May you let its wild, wonderful and still-unfolding story
intersect with and transform your own,
sending you out with the good news
of Jesus the Living Word who has not only
etched himself into the Written Word,
but is ready to write himself more deeply into your life
and into the stories of countless people
near and dear, far and wide. Amen."

EPILOGUE: THREE STORIES

I complete my book by sharing three short stories that will, I hope, make a lasting impression on you. Each demonstrates the sheer privilege of having and reading the Bible, and being read by it.

STORY ONE: FINDING EACH OTHER

Something that has helped my marriage to Julie enormously is that we sing from the same song sheet.

I still remember sitting near to her at church, and seeing her open up her Bible. It was dog-eared, and the page she was on was filled with hand-written squiggles and markings of all kinds. "Here is somebody who takes God seriously," I thought to myself.

Seventeen years into marriage, a lot of differences have complicated things at times: clashing personality elements, a mismatch of expectations, and differences of opinion. However, the Bible has tightened the bond between us in two ways:

First, it has given us the same starting point, the same assumptions about reality. God is good. Jesus is Lord. Marriage is a gift to be protected. Materialism is bad. Forgiveness is a priority. Reconciliation is a possibility. Help is a prayer away. Second, time in God's Word has softened our hearts—first towards God and then towards each other. On honeymoon, Julie and I read and discussed a chapter of the Bible together every day, inviting God to speak to us as we did so. We quickly learnt that the secret of a good marriage is to know that it's not "just the two of us"—much better, it's "just the three of us."

But it's not only marriages that benefit. It unifies entire communities. Yesterday I visited a new church. I was a little nervous. These were people I did not know, in a venue I had never been to before, singing songs I had never heard before. Yet when they opened the Bible, and read, preached from, and prayed from it. I was immediately at ease, blessed with a feeling of belonging: for their heart language is my heart language; and their home is my home.

Satan's strategy to divide Adam and Eve was to get one of them to doubt God's Word. It's still his strategy for every Christian marriage and every church. If he can cause people to sing from different song sheets, things quickly go awry.

We're told that Nehemiah would gather and unite the physically distanced groups of people encircling Jerusalem's walls with a trumpet blast. In the same way, our Heavenly Father, week after week, gathers and unites his children in every local church by the trumpet call of the Bible read and preached, and its gospel heralded.

STORY TWO: FINDING THE BIBLE

A few months before passing away from cancer, a friend of mine wanted to make the most of every opportunity. So she asked God to minister to others through her any time he liked. As she walked through a park, reveling in God's creation and presence, she noticed a homeless man digging in a bin. "Go tell that man," a heavenly whisper came to her, "that I want to speak to him through the Bible." She promptly obeyed.

He astonished her by thanking her, immediately agreeing to do so, then reaching into his pocket and pulling out a small Bible.

"Where did you get that?" she enquired.

His response startled her all the more as he pointed behind him. "I ust found it in that bin." Now he too realized the weight of the moment: "Oh, I thought you knew."

When she told me the story I was so impacted by it that I took to reflecting upon its meaning. As I did so, four questions crystalized in my mind:

How many Bibles in the world are sadly left unread or worse, tossed out as irrelevant? That binned Bible was the sign of a sad story. Someone, somehow had given up on the book whose God had not given up on them.

How many of us are, having come to the end of our resources and options, now ready to discover a God who speaks? As the homeless man found out firsthand, underneath all our needs is our need for a God who has something to say to us.

Is there a more life-changing message to hear than: "God wants to speak to you through the Bible"? For this one message, if it leads us to have an open heart before the open Book, gives way to 10,000 other things God will then show us. There is no better way to stay within the range of God's voice than to carve out daily and weekly a practice of engaging the words of the Bible. With an open heart, before the open Book, ask God to open your eyes so that you can see the wonderful things in his Word.

Is there any person in any situation at all whom God's Word cannot speak to? A homeless man and a woman nearing the end of her days: God's Word is sufficient for both. Wherever and whenever we live, whatever season of life we are in, whatever range of experiences may befall us: God's Word fits hand in glove with our lives.

This last question reminds me of another true story of the Bible's ability to meet us exactly where we are…

STORY THREE: FINDING GOD

In 1963, Christianity Today magazine published a marvelous real-life story, titled "The Book That Understands Me"[1] by Emile Cailliet, a professor of philosophy. He tells how, having never seen a Bible, he graduated as an agnostic university student in France, then enrolled as a soldier in WW1. He wrote: "The inadequacy of my views on the human situation overwhelmed me. What use is ... the philosophic banter of the seminar, when your own buddy—at the time speaking to you of his mother—dies standing in front of you, a bullet in his chest?"

He was then shot too. Recuperating in hospital, he read literature and philosophy, and started to long for, in his words, "a book that would understand me." Knowing no such book, he commited to compiling one himself. As he read widely, he decided to write out every portion that "spoke to my condition." As his pocket-size books filled up, his anticipation grew. One day he would read it in one sitting and let it "lead [him] as it were from fear and anguish, through a variety of intervening stages, to supreme utterances of release and jubilation."

The long-awaited day finally came when his book was finally complete. What a let down it proved to be. He reflected: "What a disappointment then to read it eventually, while sitting under a garden tree."

He explained that every quote merely reminded him of the circumstances in which he had chosen it. He wrote, "Then I knew that the whole undertaking would not work, simply because it was of my own making."

But this is not a sad story. Coming so anti-climactically to the end of his self-initiated search for consolation and reality proved to be the

---

[1] www.bit.ly/3o31Oro

exact moment that God's search for him would come to the fore. As he despondently put his book aside, his wife returned—now with a Bible in hand. She explained that she had met a priest on her walk. Cailliet took it and—seized with curiosity about it for the first time—read the Gospels deep into that night.

"Lo and behold," he remembered, "as I looked through [the Gospels] the One who spoke and acted in them became alive to me … *I discovered that this is the book that would understand me.*"

And of course, he was quite right. For the Book the priest gave his wife that day is the one that reads us even as we read it.

My prayer is that in it you will find everything you're searching for, even while you're found by the One who is searching after you.

APPENDICES

In order to keep this book to a manageable length, below are brief descriptions and search shortcuts to a wide range of helpful appendices. All are available in the articles section of www.terranwilliams.com.

APPENDIX 1: A CASE STUDY IN THE FORMS OF TIMELESS TRUTH

In chapter 8, I equip the Bible reader to ask and articulate what the timeless truths are in each passage by using the question, "Is there a principle to apply, example to follow, warning to heed, promise to believe, doctrine to grasp,[1] wisdom to learn, instruction to follow?" To help you understand how these forms of timeless truth arise from the reading and study of Scripture, and to provide you with a helpful case study, go to: *www.bit.ly/3fTzrJA*.

APPENDIX 2: AN ALTERNATE READING OF JAMES 2:14

In chapter 10, I argue that belief in the Bible's truthfulness does not mean that our interpretations and translations are without error. We can be confident in the Bible's "infallibility", even while we are humbled by the fact our interpretations are fallible.

I then give the example of a heavily debated text that has seen Catholic and Protestant scholars at loggerheads for centuries. I then provide an alternative reading that suggests both sides may be wrong, one that I have become convinced of.

The verse is James 2:14: "What good is it, my brothers and sisters, if

---

[1] By "doctrine" I mean what the Bible teaches about those subjects that loom largest in Scripture and describe reality, such as God, Jesus, the Holy Spirit, Scripture itself, humanity, creation, salvation, the church, the kingdom, and the future of all things. The word is often used interchangeably with theology, beliefs or teaching.

someone claims to have faith but has no deeds? Can such faith *save him?*"

To see why, based on a study of the last two words ("save him"), I believe this verse may have nothing to do with acquiring personal salvation, go to: *www.bit.ly/3o1zs0O.*

APPENDIX 3: THE FIVE MARKS GROUP BIBLE STUDY METHOD

As we study passages together with others in small groups, they will help us to see many things we have missed. For a method that I have adapted from something called *the Swedish Bible Study Method* go to: *www.bit.ly/37iJXpP.*

APPENDIX 4: HOW TO STUDY THE ORIGINAL HEBREW OR GREEK WORD IN A PASSAGE

In chapter 13, I speak about delving deeply into a Hebrew or Greek word so as to tease out its fuller meaning as it applies to its particular passage. Assuming you do not have a Bible concordance, or a knowledge of the ancient Hebrew and Greek the Bible was written in, but do have the Internet, follow this link to see how to do this: *www.bit.ly/39t0Y3i.*

APPENDIX 5: 40 BIBLE VERSES TO MEMORIZE

In chapter 14, I encourage and equip you to memorize select verses. When people ask me to suggest which ones to memorize first, I give them a list of 40 verses that enables them to celebrate and communicate the gospel of salvation, grasp the basics of new life in Christ, follow Jesus more effectively, become more like Jesus, and finally trust God in difficult times. The list is found here: *www.bit.ly/3fQpXhV.*

APPENDIX 6: LECTIO DIVINA FOR INDIVIDUALS AND GROUPS

In chapter 14, I explore an ancient way of reading the Bible that focuses attention on prayerfully listening to God and allowing him to transform us. It is known as *Lectio Divina.* To find out how to engage in this practice on your own, or in a group, go to: *www.bit.ly/36mPYCI.*

APPENDIX 7: THE SPIRIT'S GIFT OF INSIGHT AS WE REFLECT ON A TEXT

In chapter 14, I speak about reflecting on Scripture until the Spirit gives us the gift of insight. At this point, people often raise a question about the claim of "hearing God" through Scriptural meditation. Surely we are meant to find out the ancient meaning and the timeless message—both merely an intellectual exercise—then assume we have heard God? I respectfully disagree. Even with our minds properly engaged, we must not underplay the Spirit's role in our reflection on Scripture.

I argue that the Spirit may re-apply a text's timeless message to us in our situation in a fresh, timeous and even unique way. This is part of what makes it so exciting and helpful to read the Living Word in the presence of the Living God. Visit this address to see why: *www.bit.ly/37AGxyX.*

APPENDIX 8: HOW TO HELP A CHILD TO LOVE GOD'S WORD

In chapter 17, I highlight the importance of each generation passing a love for Scripture on to the next generation. If you have influence over a child, whether it is your own or not, how can you do that?

Here are some ways that my wife and I try to pass on a passion for God's Word to our five children. As you seek to do the same in your child or in the child of another, perhaps some of it will be useful for you too: *www.bit.ly/3lp0ehI.*

RELATED RESOURCES

Personal Devotional Reflection

Freely download at *www.bit.ly/2Vfqvol*

Small Group Discussion Guide

Freely download at *www.bit.ly/3od7ejR*

Personal Video Journey

This includes online access to:

- *30 streaming videos, averaging 12-minutes length*

- *30 downloadable Devo Studies with outline, reflection questions and book excerpts*

- *a downloadable Group Guide if you opt to take the journey with others*

Buy at www.terranwilliams.com.

For 50% off, use this Book Owners Half-price Video Code: BOHVC50

Church-Wide Journey

An entire community can acquire code-specific online access for a five-week long church-wide series that spans across weekend messages, small groups and personal devotions:

- *for preachers, 5 adaptable sermon scripts*

- *for small groups and leaders, 5 group videos and Leader's Guide*

- *for designers, branding elements*

- *for congregants, 15 personal devotional study online videos*

- *for congregants, a Participant's Guide*

Freely available for a time on www.terranwilliams.com